THE SOUTHERN FOODIE'S GUIDE TO THE PIG

A Culinary Tour of the South's Best Restaurants
and the Recipes That Made Them Famous

CHRIS CHAMBERLAIN

NELSON
BOOKS

An Imprint of Thomas Nelson

Published in Nashville, Tennessee, by Nelson Books, an imprint of Thomas Nelson. Nelson Books and Thomas Nelson are registered trademarks of HarperCollins Christian Publishing, Inc.

Photography by Mark Boughton Photography

Food and prop styling by Teresa Blackburn

Thanks to Porter Road Butcher in Nashville, Tennessee for providing the heritage pork for the Anatomical Survey chapter.

Thomas Nelson, Inc., titles may be purchased in bulk for educational, business, fund-raising, or sales promotional use. For information, please e-mail SpecialMarkets@ThomasNelson.com.

The Library of Congress Cataloging-in-Publication Data is on file with the Library of Congress.

ISBN-13: 978-1-4016-0502-5

Printed in the United States of America

14 15 16 17 18 19 QG 6 5 4 3 2 1

To the pigs who gave their all and to the wonderful Southern cooks who respect their ultimate sacrifice by making them taste so darned delicious.

CONTENTS

INTRODUCTION

· ·

When Ben Franklin lobbied his fellow founding fathers to consider the wild turkey as our young country's national symbol, perhaps he should have considered the pig. Arguably the most democratic of all proteins, pork is beloved across the country, from a gourmet pork belly dish on the menu of the toniest Charleston bistro to a whole hog roasting in a hole dug in the sand on a beach in LA (Lower Alabama).

During Franklin's time, the residents of the wild colonies of the South were the original locavores out of necessity. The agrarian economy depended on consuming the products of the earth that surrounded them, prepared using the methods and fuel sources that were readily available. In practical terms, pigs ran wild across the Lowcountry of South Carolina and in the forests of Arkansas, so they were a logical source of meat.

However, pigs are pretty tough on the hoof, which is why you don't see a lot of pork tartare on menus. Muscular and sturdy, the meat of the pig must be broken down to make it tender and palatable. Ingenious cooks in different areas of the South simultaneously made the fortunate discovery that one of the best ways to convert a whole hog into a delicious dish is to cook it for a long time at a low temperature. This is accomplished by maintaining a fire stoked by native wood, often constructed in some sort of pit or enclosure to protect the cooking process from the elements.

The delicious side effect of this method is that low and slow cooking over wood contributes a wonderful smoky character to the meat, and as the collagen that holds the pig together breaks down, it bastes the pork in a luscious bath of flavor. In Texas, the native mesquite wood creates a dense smoke that imparts strong, spicy aromas to pork, much to the delight of Hill Country diners. The hickory of the mid-South is sweeter and makes for a barbecue product that plays well with a sticky tomato sauce. In Mississippi, pecan trees are more common, so their version of smoked pork has a spicy, nutty character. Oak grows almost everywhere in the South, so the scraps from constructing a fence to hold a farmer's hogs in the pen are a natural fuel source for cooking those same pigs when it's time for them to make their ultimate contribution to the circle of life.

Indeed, the avid regional debates that arise over the best way to smoke a pig are actually about the native terroir of each area. When you compare a Hawaiian kalua-style pig cooked wrapped in banana leaves over acacia koa wood in an *imu* dug in the sand with a Tennessee hog smoked with hickory in a cinderblock pit constructed in a dusty parking lot behind the general store, you're actually tasting the history of the land.

Another method to help tenderize a hog is also a source of considerable controversy. To keep the meat from drying out over the course of a twenty-plus-hour cook time, pit masters discovered that basting the meat with some sort of acidic solution keeps it moist and serves as a tenderizing agent. It's also fortunate that tangy sauces make smoked pork even more delectable.

Arguments over regional sauce preferences rival battles about SEC football, with the Gamecocks fans of South Carolina preferring vinegar and mustard as the bases for their bastes. In Crimson Tide country, peppers and tomatoes are the primary acid sources of choice to flavor their pork and make the meat more succulent. Again, these preferences are the result of centuries of tradition, and despite their protestations, there is no one, correct answer. (But try to tell that to somebody from Lexington, North Carolina, and you're in for a long discussion with a stubborn debater. You'd better pack a lunch.)

Pork is also uniquely democratic in that it is a meat that is welcome at every meal. The old saw goes that when considering a breakfast of bacon and eggs, "the chicken is involved, but the pig is committed." While you may occasionally see a breakfast steak on the menu, the pig is the star of the morning meal. A thick-sliced smoked bologna sammich purchased from a gas station deli in rural Tennessee is the perfect working-man's lunch, unless you consider the ultimate demonstration of the nose-to-tail versatility of the pig, a "snoot sandwich" made from a boiled hog's nose slapped between two slices of white bread. Feel free not to consider that for too long . . .

But many restaurants are proud of the fact that they serve "everything but the squeal" when it comes to pigs. This is a way to honor the animal and a historical nod to the necessity of utilizing every bit of a hog that farmers spent time, labor, and money to raise for this purpose. Whole hog cookery introduced soul food staples like chitlins and souse that reward brave eaters with bold flavors and textures. In addition to the primal cuts like the loin and hams, pork meat lends itself well to grinding so that the other parts of the pig that aren't as recognizable as spare ribs or pork chops can still contribute to the meal in the form of a wonderful world of exotic sausages. Even the fat of a hog can be used to make lard that is a key ingredient in some darned fine buttermilk biscuits.

The Southern Foodie's Guide to the Pig will take you on several different types of journeys. An anatomic survey of the pig will introduce readers to the individual parts of this versatile animal, and you'll learn procedures and recipes to prepare all sorts of wonderful dishes. A geographic tour of the Southern states will showcase restaurants in the region that have particular talents when it comes to pork. The chefs and pit masters have shared some of their most sacred secrets, the actual recipes for the best pork, barbecue, and bacon dishes that emerge from their kitchens. The contributing chefs include world-championship competition barbecue pit masters; James Beard Foundation Award–nominated chefs; people you might have seen on television shows like *Top Chef*, *Chopped*, and *Iron Chef America*; and cooks who work in family-owned restaurants that you might drive right by if you didn't know that they make some of the most delicious food on the planet. What they all have in common is a willingness to share their talents and recipes with you.

The restaurants and recipes in *The Southern Foodie's Guide to the Pig* range from down-home to upscale, simple to complex, demonstrating the myriad ways that the pig can contribute to the Southern kitchen, but all of them have been scaled and edited to make them appropriate to try in your own home kitchen. And since man cannot live by pig alone (unfortunately), there is also a selection of recipes that are great accompaniments to the pork dishes contributed by more than fifty Southern restaurants that are featured and by some of our other favorite chefs from across the South.

So feel free to keep a copy of this book in your glove box to help you find the best place for an elegant meal in Atlanta or that hidden gem of a barbecue joint in Kentucky. Or get this book a little dirty in the kitchen as you take your own tour of the South's best pork dishes while you plan your meals for the week. Either way you use it, it's a journey well worth taking.

PART 1

AN ANATOMICAL SURVEY OF THE HOG FROM NOSE TO TAIL

THE WHOLE HOG

For an animal that doesn't provide milk to humans, can't pull a plow, and isn't particularly easy to ride, the pig is actually an extremely useful beast. From bacon to chitlins to trotters to lard to sausage, there's really not any part of the pig that somebody doesn't eat somewhere.

In Louisiana's Cajun country, whole towns come together for daylong festivals where they slaughter a hog and split up the parts into teams to make soups, roasts, ribs, and sausages to feed everyone at the party. Under the knife of a talented butcher, the pig can contribute a variety of different cuts to cook in many ways, and just about everything left over can be utilized to make any number of cured and smoked sausage products.

There's a good reason why the phrase "go whole hog" means to do something to the utmost extent. Cooking a whole hog is both a wonderful way to provide enough meat to feed a small army of friends, and a reverential way to ensure that almost the entire animal is utilized after its ultimate sacrifice.

It takes a special sort of cook to take on a whole hog. This is not a "set it and forget it" operation. Whole hog cookery requires constant attention over the course of a cook time that can take more than twenty-four hours. Whichever method you choose, it is critical to monitor and maintain the proper cooking temperature, and fiery flame-ups from dripping grease are an omnipresent danger that must be dealt with to keep your pit from burning up. That's why old-time barbecue joints always built their pits separate from the rest of their operation. It was often only a matter of time before the smokehouse burned down, so why rebuild the dining room too?

But don't let the difficulty of the process deter you. While whole hog barbecue is becoming more difficult to find in restaurants, there are still places in West Tennessee and the Carolinas that smoke eight to ten hogs a day, so you can handle just one, right?

A hog cookin' is a group activity, anyway. It requires friends to help construct the pit, load the hog onto the grill, flip the hog, take turns stoking the fire and watching the temperature of the pit and the pig, and most importantly, keep the head cook fed and "watered" throughout the process.

A pig-pickin' party is probably second only to a good crawfish boil when it comes to sociable eating activities. Once your friends and family get to choose their own pieces of pork from a pig that you spent hours preparing for them, you will forever be raised in their eyes into the pantheon of great chefs. You'll also be asked to cook another hog again soon. Follow along and learn!

THE PIT MASTER—PAT MARTIN

Pat Martin is building a barbecue empire with three restaurants in Tennessee and one in West Virginia under the Martin's Bar-B-Que Joint umbrella. His restaurants are decked out with comfortable, fun, and funky dining rooms decorated with country music and sports paraphernalia, and each is equipped with a custom-designed pit large enough to cook a whole hog in full view of the diners. The spectacle is mesmerizing as employees literally crawl on top of the grill to haul a two-hundred-pound hog into position at the start of the smoking process, flip it midway through, and remove huge chunks of succulent meat a day after the cooking began.

Martin is also a member of the Fatback Collective, a group of pit masters, gourmet chefs, writers, farmers, and restaurateurs who have banded together to raise awareness of heritage breeds of hogs that have largely been forgotten by consumers and restaurants in favor of commodity pigs. The Fatback Collective cooks whole hogs at events all over the country to feed people and show them the difference in flavor between these old-breed pigs and the typical factory hogs that have had so much of their fat and character bred out of them.

Despite this estimable pork pedigree, Martin learned his craft in the humblest of situations. As a college student in West Tennessee, he discovered the tradition of whole hog cooking that was still alive in small pockets of the region. West Tennessee barbecue operations couldn't be more basic, with pits built from cinderblocks covered with sheets of corrugated metal to hold in the heat and smoke from a wood fire while pigs cooked low and slow inside.

Martin discovered the difference between the meat pulled from a shoulder and the long, stringy, delicious belly meat, which is affectionately referred to as "redneck spaghetti." He found out that his favorite meat came from the cheek of the hog, a delicacy that you would never discover in your typical "ribs and shoulder" barbecue hut.

Martin began to hang around the smokehouse of Harold Thompson in Henderson, Tennessee, where his new mentor passed on the lore and procedures of whole hog cookery. Even after taking a position as a bonds trader at a large financial firm in Memphis, Martin couldn't shake the barbecue bug and eventually quit his job to open his first restaurant.

He still loves to build a pit in a field and put a pig in the ground to feed a group and keep the traditions of whole hog cooking alive. It's hard work, but definitely worth it!

PIG TALES

The phrase "sweating like a pig" is really untrue. Pigs do not have working sweat glands, so they roll around to cool themselves. So "dirty pig" is probably a fair description, but it's not their fault.

Pat Martin's Whole Hog Procedure

Cooking a hog isn't so scary if you basically think of the pig as a pot of water that needs to gradually be brought up to a boil and simmered slowly for hours. Since 70 percent of a pig (or most animals, for that matter) is water, this makes sense. Martin's method requires cooking the split hog skin side up over the fire for 6 hours to crisp up the skin to hold in the moisture. After flipping the hog, the tough skin serves as the cauldron to hold in all that water while you slowly bring the temperature of the meat up to 190 degrees, when all the tasty connective tissues and fats render out and add so much flavor to the meat.

In his own words, here's Martin's step-by-step method for cooking a perfect pig in your own backyard.

Buying Your Pig

You can order a whole hog from many butchers and specialty stores, or directly from a pig farmer. There's no reason to try to cook the biggest pig you can find. Smaller hogs are easier to handle, easier to cook, and taste just as delicious. Don't worry about trying to impress your friends. Anybody who can cook an entire animal is worthy of admiration.

Ask for a 150- to 165-pound dressed hog. "Dressed" means that it has been split, the organs removed, and the skin scalded and shaved. Go ahead and leave the head on for effect, and it is absolutely critical that the skin be left on and not perforated in any way. Figure that you'll get about a 40 percent yield of meat from the original weight and that the average guest will eat 1/2 to 1 pound of meat.

Build Your Pit

Materials Needed

- Measuring tape
- 100 standard cinder blocks
- 4 foot level
- Mortar
- 5 rods of ½-inch thick rebar, 60 inches long
- Hardwood
- Short-handled flat-edge shovel
- Charcoal chimney starter
- 1 4 ½ foot x 3 ½ foot sheet of expanded metal or cattle fence
- Roofing tin or sheet metal 6 feet x 5 feet

Building the pit is just like playing with Legos. In fact, you might want to make a model with Legos first before you start laying down blocks. Lay out the first layer of blocks to create a rectangle with interior dimensions of about 5 feet x 4 feet. Use a level to make sure that each layer is level. Mix up some mortar according to the directions on the bag and apply to the top of each layer as you stack more blocks on top, overlapping each level by half a block. Leave a hole in one of the long sides of the pit that is big enough to shovel coals through.

When you reach the fourth layer of blocks, lay your rebars long ways across the top of the pit, then mortar them in place. Finally, build the top layer of cinder blocks on top of the rods.

If you intend to keep the pit permanently, it's a good idea to fill the center of each block with sand before you add another layer. This will insulate the pit and reduce your wood usage by 30 percent.

Fuel

Just about any hardwood will work as a fuel source for pit cooking. Hickory, oak, and fruitwoods like apple, peach, and cherry are popular, as well as nut trees like pecan. Do not use any softwood like pine or cedar!

Note: Don't ever use lighter fluid! In my opinion, it's un-American! Only amateurs use lighter fluid, and if you're cooking a whole hog, that automatically makes you a professional. Plus, lighter fluid is bad for the environment and will make your food taste awful.

Starting Your Fire and Building Your Coals

Ideally, you want to use dry, seasoned wood. Make sure to clear yourself a safe area where you can start a huge fire—the kind that could probably get you a hefty fine. Burn the logs down to a huge pile of coals. You will need to begin the fire at least 6 hours prior to putting the hog on the fire to give yourself ample enough time to build up enough coals to begin cooking. Do not underestimate the amount of time needed to prepare your coals before you begin.

You will need to continue feeding this fire until the hog is done, so plan to keep adding wood to your burn pile for at least 18 hours to keep making enough coals to finish the cooking process.

Prepping Your Hog

▸ Hatchet	▸ Mop/baste (recipe follows)
▸ 2-pound short-handled mallet	▸ Large shaker bottle
▸ 8-inch chef's knife	▸ 5-gallon bucket with lid
▸ Dry rub (recipe follows)	▸ Small mop or pitcher

Make up a prep rub from the fantastic recipe on page 8. These are the "core" ingredients you need to obtain a great "bark," or crust, on your finished product. Use this as a base to start with and then add your own flavors to it—cayenne, nutmeg, whatever! Please note, though, that any ingredients you decide to add to this need to be added in small amounts until you get it tasting like you want it, 'cause once it's in, it ain't coming out!

Find a recipe from this restaurant on page 244.

HOW TO BUILD A PROPER BBQ SANDWICH

- ▸ Bottom of a potato bun
- ▸ 5 to 6 ounces of pulled whole hog
- ▸ 2 ounces of slaw (THIS IS NON-NEGOTIABLE! Pig sandwiches need slaw!)
- ▸ Squirt of sauce on top of the slaw (try the Memphis Barbecue Sauce on page 46)
- ▸ Top of the potato bun

PAT MARTIN'S WHOLE HOG RUB

1 cup firmly packed brown sugar

1 cup salt

1 cup garlic salt

¼ cup paprika

¼ cup lemon pepper

2 tablespoons chili powder

1 tablespoon black pepper

In a large bowl mix the brown sugar, salt, garlic salt, paprika, lemon pepper, chili powder, and black pepper. Whisk the mixture until it is completely mixed and add in batches to a large shaker bottle to apply the rub to the hog.

Next, make up a mop that you will use to keep the hog moist throughout the cook time. Buy a 5-gallon bucket with a lid at the hardware store to keep the flies out of your mop!

PAT MARTIN'S WHOLE HOG MOP/BASTE

1 ¼ gallons cider vinegar

7 cups crushed red pepper flakes (about 20 ounces)

7 ½ pounds sugar

Mix the vinegar, red pepper flakes, and sugar in a large bucket.

Cooking Process

Lay the hog on its back on the expanded metal grate or cattle fence on the ground. Place the tip of the hatchet under the neck where the top of the spine begins. Using the mallet, carefully tap the tip of the hatchet into the spine to get started. Begin tapping the hatchet with the mallet all the way down the spine. It is *very* important that you do not go too deep. You're just trying to get the hog to lay flat. The spine must not be split all the way in half in order to protect the hog and keep the skin intact as it cooks in the later hours of the process.

Using a chef's knife, cut away any organs and excess fat left inside the hog. Sprinkle all the exposed meat liberally with rub. Don't worry about applying any to the skin. You won't be eating that anyway. Flip the hog over on the grate, facedown, and lift it into the pit on top of the rebar. The hog should be spread out flat.

Place the roofing tin or sheet metal on top of the pit as a lid to hold in the heat and smoke.

Using the shovel, begin putting coals under the hog through the hole in the side of the pit. Lay an initial uniform 2-inch-deep bed under the hog from end to end, and then throw extra coals under the hams and shoulders, being careful not to put much fire at all under the middle or belly of the hog. I like to put a seasoned piece of wood on some of the coals for additional smoke, but you have to be *very careful* to avoid flare-ups, so manage your oxygen intake to the pit. Put the wood in the corner where it can't breathe air so it will smolder instead. If you don't want to risk flames, just skip that step because you're still gonna get plenty of smoke flavor.

Put your hand on the lid. If you can hold it there for two "Mississippi's," you are pretty spot-on, temperature-wise. Any less than two Mississippi's and your fire is too hot, any more and it's too cool. If you want to get technical about it and use thermometers, then manage your coals to a temperature of 225 degrees to 250 degrees. No higher!

After about 6 hours, it's time to flip the hog. This will be a two-man job, so find a buddy. One of you needs to get on one shoulder (front) leg and the other needs to get on a ham (back) leg (from the same side of course). Using paper towels to grab the legs (paper towels are awesome for getting a great grip on meat), count to three and flip the hog. You will need to go in a motion of "up and then over" with it to ensure that the other two legs don't get caught on the grate and rip or tear the other half of the hog. That would be bad.

Pour your basting liquid into the rib cavities until they are filled up. This is very important because this liquid is what's going to protect the belly meat—we call it the "middlin" meat—from overcooking while you are trying to get your shoulders and hams finished. While you're at it, splash some around the rest of the hog for good measure. This really doesn't do a dang thing, but it makes you feel good about things and makes for good drama.

Now build your fire to where you can hold your hand on the lid for 3 seconds, or 200 degrees if you are using the thermometer. This might require slowing down on the shoveling for a while until the temperature drops, but don't let your coals go out! At this point you're cooking what I call "clean." What I mean is steady, blue wispy smoke. NOT WHITE SMOKE! White smoke is heavy and choking, bitter and acrid. Blue smoke sweetens your meat, and that is what makes it BBQ!

Continue to cook until the hog is done. The total process should take you about 22 to 24 hours. A really good general rule of thumb is 1 hour per 8 pounds of meat. Your hams will be the last things to finish, so be careful not to overcook your shoulders while getting your hams done. You're looking for a temperature of 200 degrees in the hams and shoulders. During the last couple of hours of cooking you may want to put coals only under the hams so as not to overcook the thinner middle section of the pig.

When you think you are within an hour or so of it being done, quit putting coals under the pig. It's time to let it "glide." The residual heat in the blocks is your heat source now.

Note: Weather can play heck with the cook times. Humidity and cooler temps are a couple of things that can affect you, but nothing messes with you more than wind! Wind is tough on you and can extend the process by hours. That's tough to explain to a picnic full of hungry folks expecting some whole hog sandwiches! If it's windy, use an old quilt or movers blanket or even a tarp to lay over the lid of the pit—anything to keep the wind off of it.

PIG TALES

The squeal of a pig can reach an ear-splitting 115 decibels, as loud as a jet plane.

When the pig is done, baste the heck out of it with your small mop and let it sit for 30 minutes to an hour or so. You may need to crack the lid some to let additional heat out of it if you think it's still hot enough to continue the cooking process.

Get three friends and some heavy gloves and lift the entire grate off the pit and place the pig on a table you're not worried about messing up. Pull the meat from all parts of the pig and serve it. (Feel free to save the belly meat for yourself.) The only thing that should be left when you are done is bones and skin. Don't get in there and start trying to pick the fat out of the meat. First of all, most of the fat has rendered out anyway. Second, if you find yourself worrying about doing that, then you shouldn't be cooking a hog in the first place. Mix it all together and serve.

BELLY AND BACON

Without a doubt, when it comes to America's favorite portion of the pig, the bottom is tops! The belly of a hog runs from stem to stern between the shoulders and the hams, and is a lovely cut of meat, full of flavorful fat and available either skin on or off from many butchers.

Belly meat can be salted and smoked and then cut into strips to make bacon or it can be cured Italian-style to create delicate pancetta. As much as home cooks (and basically everyone else) love bacon, restaurant chefs really enjoy showing off their prowess with either pieces or the entire length of the belly.

A complete belly can weigh as much as 12 to 14 pounds and is so rich and fatty that it is best served in small bites. But crisped under a broiler or slow-braised until some of the fat renders out, the belly can be a luxurious treat that can be enjoyed at home or out to dinner.

Home chefs probably want to look for a trimmed, skinless belly somewhere in the 5- to 7-pound range to play with in your own kitchen. Whether you experiment with haute cuisine or attempt the surprisingly simple process of curing your own bacon, you won't be sorry you put some belly in your belly!

When it comes to bacon, a dedicated following of fans have discovered what used to be a simple breakfast meat and turned it into an obsession. Bacon is now a part of every meal of the day and is included in dishes that would have been unimaginable to your grandparents. You can find bacon in cocktails, soda, ice cream, donuts, and cupcakes. The sweet, smoky aroma of bacon has been injected into some crazy non-food products as well. Bacon toothpaste? Yep, you can buy that. Bacon shaving cream? Check. Scented bandages made to look like strips of bacon? Sure, cover that skinned knee with a strip of belly.

The average American reportedly consumes eighteen pounds of bacon per year, and porkaphiles literally wear their allegiance on their chests in the form of bacon T-shirts and attend entire festivals dedicated to their favorite food. But Southerners have recognized the value of smoked belly for generations, raising their own hogs and curing their own belly in backyard smokehouses. No part of the pig can add as much pure porky flavor to a recipe as bacon. No treat is as ultimately portable as a perfectly crisp strip of bacon, and nothing can put a smile on the face of someone who isn't a morning person like the smell of bacon frying in a skillet.

Don't be embarrassed by your love of the pig. Embrace the belly!

How to Cook Bacon (3 Ways)

While bacon is delicious to eat, it can be frustratingly difficult to cook properly. Because of the high ratio of fat to meat, a strip of bacon can go from limp to overcooked in seconds if allowed to steep and boil in the grease from the cooking process. While bacon grease is a wonderful flavoring agent that should be preserved after cooking and stored in a mason jar in your refrigerator for future use in dishes like cornbread or a mess of greens, it must be judiciously managed in the pan since it burns hot and can ruin a perfectly good batch of bacon.

Of course, the thickness of your slice can affect the cooking time slightly, but follow one of these methods and you'll get perfect bacon every time.

Skillet-Fried Bacon

Traditionalists love to fry up their bacon in a pan, and there's nothing wrong with that as long as you take the proper care with the process. First, always start with a cool frying pan. If you drop bacon into a hot pan, it is much more likely to stick to the skillet and scorch the meat. Remove your bacon from the refrigerator 5 to 10 minutes before cooking to give the fat a little time to warm up and soften so that as it heats up in the skillet, the rendering fat can lubricate the pan naturally. Cooking bacon in a cast-iron skillet is one of the best ways to season the pan to create a nonstick surface for cooking. Consider it nature's Teflon.

Lay out enough strips of bacon in the bottom of the pan to cover most of the cooking surface without overlapping. Figure about 6 strips at a time in a standard 10-inch skillet. If you overcrowd the bacon, the overlapping parts of the meat won't cook evenly. However, if you don't add enough bacon to fill the pan, there won't be enough grease created to keep the bacon from sticking.

Once your meat is in the pan, turn up the heat to medium. Long-handled tongs are the best tools to manipulate the meat and avoid burning yourself from splattering grease. After 2 to 3 minutes, use the tongs to move the strips around a little bit to coat the bottom of the pan with rendering fat. After this, you shouldn't have to worry about the meat sticking.

After 2 to 3 more minutes, the bacon should begin to draw up and the grease will begin to pop. If you are obsessed with perfectly flat bacon, you can use a cast-iron press to help the strips cook more evenly and reduce shrinkage. But if uniformity really matters to you, try the oven-cooking method, which follows.

Flip the bacon with the tongs and cook for 2 to 3 minutes more. If the level of grease rises above the top of the bacon, you can be in danger of boiling it instead of frying it. Move the strips toward the edges of the pan to rescue them from this fate. After 8 to 9 minutes total cooking time, remove the bacon from the pan and drain on a plate covered with paper towels. Some people prefer to drain their bacon on a brown paper bag, so if you want to go old school, that's a nice way to recycle a grocery sack. As bacon cools and the grease seeps out, it will continue to become crispier, so remove it from the pan before it is as crispy as you ultimately desire.

Allow the grease in the pan to cool for at least 10 minutes before you attempt to pour it into a glass container for storage. If you intend to cook up another batch of bacon, always drain the used grease out of the pan first and allow the skillet to cool before starting the next fry.

Oven-Cooked Bacon

Bakin' bacon has many advantages over skillet frying. You can fit twice as many strips on a rimmed baking sheet compared to a frying pan, so that doubles your productivity in the kitchen. Oven-cooked bacon shrinks up less and ends up much more uniform looking than it does when cooked in a frying pan. If you cook your bacon on top of a cooling rack placed on a rimmed baking sheet, the grease drips away from the meat and collects in the pan. This makes for a less messy process and for easier collection of those delicious utilitarian drippings.

The process is simple. Preheat your oven to 400 degrees and lay out the bacon strips on a rack that is slightly smaller than your baking sheet. Be careful not to overcrowd the bacon, and unfortunately it's difficult to cook an entire 1-pound package of bacon in a 15 x 10 standard baking sheet. Save some for tomorrow's breakfast or cook the package in two batches.

Line the pan with foil for easier cleanup, and place the rack inside the pan and in the oven. Bake for 18 to 20 minutes, checking after 15 minutes to make sure that nothing is burning. If you can avoid opening the oven by turning on the light and peeking through the window, that's the best way to check on your cooking bacon. With the oven method, flipping the bacon is unnecessary.

When the bacon is done, turn off the oven, remove the rack, and allow the bacon to drain over another baking sheet lined with paper towels for 5 to 10 minutes. Carefully remove the pan from the oven because the accumulated grease can slosh over the edges of the pan, and you'd hate to make a mess and lose any of that good grease.

Microwaved Bacon

Cooking bacon in the microwave is actually the most difficult way to get great bacon, but occasionally you may be in a hurry or just need a few strips for a recipe or a snack, so we won't judge. Cook times in microwave ovens can vary drastically according to the power of your particular model, so it's always good to consult your instructions for the manufacturer's recommendations.

Place the strips on a plate with at least two paper towels beneath the meat and one on top to control splattering. A good rule of thumb is to nuke your bacon on high for about 45 seconds per slice. If anything, err on the short side of cook times since the bacon will continue to crisp up after cooking. You can always cook it for a few seconds more if it hasn't reached your desired doneness, but you can't cook it less if you've overdone it.

8 Ways to Use Bacon Grease

1. Use a tablespoon of bacon drippings to grease the skillet when you bake cornbread.
2. Add 1/4 cup of bacon grease to the pot and cut back a little bit on the salt in your favorite turnip, mustard, or collard greens recipe.
3. Grease the griddle with 1 tablespoon of butter and 1 tablespoon of bacon drippings to make the best pancakes you've ever tasted.
4. Kids can't fathom making popcorn on the stovetop instead of in the microwave. Use an equal mix of bacon fat and canola oil to pop up a batch and teach those little whippersnappers what popcorn can really taste like!
5. Just a teaspoon of bacon drippings added to a pot of vegetable soup will add a burst of flavor without drastically affecting the healthiness of the dish.
6. Rub bacon grease on the outside of a potato before baking to help crisp up the skin. Of course it goes without saying that you should sprinkle bacon bits on top.
7. Melt 1/4 cup of bacon fat over medium heat to cover the bottom of a skillet about 1/8 inch deep. Then fry flour tortillas for 1 to 2 minutes per side until golden and crisp. Break the tortillas and sprinkle with salt and pepper to make unbelievable homemade tortilla chips.

8. Melt a tablespoon of bacon drippings in a skillet over medium-low heat and add 1/2 cup of red wine vinegar, 1 tablespoon of Dijon mustard, and 1/2 tablespoon of sugar. Whisk for 2 minutes until the sugar is completely incorporated and pour over a spinach and red onion salad for an easy hot bacon vinaigrette.

PIG EVANGELISTS—THE FATBACK PIG PROJECT

www.jimnnicks.com/community/fatback-pig-project

As the founder of Jim 'N Nick's Barbecue, Nick Pihakis definitely appreciates the value of quality pigs. His collection of excellent barbecue restaurants emphasizes the traditional recipes and methods of authentic Southern cooking, and the owner of each location is educated about much more than just how to operate a successful restaurant. Individual operators at Jim 'N Nick's in multiple states are trained in Southern hospitality, the importance of using quality, fresh ingredients, and the heritage of barbecue in the region.

Pihakis is also one of the founding members of The Fatback Collective, a group of like-minded individuals who travel the country cooking heritage hogs at various events to promote heritage-breed hogs like Mangalitsas and Ossabow Island pigs from Georgia. They also support and encourage the farmers who raise these hogs, which are prized for the fact that they have not been bred to limit the fat in the animal. These animals look more like wild hogs than the typical fast-growing, lean factory farm pigs that dominate the American market.

Pihakis has partnered with several chefs and entrepreneurs from around the South to really put their money where their snout is. They have created the Fatback Pig Project, a collaborative effort to encourage the production and availability of heritage hogs. Their goal is to revive the popularity of small pig farms and create a viable and sustainable market for animals that are raised in an environment where natural feed is encouraged and antibiotic usage is controlled. The Fatback Pig Project also seeks to raise public awareness of the real difference in quality between heritage breeds and commercial pigs.

The group purchased a shuttered emu processing facility in Eva, Alabama (you can't make this stuff up!), and employed many local residents of Cullman and Morgan Counties, an area of Pihakis's home state of Alabama that has seen an agricultural and economic downturn as large factory farms have displaced family farmers. The Fatback Pig Project immediately began working with smaller farms in the region to educate them and encourage them to consider raising heritage breeds. Many of the farmers have begun to shift their farming practices to all-natural diets and actually allowing their pigs to root in the dirt instead of living their whole life in a cage.

The Fatback Pig Project knows that this paradigm shift in farming practices may take a long time to scale up, and they also process commercial hogs in their Eva facility to keep their employees working. Their hope is that as the desire for these unique and ultimately delicious pigs grows in the marketplace, both the farmers of the region and the Fatback processing facility can shift the focus to heritage hogs. It's certainly a noble desire that could have a profound impact on rural Alabama.

Wearing plastic gloves, in a large bowl mix the kosher salt, sugar, brown sugar, red pepper flakes, black pepper, and pink salt. Massage the cure into both sides of the pork belly. In a pan large enough to hold the belly and any liquid that will accumulate during the curing process, place the belly and completely cover with remaining cure. Cover the pan with plastic wrap and let sit for 7 days in the refrigerator.

After 7 days, rinse the pork belly and then smoke with hickory wood in a smoker or on a grill over indirect heat at a low temperature (160 to 180 degrees) for 4 to 6 hours. Place the pork belly in a pan, uncovered, in a refrigerator overnight to cool. Slice, cook, and enjoy your own homemade bacon!

» MAKES 12 1-POUND SERVINGS.

* Pink Salt, also known as Prague Powder or Insta Cure #1, is a special mixture of 6 percent sodium nitrite and 94 percent table salt that is used to cure meats. The nitrite helps maintain the color of the meat during the curing process. It is colored pink to prevent confusion with regular salt, and is readily available from online stores, at specialty food stores like Williams Sonoma, or even from some outdoors stores like Bass Pro Shops.

ALABAMA BACON FROM THE FATBACK PIG PROJECT

2 cups kosher salt

1 cup sugar

1 cup firmly packed brown sugar

5 tablespoons crushed red pepper flakes

5 tablespoons black pepper

¾ teaspoon pink salt*

12 pounds pork belly

SHOULDERS AND BUTTS

robably the most popular part of the pig's anatomy for outdoor cooking is the shoulder of the front legs. A full shoulder should weigh between 12 to 18 pounds and contains two primary parts. Contrary to its name, the butt of a pig is not located in the back half of the pig but is actually the upper half of the front shoulder, while the lower part is referred to as a picnic ham. Together or separately, both cuts are excellent for smoking and can produce some excellent pulled pork.

A whole pork butt is a 6- to 10-pound rectangular roast when trimmed and should have some very nice fat marbling throughout the meat that makes for juicy barbecue as the fat renders into the barbecue during a long low-temperature cooking. Other names for the pork butt that you might encounter at the supermarket or butcher shop include a Boston butt or a pork shoulder blade roast.

The picnic ham is a slightly smaller and more pyramidal-shaped roast that can be sold either skinless or with some skin still attached to the lower foreleg. Picnic hams are not as desirable for slow smoking because their irregular shape makes for uneven cooking over the long cook time. It is possible to wrap the thinner portions of the ham in aluminum foil to slow down the rise in temperature toward the end of the cook.

More appropriate cooking methods for picnic hams are roasting in the oven, cooking in a slow cooker, or even boiling on a stovetop. Uncooked picnic hams can also be sliced into 1/2-inch steaks and then fried in a skillet or grilled outside over medium-high heat for 3 minutes per side.

Putting a well-salted and peppered pork butt in a large slow cooker with a cup of water and aromatics like onions, garlic, and rosemary or a cup of your favorite BBQ sauce is a shortcut way to create some fairly decent pulled pork for sandwiches, but nothing rivals dedicating a half day to smoking a shoulder over wood until the internal temperature reaches 190 to 200 degrees and allowing the fat and luscious connective tissues to break down to baste and flavor the meat from the inside.

If you're a fan of pulled pork, definitely take the time to tour the South to discover your own particular favorite type of meat. Experiment with the different styles and don't be afraid to ask the pit masters for advice. While they might not give up the recipe for their secret sauce or every detail of their cooking process, for the most part barbecue people are some of the friendliest and most dedicated folks in the entire restaurant industry. Show a sincere interest in their life's work, and they'll usually be happy to teach you a trick or two.

Then head home and give it a try in your own backyard. Even if you don't have a home smoker, you can cook a pretty good version of pork butt by building a small fire on one end of your charcoal grill and cooking over the opposite half of the grate surface.

PIG TALES

Wild hogs used to roam the fields of the lower end of Manhattan. Farmers had to build a wall to keep the pigs from digging up their crops. The street that ran alongside this wall became known as Wall Street.

THE COMPETITIVE PIT MASTER—CHRIS LILLY

www.bigbobgibson.com

Back in 1925, the idea of selling barbecue in a restaurant was pretty foreign. But Bob Gibson was clearly a bit of a visionary and began vending his wares from a picnic table in his front yard. They say, "Never trust a skinny cook," and at six foot four and weighing in at over three hundred pounds, "Big Bob" was immediately trustworthy.

Big Bob moved his restaurant around several locations in the Decatur, Alabama, area and opened several new outposts along the way. In 1992, the fourth generation of the Gibson family entered the business as Bob's great-granddaughter, Amy, and her husband, Chris Lilly, planted their flag in a new operation south of town. The rest, as they say, is barbecue history.

Big Bob's unique tangy white sauce had always been the calling card of the restaurant. This mayonnaise-based dressing perfectly complements the hickory-smoked chickens that emerge from the pits, and also works quite nicely as a condiment for smoked turkey or even pork shoulder.

Lilly, however, wanted to add a truly special red sauce that could stand alongside the famous peppery white version. With his father-in-law, Don McLemore, Lilly set out on a year-and-a-half quest to create the perfect tomato-based sauce. The result was named "The Best Sauce on the Planet" in a competition featuring over five hundred other entries at the American Royal International Barbecue Sauce Contest in 1998. Despite the overwhelming success of their red and white sauces, McLemore promises, "A blue sauce is not in the works."

In addition to operating three very successful barbecue restaurants in Alabama and North Carolina, Big Bob Gibson's frequently puts their reputation on the line as a member of the competitive barbecue cooking circuit. The team has won scores of awards, including being named Grand Champion four times at the prestigious Memphis in May World Championship BBQ Cooking Contest, most recently in 2014. Their sauces and rubs are very popular online purchases among barbecue aficionados, and the *Big Bob Gibson's BBQ Book* is a must-have addition to any serious smoker's kitchen library.

Though Lilly is a tough competitor on the barbecue contest circuit, he is also well known as an ambassador for barbecue and has been invited to bring his brand of Alabama barbecue to Manhattan as a special guest at the annual Big Apple BBQ Block Party each July. He has served as a celebrity judge on television's *BBQ Pitmasters* show and as the corporate pit master for Kingsford Charcoal. Lilly is also recognized for his readiness to share his techniques and some of his recipes. (Well, maybe not *every* secret recipe . . .)

PIG TALES

The skin of all pigs is pink, but their hair can be many different colors.

BIG BOB GIBSON BAR-B-Q CHAMPIONSHIP PORK BUTT

Injection

⅓ cup apple juice

⅓ cup white grape juice

¼ cup sugar

1 ½ tablespoons salt

1 (6- to 8-pound) pork butt

Dry Rub
(enough for 2 butts)

4 teaspoons seasoned salt

2 teaspoons dark brown sugar

1 ½ teaspoons white sugar

1 ½ teaspoons paprika

¼ teaspoon garlic powder

¼ teaspoon black pepper

⅛ teaspoon mustard powder

⅛ teaspoon cumin

1/16 teaspoon ground ginger

2 cups of barbecue sauce

Build a fire (wood or combination of charcoal and wood) for indirect cooking. Preheat the cooker to 250 degrees.

TO MAKE THE INJECTION: In a medium bowl combine the apple juice, grape juice, sugar, and salt and mix well. Inject the pork butt evenly with this solution using a syringe.*

TO MAKE THE DRY RUB: In a small bowl combine the salt, brown sugar, sugar, paprika, garlic powder, black pepper, mustard powder, cumin, and ginger and stir to mix. Coat the pork butt with the dry rub, patting gently until the mixture adheres to the meat.

Place the pork butt in the cooker and cook over indirect heat for 8 to 10 hours. Add hot charcoal or wood coals as needed during the cooking process to keep the smoker temperature stable. The internal temperature of each pork butt should reach 195 degrees when done.

Slice, pull, or chop the meat and drizzle with your favorite barbecue sauce.

>> MAKES 10 TO 12 SERVINGS.

*Find a food-safe syringe at cooking supply and sporting goods stores.

HAMS

Take a look at some pigs rooting around in a pen, and it's readily apparent that these are some sturdy animals. The meat to total weight ratio of a hog is very high compared to most food animals, making the pig a very efficient form of livestock to raise. Pigs put on weight quickly and can be ready to eat within a year of being born.

This also means that it takes a dense musculature to hold up such a brawny beast. In general, the closer to the nose or the tail a muscle is located, the tougher the muscle. For a pig, the biggest muscle group is the rear haunch that is generally referred to as the ham. Because the ham is such a strong muscle, it lends itself better to being served as a steak or a roast instead of trying to break it down into pulled pork. An uncooked, uncured cut from the hind leg of a pig is called a "fresh ham," and is excellent for slow-cooking or roasting. Most hams sold in the supermarket are either precooked or cured and simply require reheating. Or you can slice it and serve it on a sandwich if that's your preference.

The real character of a ham comes out when it is cured over an extended period of time. Originally, hams were cured in salt and cold-smoked in smokehouses to dry the meat and eliminate any bacteria that might spoil the meat before a family could finish eating a whole hog that they had raised to get them through the winter. The best American hams are still treated with these old-school methods, although many commercially processed hams are quick cured with injections of a brine of salt, sugar, seasonings, and water to create what is called a "city ham." You can definitely taste the difference and note the disappointing texture that results from a quick brine versus the artisan methods.

In the South, country ham rules. Although some consider the salty taste and chewier texture of a country ham to be too aggressive compared to the honey-glazed holiday hams they might have grown up with, real connoisseurs will compare a Smithfield ham with the best Iberico out of Spain. According to Virginia law, Smithfield hams must be produced in or around the town of Smithfield and must be cured for a minimum of six months. However, similar methods are used in Kentucky, Tennessee, and the Appalachians to produce some excellent country hams to rival the best of Virginia.

Traditionally, hams were rubbed with a cure of salt and sugar to draw out water from the meat and kill surface bacteria. Then they were literally "hung out to dry." The seasonal variations of temperature would impart unique flavors to the meat, similarly to how the hot summers and cold winters of Kentucky draw the flavors of a charred oak barrel into a fine bourbon.

PIG TALES

Iowa is by far the top pork producing state, and combined with North Carolina, Minnesota, and Illinois, the top four states produce over 60 percent of the nation's pork.

Modern country ham producers simulate the natural seasonal changes by curing the outside of the meat with their own proprietary sugar, salt, nitrite, and seasoning mixtures and then storing the hams in huge refrigerated rooms. After the water has been drawn out and the flavors of the cure have been absorbed by the meat, the hams are exposed to smoke that has been cooled so as not to start cooking the meat. Then the hams are aged in an environment that simulates spring and summer weather, usually somewhere between 75 to 95 degrees, to allow the flavors to further develop. This process is not unlike the aging of cheeses, where the texture and intensity of aromas become more complex with age. Also like cheese, an aged ham sometimes grows a layer of harmless mold on the outside rind that can be rinsed off before eating.

Since the flavors of a country ham can be more intense and saltier than a city ham, it's usually appropriate to use less of it in a recipe. Country ham is wonderful on its own, fried in a skillet with a sprinkling of brown sugar to form a crust and served with redeye gravy for breakfast, or added to vegetable dishes for a wonderful complexity of flavors.

KING OF THE CURE— ALLAN BENTON

www.bentonscountryhams2.com

Allan Benton is a humble man. Despite the fawning admiration of chefs and diners from all over the world, he is fond of describing his eastern Tennessee ham and bacon-curing operation this way: "It's not a difficult business. It's not rocket science, or I certainly couldn't do it."

This self-effacing proclamation belies the success of Benton's operation in tiny Madisonville, Tennessee, that is renowned for producing some of the most amazing country hams and bacon in the world. His products are featured on menus in some of the most famous restaurants across America, and Benton is treated like a rock star when he walks into a room full of chefs and foodies. Even in the face of such acclaim, Benton always carries himself with quiet dignity and insists that the pig is the star of the show.

Benton was born "deep in the hollers" of Scott County, Virginia, where his grandfather used to raise huge hogs, up to seven hundred pounds, to feed his family. Out of necessity, after butchering the pigs the family would cure their meat so that it would last through the year. Once his grandparents grew too old for that labor-intensive process, they began to purchase their meat from a neighbor named Albert Hicks who cured and smoked hams and bacon in a tiny smokehouse.

By this time, Allan Benton had graduated from college and moved to Florida to teach school, but he missed his home. He returned to Tennessee and earned a master's degree, but soon discovered that working at a high school was not what he wanted to do for his life's work.

Benton's father told his son that Albert Hicks was retiring and might want to sell his smokehouse. Remembering the fond times he had spent working with his family, Benton decided to make the leap and become a ham maker. He leased the small smokehouse from Hicks, who also taught Benton more about the process of curing and smoking.

Benton continued to slowly expand his business over the years, putting out thousands of his intensely smoky hams and bacon bellies, but primarily his customers were individuals from the surrounding area. Then a few culinary and lifestyle magazines took notice, and suddenly chefs like John Besh, Sean Brock, and David Chang were clamoring for Benton's pork products.

A whole new market of restaurant customers certainly increased Benton's visibility, but he steadfastly clings to his same old traditional methods. Although he is quiet and unassuming, Benton has a sharp scientific mind. He has developed techniques through the years that combine the best of the regional heritage of curing with practices that assure he has a very low spoilage rate, which is the key to making a profit in the ham business.

After applying a simple cure of salt, brown sugar, and sodium nitrite to the outside of the hams, Benton stacks them in maple racks that he built himself. The hams rest in cure at a temperature just above freezing for about two months. Then he pulls the hams out of the racks and hangs them shank down to help shape them into a traditional country ham. After a short spell in the intense environment of the smokehouse, the hams continue to age for up to a year in a cooler.

Benton still uses a rotary telephone in his office, and if you call to order a pound of bacon, you'll either speak to Allan or hear a message saying that he's probably back in the smokehouse and he'll call you back.

Chefs who are able to purchase Benton's products tell stories of delivery drivers who ask if they can keep the box that the bacon shipped in just so that their trucks will continue to smell so good. Benton even hangs the T-shirts that he sells in his store in the smokehouse for a little while so that you can take the aroma home with you. Don't be surprised if a few stray dogs follow you home the first time you wear it.

PIG TALES

During the War of 1812, a New York pork packer named "Uncle" Sam Wilson was a huge supplier of pork to U.S. troops. Each barrel was stamped "U.S." for Uncle Sam, who had sent enough food "to feed an entire army." Eventually, "Uncle Sam" came to represent the U.S. government itself.

RIBS

∙∙∙

There may be no more user-friendly food in nature than a well-cooked pork rib. Think about it: a spare rib can carry the flavor of the pig, a zesty rub, and a glaze of sweet sauce, and it comes with its own set of handles to eat it with.

Ribs are versatile as well. A rack of country-style ribs simmered all day in a slow cooker flavored with your favorite barbecue sauce can make a perfect evening meal that's ready when you walk through the door after a hard day's work. In a hurry? Baby back ribs can be baked or parboiled and then grilled over charcoal for a quick and delicious main course. Or if you have some time, a rack of spare ribs smoked slowly until the meat falls off the bone is a thing of beauty.

Probably the most utilitarian of the different rib cuts from the pig are spare ribs. Cut from the side of the belly after the bacon and belly have been removed, a full rack of spare ribs should contain between eleven and fourteen bones from between the sternum and back ribs. This particular cut includes an extra layer of lean meat on top of the larger bones and the short, dense meaty rib tips attached to the lower end of the spare ribs. Because there are different types of meat attached to the full rack of spare ribs, they can be cooked in a variety of ways from grilled to smoked to roasted.

Since spare ribs are so irregular in shape, they can be difficult to cook evenly, so many people prefer what is called the St. Louis style of ribs. This style is made more rectangular by cutting away the rib tips and the portions of the spare rib bones and sternum that have little or no meat. Competitive barbecue contestants often cook St. Louis ribs because they cook more consistently and look very neat and orderly when presented to judges.

Other rib lovers swear by baby back ribs, cut from the top of the rib cage between the spine and spare ribs. Because the meat attached to the baby backs comes from the loin section of the pig, they are much leaner than spare ribs and tend to dry out during long cooks. On the plus side, baby back ribs can have more meat on them than spares depending on how much of the loin the butcher chooses to trim off with the bone. If you were to cut across the rack of

AN ANATOMICAL SURVEY OF THE HOG FROM NOSE TO TAIL

baby backs through the loin, you would actually be cutting loin chops, which is why some butchers won't sell back ribs for fear of wasting perfectly good pork chops.

The equivalent to loin chops from the shoulder blade end of the spine are called country-style ribs. This is a bit of a misnomer because they normally don't actually contain any rib bone at all. Instead, the bone in a country-style rib is part of the shoulder blade. Regardless of whether they are misnamed, country-style ribs are meaty and flavorful and usually a great value compared to some other butcher cuts. Cook them on the grill, in your slow cooker, or braised in the oven for a real country-style treat.

The Vergos family of Memphis developed their world-famous Rendezvous dry rib rub from a base of a lamb seasoning recipe from their Greek heritage. To make it more Southern, they added chili powder to traditional Greek ingredients like lemon, vinegar, oregano, and garlic. Squeeze a lemon on your dry ribs to taste what they were going for. Opa!

BARBECUE ENTREPRENEUR— CAREY BRINGLE

www.peglegporker.com

Carey Bringle is a hard-working man and a genuine character. He's the kind of guy whose tongue-in-cheek business card reads, "Wars Fought—Stud Service—Revolutions Started—Tigers Tamed—Assassinations Plotted—Bars Emptied—Uprisings Quelled, etc." Depending on when you ask him, he will tell you that he lost his leg to a shark attack or in a bar fight or that he donated it to an Olympic marathoner who needed a spare tire. The truth is that he lost his right wheel to bone cancer when he was still in high school in Nashville, but Bringle's attitude is always optimistic and contagious.

As a competition cooker, Carey is a multi-time medalist in the Memphis in May World Championship BBQ Cooking Contest and at other contests, and he likes to claim that his Peg Leg Porker Barbecue Team has never lost a party. Another facetious claim about that missing leg was that when the team was named years ago, they all pledged to cut off a leg to show their dedication to the Peg Leggers. Bringle says he unfortunately volunteered to go first, and everyone else chickened out.

Bringle is also a media darling, with *Bon Appétit* magazine naming his sauce as one of their top five favorites in the entire country, and he has made several appearances on national television including *Chopped*, *BBQ Pitmasters*, and *BBQ Crawl*. His rise to national attention has followed an unorthodox path. Many barbecue celebrities start out by opening a restaurant, gaining a reputation as a pit master, releasing a line of sauces, rubs, and souvenirs, and then maybe appearing in cooking competitions and on television. Bringle turned that progression on its head.

First, he created his clever team name and persona. Then as his team grew in success and popularity, he began to sell shirts and hats emblazoned with his clever logo of a three-legged pig with a wooden peg leg strapped on in place of a ham. That led to a public demand for his Memphis-style rub, barbecue sauces, and a do-it-yourself barbecue cooking kit for beginners that he sold on his website and on television.

Finally, after two decades in the amateur barbecue biz, Bringle opened his own joint in the burgeoning Gulch neighborhood of Nashville in a cinderblock building, decorated with pictures of friends and members of his family who have been cooking West Tennessee-style barbecue for generations. Boisterous music entertains the lines of patrons who flock for a taste of Peg Leg's ribs, sandwiches, and whole hog barbecue. The play list is usually a mix of classic country and Southern rock, except for "Barry White Wednesday," which features the basso profundo tones of the master of seductive soul.

The next element of the "Peg Leg Porker lifestyle brand" is the release of his own Tennessee Bourbon. Based on Bringle's past track record, it should be a hit!

AN ANATOMICAL SURVEY OF THE HOG FROM NOSE TO TAIL

Peg Leg Porker's Guide to Cooking Baby Back Ribs

At the Peg Leg Porker restaurant, Carey Bringle offers Memphis-style ribs in both the traditional dry rib style of the Bluff City and the wet rib style glazed with his delicious, tangy sauce. As a competition cooker, he has lots of experience cooking outdoors as well. Here's his procedure for smoking baby back ribs at home, written in his inimitable style.

First make up a mop sauce.

MOP SAUCE

2 cups cider vinegar
2 cups apple juice
2 cups water

½ cup dry seasoning (preferably Peg Leg Porker, available online, or use the Memphis Finishing Rub on page 56)
2 racks baby back ribs

Mix the vinegar, apple juice, water, and dry seasoning in a large bowl.

Now get your smoker ready. I use hickory to smoke ribs, but also sometimes use apple or cherry wood. You can also use a combination of lump charcoal and wood chunks for a nice, even heat. It is best to start your grill or smoker with a charcoal chimney instead of using lighter fluid so that you don't get a chemical taste or smell in your ribs. If you're using a grill instead of a smoker, build the fire with the coals on one side and place the ribs on the other.

How to Cook Baby Back Ribs

Take the racks of ribs and turn them over, meat side down on a cutting board. With a paring knife, remove the tough silvery membrane from the backside of the ribs so that the flavors of the rub and the smoke can penetrate the meat better. Plus, nobody likes to have to chew through that tough layer of silver skin anyway.

You can do this by starting at the end of the rack and sliding the knife under the membrane right next to the bone to give you better leverage to pull it up and get a handle on it. Once you get a grip on it, pull it all the way down the rack. If it doesn't pull off, then you can always score the back of the ribs so that the membrane is broken up and peel it off after cooking.

I smoke my ribs at a temperature between 300 and 325 degrees, which is hotter than I do a pork shoulder or butt. I put them in the smoker with nothing on them except for a sprinkling of about a tablespoon of kosher salt per rack and mop them every 30 minutes with a brush or small mop. I do this until they are the color that I want them, a nice golden brown/mahogany shade. If you don't have anything to mop them with, I sometimes use cola or beer. Just something to keep them moist.

After they are the color that I want them (should be about 2 to 3 hours), I stack them up in stacks of two and mop the ribs again, then seal them up in aluminum foil. This helps put some liquid in the foil to steam the ribs a little. It is not necessary to wrap the ribs if they are not getting too dark. Wrapping with foil keeps them from taking on too much smoke, which will make the color too dark.

Put them back on the smoker. There's no need for any more smoke at this point, so just let them keep rolling at 300 degrees for about another hour. After that time, open the foil, and with a pair of tongs try to lift a rack from the end, sliding the tongs up about halfway. If they start to break in the middle, they're done. If they just bend a little bit instead of pulling apart, give them another 15 minutes and test them again until they are ready.

Once done, pull them out and either sprinkle them with dry seasoning or slather them with your favorite sauce. Now they will not only be nice and tender, but they will also look great. Make sure that you know the difference between a rub and a BBQ seasoning. Peg Leg Porker and Rendezvous make BBQ seasonings, but most people make a rub that is meant to be applied before cooking. A rub is usually heavy on salt or sugar, while a BBQ seasoning is not.

 PIG TALES

In seventeenth-century England, it was common to buy a baby pig in a sack, called a "pig in a poke." Unscrupulous merchants who tried to swap out another animal for the suckling pig were discovered when someone "let the cat out of the bag."

LOINS AND CHOPS

. . . .

The part of the pig that runs along the spine on top of the rib cage between the shoulder and the ham is called the loin. The muscles of the loin are not really critical to the ambulation of the animal, so they tend to be much more tender than the hardworking muscles of the legs. Whether you care about the specific anatomy or not, this is important because the lean, tender meat of the loin is quite delicious.

If cut across the ribs with the bones included, consumers call these pork chops, although the USDA has recently decided that the nomenclature should follow that of beef, so it's officially a pork porterhouse. You can compare it to a T-bone steak with a small piece of tenderloin divided from a strip steak by a large T-shaped bone. The same cut can be made without bones for a boneless pork loin chop that is very easy to cook and makes a great breakfast cutlet.

The full boneless loin can be cut into various roasts named after which particular portion of the pig it comes from: blade loin (front), center loin, and sirloin (rear). These roasts cook well in the oven or on the grill and can also be smoked and cut into steaks. Particularly popular in Canada are cured strips of loin cut from the top of the loin closest to the fat of the back. Canadians logically call this product "back bacon," while Americans instead refer to it as "Canadian bacon."

Deep inside the already lean loin section of the pig is the almost fatless tenderloin. The equivalent of a filet mignon in a cow, this is the most naturally tender muscle in the entire pig. Scientifically, this is because the *psoas major* muscle is not used at all for locomotion, but instead is just what anatomists call a "posture muscle." If you've ever seen a pig wallowing in the mud, you know that good posture is not the first thing on his mind.

Since it is a small muscle with almost no fat or connective tissue, the tenderloin cooks very quickly. Unlike denser cuts, this allows for tenderloin to be grilled and then sliced into medallions or sliced thin and deep-fried as the star attraction of a pork tenderloin sandwich, a lunchtime staple in many parts of the Midwest. In the South, fried tenderloin is more popular on top of a biscuit as a breakfast dish, but either way it is delicious.

Pork in general gets a bad rap as being unhealthy. While there's certainly enough fat in the belly of a pig to make you check your cholesterol numbers if you eat bacon every day, pork tenderloin is as lean and healthy as a boneless chicken breast. Don't be afraid to add pork to a balanced diet.

Top left: Memphis, Tennessee Whiskey, Louisiana, Kansas City, and St. Louis sauces

Top right: Texas Barbecue & Brisket and Kentucky Mops sauces

Right: Lexington Dip & Eastern North Carolina Sauce

SAUCES, RUBS, AND BRINES

Without a doubt, pork is a very delicious meat, but as America has become more health-conscious, pork producers have sought to breed the natural fat out of hogs. This leaner version of "The Other White Meat" can tend to be drier and have less intense flavors than heritage hogs used to feature.

So it's more important than ever to take steps to keep pork from drying out over the course of a long, slow cooking process or a blazing sear over a hot grill. Barbecue sauces come in all sorts of regional styles but share the characteristics of adding sweetness and/or acidity to the mild flavor of the meat.

Rubs are usually used to form a sweet crust on ribs to add flavor and color to the smoked meat, but they can accomplish the same tasks on a pork shoulder or chop. While sugar and salt are important components of most rubs, it's important not to let the sugars burn since that can add an unpleasant flavor to the meat. Other spices and herbs like cumin, chili powder, and paprika are standard additions to most rubs. The addition of your own favorite herbs and spices like dry mustard, garlic powder, celery salt, ginger, and onion powder can help you create your own signature rub. Part of the fun is experimenting, since there's really no such thing as a bad rib as long as you smoke it slowly and make sure not to overcook it.

Brines can be a great way to help keep pork from drying out, and they are very easy to make and use. Without going too deeply into the science of osmosis, just rest assured that submerging your pork in a salt and water solution overnight will draw the moisture through the meat to give you a more tender and juicy result. This is especially useful for the leanest cuts like pork tenderloin and pork chops that don't have the advantage of internal fat and collagen that can render out during a long cook to help keep the meat from getting too dry.

In a piece of beef, the amount of marbling is an important characteristic by which steaks are graded into categories like USDA Prime, Choice, etc. Since most of the fat on a pig is situated between the skin and the meat, you can't expect it to add much flavor to anything but the belly and bacon.

Use a combination of these recipes and techniques to help create the most flavorful pork dishes imaginable.

Sauces

The topic of barbecue can raise some great debates between friends. In Texas, beef is king, but Texans also appreciate a good pork shoulder that has been smoked well. Pulled pork aficionados swear by their favorite method of presentation, but chopped meat fans think they are just shredding good pork. Ribs can be cooked as a full spare rack or trimmed to a neat rectangular St. Louis style and then grilled, smoked, wrapped in foil, or even (horrors!) parboiled. Some folks swear by tender baby back ribs, but others claim that particular cut ruins a bunch of perfectly good pork chops since they are essentially cut from the same primal parts of the pig.

But no element of the barbecue process engenders as much conversation as the regional choices of barbecue sauce. While the general public across the country demonstrates a strong predilection for thick, sweet tomato-based sauces, Southerners are much more specific in their favorite styles of sauce.

Many of these varieties have characteristics that are based in history that stretches back from when the first settlers started cooking in a particular region. The Scotch-Irish who moved into the hills of Kentucky had a heritage of cooking sheep in their homeland, while the Germans who populated colonial South Carolina brought their love of mustard to the table when they first began smoking the feral hogs they encountered in the bushes of the scrub forests of coastal Carolina.

PIG TALES

Politicians love to talk about pigs and "pork barrel politics." Winston Churchill said, "Dogs look up to man. Cats look down to man. Pigs look us straight in the eye and see an equal." Harry Truman believed, "No man should be allowed to be president who does not understand hogs."

Fortunately, there really are no right or wrong answers when it comes to your choice of barbecue sauce. Feel free to experiment on your own and take a different culinary journey every time you try one of these recipes. Once you learn how easy these are to make, you'll never use store-bought sauces again.

SOUTH CAROLINA MUSTARD SAUCE

South Carolina is one of the few states that have four distinct styles of barbecue sauce that are widely popular. Probably the best-known version is the South Carolina Mustard Sauce that traces its heritage to the large population of Germans who settled in the central and southern regions of the state centuries ago.

Western South Carolina generally prefers a thicker ketchup-based sauce that spills over from their Georgia neighbors to the west (see page 40). Eastern South Carolina is known as the "Pee Dee" region, and shares a simpler vinegar and red pepper concoction that is very similar to eastern North Carolina sauce (see page 42).

Finally, the northwestern corner of the state prefers a sauce that is close to North Carolina's Piedmont-style sauce, or Lexington Dip (see page 43). This sauce is very similar to the Pee Dee red pepper and vinegar sauce with addition of some tomato, but not enough to make it thick and sticky.

3 cups prepared mustard

½ cup cider vinegar

6 tablespoons brown sugar

2 teaspoons Worcestershire sauce

¾ tablespoon crushed red pepper flakes

¾ tablespoon black pepper

1 ½ teaspoons salt

1 ½ teaspoons garlic powder

In a medium saucepan add the mustard, vinegar, brown sugar, Worcestershire, red pepper flakes, black pepper, salt, and garlic powder and heat over medium heat, stirring frequently. When the sauce begins to boil, lower heat to a simmer. After 10 to 15 minutes, the sauce should begin to thicken slightly. Remove from the heat and allow to cool or serve warm over pulled pork. Store in a sealed bottle or jar in refrigerator for up to a month.

>> MAKES 4 CUPS.

GEORGIA SWEET TOMATO SAUCE

The first commercially produced barbecue sauce was manufactured in Georgia, but the Peach State really doesn't have a particularly famous style of sauce (unless you count some novelty peach varieties). The part of the state nearest to South Carolina does like mustard-based sauces, but you are more likely to encounter a fairly traditional sweet tomato and brown sugar sauce in most restaurants around the rest of the state.

2 cups ketchup

1 (6-ounce) can tomato paste

1 cup firmly packed dark brown sugar

3 ½ tablespoons cider vinegar

1 tablespoon Worcestershire sauce

1 tablespoon dry mustard

2 teaspoons salt

2 teaspoons paprika

1 teaspoon onion powder

½ teaspoon garlic powder

¼ teaspoon ground cloves

¼ teaspoon ground red pepper

In a medium saucepan add the ketchup, tomato paste, brown sugar, vinegar, Worcestershire, dry mustard, salt, paprika, onion powder, garlic powder, ground cloves, and ground red pepper and heat over medium heat, stirring frequently, for 15 minutes. Be sure that all the dry ingredients are fully incorporated into the sauce and that the tomato paste has no chunks left. Remove from the heat and allow to cool or serve warm over pulled pork. Store in a sealed bottle or jar in refrigerator for up to a month.

≫ MAKES 4 CUPS.

ALABAMA WHITE SAUCE

Alabama serves both red and white sauces with its barbecue, but white sauce
is even more popular with smoked chicken and turkey. Many northern Alabama
restaurants will serve their secret white sauce as a condiment for french fries, like
a Southern version of Europeans dunking their *pommes frites* in mayonnaise.

In a food processor or blender place the mayonnaise,
black pepper, salt, cayenne pepper, lemon juice, cider
vinegar, horseradish, and sugar. Blend (in batches if
necessary) until the mixture is smooth. Store in an
airtight container in the refrigerator for up to 3 months.

≫ MAKES 4 CUPS.

3 cups mayonnaise

3 tablespoons freshly ground black
pepper

3 tablespoons salt

½ tablespoon cayenne pepper

½ cup lemon juice

½ cup cider vinegar

1 tablespoon prepared horseradish

1 teaspoon sugar

EASTERN NORTH CAROLINA SAUCE

The virtual dividing line between the two major barbecue regions of North Carolina is Interstate 95, which bisects the state from north to south. Barbecue east of I-95 is traditionally prepared whole hog style, cooked over oak, hickory, or pecan wood. Long, slow cooks of massive pieces of meat necessitate an acidic sauce to help break down the muscles of the hog, so eastern North Carolina barbecue sauce is a red pepper flake, black pepper, and vinegar mixture that has its roots in the cooking by African slaves who used the sauce to mop the pig as it roasted in a pit. The mop helped keep the meat from drying out and added a wonderful peppery flavor to the pork.

3 cups white vinegar
1 cup cider vinegar
½ cup crushed red pepper flakes
⅓ cup sugar
1 tablespoon kosher salt

In a large bowl whisk the white vinegar, cider vinegar, red pepper flakes, sugar, and salt together until thoroughly mixed. Pour the mixture into a saucepan and simmer over medium heat for 10 minutes. Remove from heat, allow to cool to room temperature, and return to the bowl. Cover the bowl with plastic wrap and allow to stand at room temperature for 4 hours until flavors have combined.

The sauce can be stored in the refrigerator with the pepper flakes included for up to a month, but it will continue to get even hotter over time. You can also strain the sauce through a fine sieve to remove the pepper flakes and create a clearer sauce.

This pepper sauce is of course great with smoked pulled pork but also adds a nice kick to bitter greens like mustard or turnip greens.

≫ MAKES 4 CUPS.

LEXINGTON DIP (PIEDMONT BARBECUE SAUCE)

West of I-95 is the Piedmont region, epitomized by the barbecue mecca around Lexington, North Carolina. Lexington Dip is similar to the eastern pepper sauces of the state, but tomato sauce, tomato paste, or ketchup is added to thicken the sauce and soften the bite of the vinegar. Smoked pork butts and shoulders are more popular than whole hog cooking in the western region of North Carolina, and Lexington Dip is an excellent addition to any shoulder sandwich.

2 cups white vinegar

1 cup cider vinegar

1 cup ketchup

1 tablespoon hot sauce

½ cup firmly packed light brown sugar

1 tablespoon salt

1 tablespoon crushed red pepper flakes

1 tablespoon black pepper

Whisk together the white vinegar, cider vinegar, ketchup, hot sauce, brown sugar, salt, red pepper flakes, and black pepper in a large bowl. Cover the bowl with plastic wrap or foil and allow to steep overnight in the refrigerator. Use as a mop on pork while cooking, brush on top of meat after cooking, or serve on the side with smoked meat. This sauce will last 6 to 8 weeks in an airtight container if refrigerated.

>> MAKES 4 CUPS.

TEXAS BARBECUE MOP/DIP

Barbecue in Texas usually revolves around beef, and instead of using complex sweet and savory rubs, most Texans believe in simply seasoning with salt and pepper. However, Texas barbecue sauces can work well with beef ribs, brisket, sausages, or pork. Sauces that are specifically formulated for lean beef briskets are usually a little richer than typical barbecue sauces in order to better complement the bold flavors of smoked beef.

2 teaspoons chili powder

1 teaspoon cumin

¾ tablespoon smoked paprika

2 teaspoons black pepper

1 tablespoon butter

1 large onion, finely chopped

2 cloves garlic, minced

1 green bell pepper, chopped

1 cup lager beer

½ cup ketchup

½ cup cider vinegar

2 tablespoons Worcestershire sauce

2 tablespoons brown sugar

1 tablespoon hot sauce

2 cups chicken stock

In a small bowl mix the chili powder, cumin, paprika, and black pepper with a fork. Melt the butter in a small saucepan over medium heat. Add the onions and cook for 5 minutes until they turn translucent. Add the garlic, green pepper, and the chili powder mixture to the onions and cook 3 to 4 minutes until the garlic becomes aromatic. Add the beer, ketchup, cider vinegar, Worcestershire, brown sugar, hot sauce, and chicken stock and stir until blended. Simmer for 20 minutes over medium-low heat. If you prefer a smooth sauce, allow the mixture to cool and puree in a blender for 30 seconds. Store in an airtight container for up to a month in the refrigerator.

≫ MAKES A LITTLE OVER 4 CUPS.

TEXAS BRISKET SAUCE

....

¼ cup (½ stick) butter
1 large sweet onion, chopped
4 cloves garlic, minced
1 cup tomato sauce
1 cup ketchup
1 cup cider vinegar
¾ cup firmly packed brown sugar
1 cup apple juice
3 tablespoons Worcestershire sauce

3 tablespoons lemon juice
1 tablespoon honey
1 tablespoon paprika
1 tablespoon dry mustard
1 tablespoon chili powder
1 tablespoon black pepper
1 teaspoon garlic powder
1 teaspoon ground allspice

Melt the butter in a saucepan over medium heat and add the onions. Sauté the onions for 5 minutes until translucent and then add the garlic. Sauté the garlic for 2 minutes and then add the tomato sauce, ketchup, cider vinegar, brown sugar, apple juice, Worcestershire, lemon juice, honey, paprika, dry mustard, chili powder, black pepper, garlic powder, and allspice. Mix well and raise heat to medium-high until a gentle boil is achieved. Reduce heat to low and simmer for 15 to 20 minutes until the sauce thickens. Apply to brisket (or even ribs) as a mop while cooking. Store covered in refrigerator for 2 to 4 weeks.

» MAKES A LITTLE OVER 4 CUPS.

TENNESSEE WHISKEY SAUCE

....

2 tablespoons vegetable oil
½ cup onion, minced
1 cup Tennessee whiskey or Kentucky bourbon (if you must)
1¼ cups ketchup

½ cup dark molasses
1 cup cider vinegar
2 tablespoons hot sauce
1 tablespoon Worcestershire sauce

In a medium saucepan heat the oil over medium heat. Add the onions and cook for 5 minutes until the onions begin to turn translucent. Add the whiskey to the pan and deglaze the pan by scraping the sides of the pan with a spoon to incorporate the onion into the sauce. Whisk in the ketchup, molasses, cider vinegar, hot sauce, and Worcestershire and bring the mixture to a boil. Reduce the heat to low and allow the sauce to simmer uncovered for 30 minutes until it reduces by a third. It is important that you allow the sauce to thicken as the whiskey cooks off. Store up to a month in the refrigerator in a sealed container.

» MAKES 4 CUPS.

MEMPHIS BARBECUE SAUCE

While Memphis dominates the Tennessee barbecue scene, there are many different styles of sauce and cooking across the state. Memphis concentrates on ribs and pulled or chopped pork, but there are still pockets of whole hog cooking remaining in other small west Tennessee towns like Lexington and Henderson. Since Tennessee is such a long state from west to east, barbecue styles shift and overlap depending on the influences of the eight adjoining states. In southern middle Tennessee, you might encounter Alabama white sauce on the table of your favorite barbecue restaurant, but by the time you reach Johnson City in the east, you'd think you were eating in the Piedmont of North Carolina.

2 tablespoons vegetable oil
1 medium onion, chopped
2 cloves garlic, minced
2 cups ketchup
1 cup water
¼ cup firmly packed light brown sugar
2 tablespoons Worcestershire sauce
½ cup cider vinegar
3 tablespoons prepared mustard
2 tablespoons molasses
2 tablespoons lemon juice
1 teaspoon onion powder
½ teaspoon celery salt

In a medium saucepan heat the vegetable oil over medium heat. Add the onions and sauté for 5 minutes until they begin to turn translucent. Add the garlic and cook for 2 additional minutes. Add the ketchup, water, brown sugar, Worcestershire, cider vinegar, mustard, molasses, lemon juice, onion powder, and celery salt and heat until boiling, stirring frequently. Once the sauce reaches a boil, lower the heat to medium-low and simmer for 20 minutes until the onions are tender. Remove from the heat and run sauce through a strainer to remove any solids. Store refrigerated in an airtight container for up to a month.

≫ MAKES 4 CUPS.

KENTUCKY MOP/DIP

Kentucky is probably underappreciated for its excellent barbecue. No other state smokes as many different cuts of meat as the Bluegrass State, where you're liable to find pork, beef, chicken, lamb, mutton, and even goat on the menus of tiny little barbecue shacks spread across the state.

In a large saucepan mix the white vinegar, water, beer, Worcestershire, black pepper, salt, garlic powder, cayenne pepper, brown sugar, and hot sauce and simmer over low heat for 15 minutes.

This mop is designed for mutton, but also works great with pork or brisket. Set aside a cup to serve as a dip or sauce after cooking and use the remainder to mop your meat with a brush every hour or so during the smoking process.

>> MAKES 4 CUPS.

1 ½ cups white vinegar

1 ¼ cups water

1 cup beer (or beef stock)

½ cup Worcestershire sauce

3 tablespoons black pepper

1 tablespoon salt

1 tablespoon garlic powder

1 teaspoon cayenne pepper

1 ½ tablespoons light brown sugar

1 teaspoon hot sauce

LOUISIANA CAJUN BARBECUE SAUCE

They like their barbecue spicy in Louisiana, and the ready availability of outstanding local hot sauces makes it easy to fire up any sauce recipe. A different sort of barbecue sauce is reserved for the wonderfully messy and buttery BBQ shrimp dishes made famous by restaurants like Mr. B's Bistro and Pascal's Manale. Spiked with pepper and Worcestershire, it ain't pig, but it sure is tasty.

2 cups ketchup

1 ½ cups water

½ cup Worcestershire sauce

1 cup chopped red onion

½ cup firmly packed light brown sugar

1 tablespoon paprika

1 ½ tablespoons red wine vinegar

2 tablespoons Creole mustard

1 ½ teaspoons cayenne pepper

½ teaspoon black pepper

1 teaspoon hot sauce

In a large saucepan combine the ketchup, water, Worcestershire, red onions, brown sugar, paprika, red wine vinegar, Creole mustard, cayenne pepper, black pepper, and hot sauce over medium heat. Heat until boiling, stirring frequently. Lower the heat to low and simmer uncovered for 1 hour until the sauce thickens and reduces to about 4 cups. Allow to cool and store up to 1 month in a sealed container in the refrigerator. This sauce is a nice change of pace on chicken wings instead of your regular Buffalo sauce.

≫ MAKES 4 CUPS.

KANSAS CITY RIB SAUCE

While some may debate whether Missouri is really part of the South, there's no question that they make some serious ribs in the Show Me State. The primary difference in style between St. Louis and Kansas City-style ribs is in the cut of the meat, with St. Louis ribs squared off by the removal of the rib tips. Many competitive barbecue cookers prefer this tidy presentation, but make sure to save those tips to grill up separately. They make for an outstanding sandwich!

Sauce-wise, Kansas City pit masters prefer a thick, sweet sauce that has become the standard across the country thanks to the popularity of KC Masterpiece Sauce, available in grocery stores everywhere.

Melt the butter in a saucepan over medium heat. Add the garlic and sauté for 2 minutes until aromatic. Be careful not to let the garlic burn. Whisk in the ketchup, water, cider vinegar, brown sugar, olive oil, honey, paprika, chili powder, and cayenne pepper and simmer for 20 minutes until the sauce thickens.

Since this sauce contains quite a bit of sugar, do not apply to ribs until the final 30 minutes of cooking, or even after cooking, to avoid over-caramelizing. You can also use it as a finishing sauce after the cooking process is completed.

≫ MAKES 4 CUPS.

2 tablespoons butter

4 cloves garlic, minced

2 cups ketchup

½ cup water

½ cup cider vinegar

½ cup firmly packed dark brown sugar

¼ cup olive oil

¼ cup honey

3 tablespoons smoked paprika

2 tablespoons chili powder

½ tablespoon cayenne pepper

ST. LOUIS RIB SAUCE

St. Louis rib sauce is generally a little thinner and tangier than its neighbor on the western end of the state.

3 cups ketchup

¾ cup water

¾ cup cider vinegar

½ cup firmly packed light brown sugar

¼ cup prepared mustard

2 tablespoons minced onion

2 tablespoons granulated garlic

1 teaspoon cayenne pepper

1 teaspoon celery seeds

1 teaspoon smoked paprika

In a large saucepan whisk the ketchup, water, cider vinegar, brown sugar, mustard, minced onion, granulated garlic, cayenne pepper, celery seeds, and paprika over low heat. Do not allow the sauce to come to a boil so that it does not thicken up. Heat through for 10 to 15 minutes, stirring frequently. Remove the sauce from the heat and allow to cool. Store refrigerated in an airtight container for up to a month.

≫ MAKES A LITTLE OVER 4 CUPS.

Rubs

While most people associate dry rubs with ribs, these recipes can contribute nuances of flavors and help hold in the moisture to just about any cut of pork. Try a rub on a grilled pork chop to add a nice crispy crust. Cover a pork shoulder with a healthy helping of spice mix to create a lovely bark that will add a little crunch to your pulled pork. If you give guests a choice of their meat, you'll notice that most of them grab the pieces of the sweet outside meat.

Slices of tenderloin benefit from the herbs and spices of a good rub, especially one that includes a little zing of citrus from some lemon rind or a healthy addition of lemon pepper. The innate juiciness of a well-prepared tenderloin can mix with the spices of the crust to create a delicious jus for flavoring each bite of loin.

Rubs are also easy to mix up and even easier to use, so they are a great addition to your kitchen arsenal. Toss the ingredients in a large bowl, mix them up with a fork until well blended, and store them in an airtight container or plastic freezer bag, and they'll keep for 2 to 3 months in a cool, dark storage place or up to 6 months in the freezer.

It's helpful to buy a large shaker like the kind that pizza restaurants use for Parmesan cheese or red pepper flakes to help you liberally apply your rub to whatever meat you want to experiment with. Don't store your rub in the shaker, though, or the spices will lose some of the intensity of their flavors over time.

The base ingredients of most rubs are salt and sugar, but there are lots of variations that you can play with as you design your own signature recipe. Salt can be fine-grained or coarse like kosher salt. Substitute seasoned salts for a portion of the recipe to add additional nuances like garlic salt, onion salt, or celery salt. Be careful not to use too much of these seasoned options since their flavors can overpower the rest of the mix.

Pork responds especially well to rubs that have a higher percentage of sugar, so either white refined sugar, unrefined turbinado sugar, or light or dark brown sugar can contribute unique characteristics to a rub recipe.

Beyond the bases of salt and sugar, you'll probably want some pepper in the mix to add some sharper flavors to your rub. Play around with the ratios of white, black, cayenne, and chili peppers in your rub, and there's nothing wrong with tasting your recipe as you go along. Other spices that are key elements of many rub recipes are chili powder, cumin, and paprika, either smoked or unsmoked. Each contributes unique nutty and smoky characteristics to the rub, and ultimately your pork.

Finally, experiment with more exotic spices like coriander, garlic or onion powder, dry mustard, thyme, ginger, cloves, or allspice to personalize your own recipe. Feel free to use any of the following recipes or add and subtract your own ingredients at will.

BASIC RIB RUB

This basic rub works well on ribs, but also can coat the outside of a pork shoulder before smoking. Apply the rub liberally to both sides of a rack of ribs at least 2 hours before cooking and wrap the ribs in plastic wrap to allow the flavors to penetrate the meat. Some pit masters coat their ribs with mustard before shaking on the rub to help the spices stick to the surface of the ribs. Don't worry about the mustard flavoring your meat. At most it will contribute just a slight bit of tanginess since it will cook off over the course of the smoking process.

⅓ cup smoked paprika
¼ cup sugar
2 tablespoons black pepper
2 tablespoons sea salt
1 tablespoon dry mustard
2 teaspoons cayenne pepper
1 teaspoon white pepper
1 ½ teaspoons cumin
1 ½ teaspoons ground thyme

In a small bowl add the paprika, sugar, black pepper, salt, dry mustard, cayenne pepper, white pepper, cumin, and ground thyme and mix thoroughly with a fork or small whisk. Store in a zippered plastic bag or an airtight container in a cool, dry place.

» MAKES ABOUT ¾ CUP, ENOUGH FOR 2 RACKS OF RIBS.

KANSAS CITY RUB

They definitely know their ribs in KC, and this rub has a very nice sweet and heat flavor profile. As with just about any rub, you should save a few tablespoons to add to your barbecue sauce to help the flavors of the rub and the sauce better complement each other.

In a small bowl add the sugar, paprika, black pepper, salt, chili powder, garlic powder, onion powder, dry mustard, and cayenne pepper and mix thoroughly with a fork or small whisk. Store in a zippered plastic bag or an airtight container in a cool, dry place.

≫ MAKES 1 ¾ CUPS, ENOUGH FOR 4 RACKS.

1 cup firmly packed brown sugar

½ cup paprika

2 tablespoons freshly ground black pepper

2 tablespoons kosher salt

2 tablespoons chili powder

2 tablespoons garlic powder

2 tablespoons onion powder

1 tablespoon dry mustard

1 tablespoon cayenne pepper

CAROLINA PORK SHOULDER RUB

Carolina is not especially famous for ribs, but this recipe is excellent for coating a pork shoulder. Use a shaker to liberally cover the outside of the entire shoulder and allow to rest in a disposable aluminum pan for at least an hour before cooking. It's also great as a seasoning for smoked or fried chicken wings or even sprinkled over popcorn for a snack.

¼ cup paprika

3 tablespoons kosher salt

3 tablespoons sugar

2 tablespoons ground cumin

2 tablespoons freshly ground black pepper

1 ½ tablespoons brown sugar

1 tablespoon chili powder

1 tablespoon cayenne pepper

1 tablespoon garlic powder

In a small bowl add the paprika, salt, sugar, cumin, black pepper, brown sugar, chili powder, cayenne pepper, and garlic powder and mix thoroughly with a fork or small whisk. Store in a zippered plastic bag or an airtight container in a cool, dry place.

≫ MAKES 1 CUP, ENOUGH FOR A 10- TO 12-POUND SHOULDER.

MEMPHIS RUB

In Memphis, it's traditional to serve ribs dry and without sauce, or perhaps with the sauce on the side if you prefer wet ribs. Without sauce to contribute extra flavors, the ingredients of a Memphis rub benefit from a heavier hand with bolder spices like paprika and chili powder.

In a small bowl add the paprika, salt, chili powder, onion powder, black pepper, cayenne pepper, turmeric, and nutmeg and mix thoroughly with a fork or small whisk. Store in a zippered plastic bag or an airtight container in a cool, dry place.

>> MAKES 1 CUP, ENOUGH FOR 2 RACKS OF RIBS.

½ cup paprika

¼ cup salt

4 tablespoons chili powder

2 tablespoons onion powder

2 tablespoons ground black pepper

2 tablespoons cayenne pepper

1 teaspoon turmeric

¼ teaspoon ground nutmeg

MEMPHIS FINISHING RUB

Many traditionalist Memphis pit masters prefer to cook their ribs with no rub at all, utilizing just a sprinkle of 3 tablespoons of kosher salt and 2 tablespoons of coarse black pepper per full rack of ribs while they are on the grill or the smoker. The flavor comes after the ribs emerge from the heat in the form of a bold finishing rub. Try a rack or two of ribs using this method for a taste of the Bluff City.

½ cup paprika

¼ cup garlic powder

¼ cup chili powder

¼ cup black pepper

¼ cup kosher salt

2 tablespoons unrefined turbinado sugar

2 tablespoons whole mustard seeds

2 tablespoons crushed celery seeds

2 tablespoons dried oregano

1 tablespoon dried thyme

1 teaspoon ground coriander

1 teaspoon ground allspice

1 teaspoon cumin

In a small bowl add the paprika, garlic powder, chili powder, black pepper, salt, turbinado sugar, mustard seeds, celery seeds, oregano, thyme, coriander, allspice, and cumin and mix thoroughly with a fork or small whisk. Store in a zippered plastic bag or an airtight container in a cool, dry place.

≫ MAKES 1 ¾ CUPS, ENOUGH FOR 4 RACKS.

TEXAS BRISKET RUB

While brisket isn't pork, there comes a time in every home barbecuer's life when he or she wants to try cooking a Texas-style brisket. A notoriously difficult piece of meat to trim and cook well, brisket definitely benefits from a good spice rub, though purists will say that only salt and pepper should be used to season a properly trimmed piece of beef. It's also fine for a spicy version of smoked butt or shoulder.

In a small bowl add the paprika, brown sugar, garlic powder, onion powder, oregano, salt, black pepper, cayenne pepper, cumin, and chili powder and mix thoroughly with a fork or small whisk. Store in a zippered plastic bag or an airtight container in a cool, dry place.

≫ MAKES 1 CUP, ENOUGH FOR A 6- TO 7-POUND BRISKET OR
   PORK BUTT.

½ cup paprika

⅓ cup firmly packed brown sugar

3 tablespoons garlic powder

3 tablespoons onion powder

2 tablespoons dried oregano

2 tablespoons salt

2 tablespoons ground black pepper

1 tablespoon cayenne pepper

2 teaspoons ground cumin

⅓ teaspoon chili powder

Brines

Brines are an important trick to help keep larger cuts of pork juicy during the hours that it takes to bring a tenderloin or shoulder up to temperature slowly. During the 12 to 14 hours that it can take to smoke a large pork shoulder, the goal is to bring the internal temperature up to about 190 degrees as slowly as possible. When the thermometer reaches 175 to 180 degrees, you might see the increase in temperature begin to slow down as the collagen that holds the fibers of muscle together starts to break down.

This process provides for two wonderful side effects. Once the collagen boils out, the individual fibers release and allow you to pull the meat apart with your fingers or two large forks positioned with the tines facing out. Second, the rendering collagen distributes itself throughout the meat to impart a lovely creamy texture to the pulled pork. Since pork is best when it takes a long time to cook, it's crucial to do whatever you can to help retain the juices in the meat in the relatively low humidity environment of a smoker. Brines are a great way to accomplish this.

Whether you make up a batch of brine in advance and allow the meat to soak covered in the liquid overnight in a pan or use a special syringe to inject the brine directly into the meat, nothing improves the juiciness of a pork dish like brining.

The basic components of a brine are water and salt, which through a fairly complex scientific process draw liquid through the meat as individual cells of the meat fibers seek to equalize the salinity inside and outside the outer membranes of each cell. The simple explanation is that the cells will actually pump water from outside to inside and can increase the weight and moisture content of a piece of meat by as much as 15 percent during an overnight soak.

An easy rule of thumb for any brine is 1 cup of salt to 1 gallon of water. As an aside, any of these brines will also be beneficial to chicken or turkey, two other meats that are notorious for drying out in the oven or smoker. You can substitute fruit juices like apple or pineapple for all or part of the liquid content of a brine for a little extra flavor, and brines made with juice are even better as a mop during the cooking process to keep the meat from drying out on the grill or in the smoker.

Bring all the ingredients of any of these brines to a boil in a saucepan and be sure to allow it to cool completely in the refrigerator for at least an hour before adding the meat or injecting so as to avoid raising the temperature of the meat to unsafe levels.

Many people add other ingredients like sugar, pepper, spices, and vinegar for nuanced flavor profiles, but it's important to be sure to thoroughly rinse and pat dry the meat before cooking, since the salt of the brine is too intense for most dishes. Any amount of brining will improve a piece of pork, but between 8 to 24 hours is ideal to ensure the best effect without actually starting to break down the fibers of the pork, which can leave it mushy.

PORK TENDERLOIN BRINE

....

½ gallon of water, divided
½ cup kosher salt
½ cup sugar

½ cup whole black peppercorns
8 cloves garlic, crushed
2 bay leafs

Bring 4 cups of water in a large saucepan or pot to a boil. Add the salt and sugar and stir until dissolved. Add the remaining 4 cups of water and mix in the peppercorns, garlic, and bay leaves. Remove from the heat and allow the brine to cool to room temperature, and then move to the refrigerator for at least an hour. Brine the tenderloin for 8 to 24 hours refrigerated, either in a gallon plastic freezer bag with excess air removed or in a sealed plastic tub with the loin completely covered by the brine.

>> MAKES ENOUGH BRINE FOR A 5- TO 6-POUND PORK LOIN.

PORK CHOP BRINE

....

½ cup kosher salt
½ cup sugar
4 cups boiling water
2 cups apple juice

2 cups cider vinegar
1 tablespoon black pepper
1 teaspoon crushed red pepper flakes

Dissolve the salt and sugar in the 4 cups of boiling water in a large saucepan over medium-high heat, stirring constantly. Add the apple juice, cider vinegar, black pepper, and red pepper flakes and whisk to dissolve. Lower the heat to low and simmer for 5 minutes, then remove from the heat. Allow to cool to room temperature in the pot and then transfer to refrigerator until temperature reaches 40 degrees. Add the pork chops to the bowl of brine and place a small plate on top if necessary to weigh down and completely submerge the chops. Cover the bowl with aluminum foil or plastic wrap and allow chops to steep in the brine overnight or for at least 8 hours before removing, rinsing, and patting dry with a paper towel before cooking. Brined pork will cook slightly faster than unbrined meat, so pay close attention to internal temperatures and cooking times.

>> MAKES ½ GALLON, ENOUGH FOR 6- TO 8 THICK PORK CHOPS.

PORK SHOULDER BRINE

2 cups water
¼ cup kosher salt

¼ cup firmly packed dark brown sugar
1 ½ cups pineapple juice

In a saucepan over medium heat, bring the water to a boil. Dissolve the salt and brown sugar in the boiling water, stirring constantly. Remove from heat and whisk in the pineapple juice. Allow to cool to room temperature. Place a pork shoulder in a large turkey roasting bag and add the brine over the top. Carefully squeeze out any excess air and seal up the bag. Just in case of leakage, place the bag in a large disposable foil pan and allow shoulder to brine overnight in the refrigerator or in a cooler covered with ice to keep the pork at a safe temperature. Pour out the brine, rinse the pork shoulder completely, and pat dry before applying spice rub.

>> MAKES 4 CUPS, ENOUGH FOR AN 8- TO 10-POUND PORK SHOULDER.

PORK SHOULDER INJECTION

1 cup apple juice
1 cup chicken stock
½ cup cider vinegar
½ cup Worcestershire sauce
2 tablespoons melted butter

2 tablespoons finely ground salt
2 tablespoons barbecue rub, optional (check out the recipe for the Carolina Pork Shoulder Rub on page 54)

Heat the apple juice, chicken stock, cider vinegar, Worcestershire, butter, salt, and rub in a medium saucepan over medium-low heat, stirring until the salt is completely dissolved. Move the ingredients to a tall bowl and allow to cool completely in the refrigerator. Place a pork shoulder in a large tall-sided pan like an aluminum turkey roaster pan. Using a syringe, inject the pork shoulder all over both sides, slowly pulling the needle out and moving it around as you inject to distribute the brine. Be careful since the brine can squirt out of previous injection points, making it messy. Wear an apron! After injecting, cover the shoulder in the pan with foil and move to the refrigerator or a cooler full of ice for 8 to 12 hours before cooking. Since this brine isn't nearly as salty as others, there is no need to rinse the shoulder, but do dry it off with paper towels before applying the rub.

>> MAKES 3 CUPS, ENOUGH FOR ONE 10- TO 12-POUND PORK SHOULDER.

PORK STOCK

It's acceptable to substitute chicken or beef stock in recipes that call for pork stock or ham stock, but a real broth made from roasted pig bones can add a depth of flavor that store-bought just can't match. In a pinch, you can also find ham base in the bouillon section of many grocery stores or online that can also serve as a decent substitute for pork stock. But if you've got some leftover bones and an afternoon to kill, nothing will make your kitchen smell better than an aromatic pot of pork stock simmering on the stove.

3 pounds pork side ribs, sawed into 2- to 3-inch sections

1 (6-ounce) can tomato paste

1 cup red wine

½ gallon water

¼ teaspoon black peppercorns

1 cup chopped onions

½ cup chopped carrots

½ cup chopped celery

6 large garlic cloves, halved

½ tablespoon kosher salt

Preheat the oven to 450 degrees.

Place the bones in a large, shallow roasting pan. Using a brush, lightly coat both sides of the bones with the tomato paste. Roast the ribs for 45 minutes and then remove from the oven. Flip the ribs with tongs and return to the oven for 30 more minutes until they are browned but not burned. Remove the ribs from the roasting pan and move to a large pot. Pour off any excess fat from the roasting pan and place the pan over a stovetop burner on high heat. Add the red wine and deglaze the pan, scraping off any brown bits of meat that stick to the pan with a wooden spoon. Pour the wine and pork bits into the pot and add water to completely cover the ribs.

Add the peppercorns, onions, carrots, celery, garlic, and salt to the pot and bring to a simmer over medium-high heat for 15 minutes. Use a spoon to skim off any foam that accumulates on the surface of the broth. Turn the heat to low and simmer gently for 4 hours. Remove the pot from the heat and allow to rest on an unheated burner for 90 minutes. Use a ladle to scoop out and discard any fat that accumulates on top of the broth after cooling. Remove the bones from the stock with tongs and strain the broth through a fine strainer into a large bowl.

Pork stock may be kept in the refrigerator for up to 3 days or frozen in smaller portions for future use for up to 6 months.

» MAKES 8 CUPS.

PART 2

··

RESTAURANT
PROFILES

American Grocery Restaurant

Brookville Restaurant

Brother Juniper's

The Cask and Larder

Central BBQ

Chef and the Farmer

Chef's Market Cafe

City Grocery

Comfort

Cotton Creative Southern Cuisine

Crescent Pie and Sausage Company

Delta Bistro

Doc Crow's Southern Smokehouse and Raw Bar

Dudley's on Short

Edley's Bar-B-Que

Empire State South

Felicia Suzanne's

FIG

Fox Brothers Bar-B-Que

The Green Room

Halcyon, Flavors from the Earth

Hammerheads

High Cotton

IvyWild

Louis's at Sanford's

The MacIntosh

Mama J's Kitchen

Memphis Barbecue Company

Neely's Sandwich Shop

NoFo @ the Pig

Nose Dive

Old Hickory Bar-B-Que

Parlor Market

Pasture

Poole's Downtown Diner

Purple Parrot Cafe

The Ravenous Pig

Restaurant Eugene

Ruffino's

Ruka's Table

The Shed BBQ and Blues Joint

Slightly North of Broad

Soby's New South Cuisine

Something Different

South on Main

Southern Soul Barbecue

St. John's Restaurant

Stella's Kentucky Deli

Swine Southern Table and Bar

Table 100

Tanglewood Ordinary Country Restaurant

Toups' Meatery

AMERICAN GROCERY RESTAURANT

732 South Main Street
Greenville, SC 29601
(864) 232-7665
www.americangr.com

Joe Clarke, the chef/owner of American Grocery Restaurant in Greenville's West End, learned how to cook from his grandmother while visiting her farm in the hills of upstate South Carolina. She introduced him to the ingredients of his native state that would become integral in the cuisine at his own restaurant. Clarke believes that the best food comes from chefs who understand where their products come from and who strive to share the story of the region and the farmers who work the fields.

At American Grocery, Clarke has created an intimate classroom to educate diners about the bounty of South Carolina produce. An early advocate of the farm-to-table movement, the chef only allows two canned items in his kitchen, tomato paste and whole peeled tomatoes, to use as concentrated flavoring agents. Everything else comes through the door fresh.

The creativity of the menu starts at the bar, where the cocktail list includes American Grocery's signature Pig on the Porch made with bacon-infused bourbon. Another striking drink that also features a degree of smokiness is The Smoky Blue. This cocktail contains actual hickory smoke that is added to what is basically a martini, and even uses smoked blue cheese–stuffed olives to take it up another notch.

Two of the best items on the menu are small plates listed in the "For the Table" section. A remarkable Fried Deviled Egg is crispy and golden out of the fryer, but still creamy on the inside. If the inventor of the Scotch egg had known about this, he might have flipped his kilt. An order of Herbed Buttermilk Biscuits with bacon butter and peach chutney is an excellent accompaniment to the egg, or really to just about any dish on the menu.

Addictive Honey-Sriracha Fried Chicken Skins would also be excellent for sharing if you have the self-control not to eat them all yourself, so you might need two orders. The charcuterie menu features patés, mousses, and sausages made from local pork, rabbit, and beef accompanied with house-made pickles, mustards, and breads.

The rotating list of entrées at American Grocery focuses more on local meats and vegetables, including a Chef's Choice of Seasonal Local Vegetables that might sound mundane, but is actually a highlight. Meat eaters will probably prefer the Greenbrier Farms Pork Belly with local chanterelles, arugula, and tangy horseradish gnocchi or even the veal sweetbreads topped with a sunny-side egg and bacon brown butter. While sweetbreads might be a little adventurous for some, when they are cooked by a master like Clarke, they reward the bravery of intrepid diners. Put yourself in his able hands for a creative tour of South Carolina's best.

SPECIALTIES: Fried Deviled Egg, Pork Belly, Crazy Cocktails

INSIDER TIP: Ask for a table by the window for some excellent people watching as the citizens of Greenville amble along Main Street.

Find recipes from this restaurant on pages 129 and 183.

BROOKVILLE RESTAURANT

225 West Main Street
Charlottesville, VA 22902
(434) 202-2791
www.brookvillerestaurant.com

If you're not a fan of pork and bacon, then don't even bother walking up the steps to the Brookville Restaurant, because Chef Harrison Keevil is absolutely obsessed with the pig. At Brookville, he has created a quirky, casual atmosphere where others that share his porky predilection can enjoy a menu filled with creative dishes that also feature locally sourced ingredients. He is proud of the fact that over 90 percent of his ingredients come from within one hundred miles of Charlottesville, and a chalkboard map of Virginia hanging on the exposed brick walls of the cozy restaurant point out the locations of the contributing farms.

Because of this commitment to fresh local produce, the menu changes almost daily, but diners can always expect a selection of intriguing pork dishes served with great vegetable preparations. The menu kicks off with a selection of "Munchies," small plates that can be starters or combined as part of a tasting menu. Highlights that periodically appear are Virginia Ham Fritters and an exotic dish of Buffalo Pig Tails served with micro greens and ranch dressing.

The showcase dish at Brookville isn't always on the menu, but can be ordered by request if you're in the know. The Brookville Burger is a half-pound of ground hanger steak, sirloin, and bacon cooked with caramelized onions and served on a house-made bun with the option of a fried egg and more bacon on top. You'll want to take them up on the bacon option, and consider cutting that bad boy in half for easier handling.

Even though Charlottesville's University of Virginia is in the Atlantic Coast Conference, Brookville serves an excellent SEC Sandwich, although in this case it stands for Surry Sausage and fried Eggs served on a Ciabatta bun. It's enough to make you change your conference allegiance.

The pig is also featured in an excellent Pig Ear Salad made with frisée lettuce, yet another fried egg, and hot sauce to give it some punch. Even Italian food gets a piggy Southern twist with Belly, Bacon, and Brisket Meatballs covered in marinara sauce and served over polenta. Oh heck, just call them grits.

SPECIALTIES: Brookville Burger, Pig Ear Salad

INSIDER TIP: Brookville offers a to-go and catering menu called "Brookville Brings It." In addition to all sorts of delicious meats, diners can select from a vast rotating selection of seasonal vegetables, and every meal comes with one of Brookville's famous Bacon Double Chocolate Cookies for dessert.

Find recipes from this restaurant on pages 216 and 278.

BROTHER JUNIPER'S

3519 Walker Avenue
Memphis, TN 38111
(901) 324-0144
www.brotherjunipers.com

Brother Juniper's serves the best breakfast in Memphis. You can believe it because it says so right there on the sign hanging over the front door. The original Brother Juniper was the cook for St. Francis of Assisi, and he created simple food for the brotherhood of monks. In that tradition, the chefs at Brother Juniper's of Memphis use fresh ingredients to make hearty but healthy breakfasts and artisan baked goods that have earned them a national reputation.

Located in the university area of Memphis, Brother Juniper's is still called by its former name, The College Inn, by many locals, so don't get confused if you hear that instead. While the menu does have many expected breakfast specials like two eggs any style or scrambles with different cheeses and meats mixed in, the creativity really starts to shine through when you look at Brother Juniper's omelet menu.

These omelets are made with three eggs apiece and served with your choice of grits on the side or on a bed of home fries. Biscuits or toast also come with each dish and are perfect for sampling Brother Juniper's fresh spreadable fruits. With no added sugar, these healthy spreads are like eating fresh blackberries, blueberries, raspberries, strawberries, or peaches right out of a jar.

The traditional omelet options include a Denver Omelet and a Mexican Salsa Omelet. At Brother Juniper's, though, diners can try egg creations that are inspired by more exotic locales than just Colorado or Mexico. The Greek Omelet is stuffed with spicy gyro meat as well as feta and mozzarella cheese. Staying in the Peloponnese with the Spanakopita Omelet, the gyro meat in the Greek Omelet is replaced with fresh spinach, onions, and spices. Vegetarians will be pleased by the Tofu Vegi with pesto, spinach, roasted red peppers, and mushrooms or by Fahim's Special, a monster of an omelet with tofu, red and green bell peppers, green onions, tomatoes, portobello mushrooms, Kalamata olives, and a secret dressing.

Also unique at Brother Juniper's are their open-faced omelets. All the ingredients of these dishes are stacked on top of the egg and served with the same side options as the regular omelets. With no fear of overstuffing the omelet, the kitchen can really go crazy with these huge plates. The San Diegan lies upon a bed of sour cream and home fries and is topped with portobellos, tomatoes, bacon, green onions, feta, and Cheddar cheese. The Coastal Delight is served atop a thick smear of avocado chipotle spread and layered with ham, black beans, tomatoes, green onions, mozzarella, and Cheddar.

With creative, affordable morning meal options like these, it's easy to see how Brother Juniper's has earned its reputation for serving the best breakfast in Memphis. They certainly deserve to paint it on that sign.

SPECIALTIES: Mama's Lil's Special, The Fireman, San Diegan

INSIDER TIP: Brother Juniper's sells many of their fruit spreads and hot sauces to-go in a small shop.

Find a recipe from this restaurant on page 140.

RESTAURANT PROFILES

THE CASK AND LARDER

565 West Fairbanks Avenue
Winter Park, FL 32789
(321) 280-4200
www.caskandlarder.com

The name of this restaurant tells you what it is all about. As a self-styled "Southern Public House," the Cask portion of the name refers to the kegs of beer that have been served in the various taverns that occupied this location since the end of Prohibition. The current owners have built a brewpub on the premises so that they can serve the very freshest available craft beers.

Kids these days may not know what the heck a larder is, but some of us of a certain age remember storing meats and produce in the coolest room in the house. The dawn of modern refrigeration has rendered most larders unnecessary, and they've probably been converted to rec rooms with big screens in the basements of many refurbished houses.

At The Cask and Larder, they pay tribute to the old days when trips to the larder were a regular part of crafting any meal's menu. The kitchen is known for their cured meats, pickled vegetables, and preserved fruits that they employ in clever dishes that emphasize seasonal Southern sensibilities. A playful attitude is very apparent in some of their menu choices, to the benefit of hungry diners.

The very first item on the lunch menu is the Hillbilly Basket. The fryer works overtime to prepare this excellent appetizer with hush puppies, green tomatoes, garlic-dill pickles, and okra all emerging golden brown out of the oil to be served with a hot sauce aioli and savory scones. (Go ahead and call them biscuits if that makes you feel better.) For a more substantial starter, order up the Southern Picnic, a smorgasbord of deviled eggs, barbecued summer sausage, pickled vegetables, and olive loaf served with blue cheese, beer mustard, and ham butter for dipping. That's right . . . ham butter!

Other lunch highlights include a traditional New Orleans muffuletta, a unique clam and pork belly po' boy, and The Cask and Larder's homage to Nashville hot chicken, an infernally spicy bird covered with cayenne until it is dark crimson with pepper. Proceed with caution.

At dinner, the menu features more seafood thanks to the proximity of fresh product from the Gulf of Mexico and the Atlantic. Fear not, pork lover, for there is plenty for the avid carnivore to enjoy at the evening meal at The Cask and Larder. A snack known boldly as The Sandwich features smoked pork topped with salsa verde, pickled watermelon rind for some sweet snap, and a down-home collard green slaw.

Like a flight of wines showcasing single-vineyard grape varietals, The Cask and Larder offers an innovative country ham tasting, featuring cured meats from different Southern farms so that diners can taste the individual styles of each smokehouse. Other excellent entrées include imaginative dishes like Country Fried Venison and a hot short rib coated with the same paprika-cayenne glaze that torques up the Nashville chicken dish.

Even though the artificial fantasy lands of Disney World are just a half-hour away, everything at The Cask and Larder is as genuine as can be. It's the real deal.

SPECIALTIES: Ham Tasting, The Sandwich
INSIDER TIP: A sister restaurant, The Ravenous Pig, is just down the street. Their menu reads almost like an extension of The Cask and Larder's. You might want to try one spot for lunch and the other for dinner.

Find a recipe from this restaurant on page 205.

CENTRAL BBQ

2249 Central Avenue
Memphis, TN 38104
(901) 272-9377
www.cbqmemphis.com

In a town full of barbecue goodness, Central BBQ has rapidly earned a reputation as one of Memphis, Tennessee's favorite destinations. In fact, since opening their anchor location in the Cooper-Young neighborhood, there are now two other Central BBQ outposts in downtown and East Memphis, plus a food truck to spread the barbecue love all over town.

The primary Midtown location offers a fun and funky feel with a huge outdoor deck that is almost as big as the entire inside dining area. With blues and soul music pumping through the speakers, the patio at Central BBQ is a wonderful place to while away an evening enjoying some iced tea or a cold beer and some of the most fantastic smoked meats in town.

The menu isn't very long, but every item is a winner. It's hard to get past the appetizers when even a simple Sausage and Cheese Plate with pickles, pepperoncini peppers, honey mustard sauce, and crackers is worthy of a try. But then you'd miss out on Central BBQ's famous BBQ Nachos, a decadent platter of tortilla chips piled high with pulled pork topped with BBQ sauce, cheese sauce, shredded cheese, and jalapeños. The nachos are finished off with a light dusting of Central BBQ's seasoning mix.

An order of chicken wings is great as an appetizer or a meal, thanks to a wonderful smoky flavor and a crisp exterior from a quick trip through the deep fryer. These delicious wings are available dry (dusted with Central BBQ's hot rib rub), wet with hot wing sauce, or jerk-style with Caribbean dry seasoning. You can also order them naked and unseasoned, but really, what's the point of that?

Ribs are also served either wet or dry, so don't feel like you must follow the Memphis tradition of dry ribs. Although Central BBQ's dry ribs are excellent, with sweet notes of brown sugar and cumin and black, white, and cayenne pepper to add some heat, their version of wet ribs is worth the mess.

Diners can choose from four different barbecue sauces available for self-serve at Central BBQ: mild, hot, vinegar, or mustard, and any of them offer interesting nuances to their pulled pork sandwiches topped with shoulder meat that has enjoyed a fourteen-hour smoky repose before serving.

Other excellent smoked meat sandwiches offered include turkey, chicken, beef brisket, and spicy sausage. Vegetarians (and even some meat lovers) enjoy a novel Portobello Sandwich featuring a huge mushroom cap that has been marinated in balsamic vinegar, olive oil, and spices, then grilled and topped with smoked gouda cheese.

Like any great barbecue joint, Central BBQ serves a delicious banana pudding for dessert, so try your hardest to save room, unless it means missing out on a plate of those wings or nachos.

SPECIALTIES: Smoked Pork, Ribs, and Chicken Wings
INSIDER TIP: Diners who are in the know order their BBQ Nachos served on top of Central BBQ's homemade potato chips instead of tortilla chips.

Find a recipe from this restaurant on page 200.

CHEF AND THE FARMER

120 West Gordon Street
Kinston, NC 28501
(252) 208-2433
www.chefandthefarmer.com

Chef Vivian Howard was born in Deep Run, North Carolina, to a family of tobacco and hog farmers, so seasonal eating and the value of preserving vegetables to enjoy all year round is second nature to her. When she asked her husband, Ben Knight, to move from New York to Kinston, North Carolina, the biggest town near her native home, he needed a little persuading. Eventually, Ben fell in love with the people and pace of life of rural North Carolina, and the two decided to open their dream restaurant in a hundred-year-old mule stable across from the Lenoir County farmers' market.

The network of farmers in the market has become a crucial part of the philosophy at Chef and the Farmer, their farm-to-fork eatery. The modern, cozy dining room seats only about seventy patrons at a time, but the experience makes it easy to forget that you are in a small town in North Carolina's coastal plain. That is until you start to read the menu and recognize the names of so many area farms that provide the bounty of ingredients that the kitchen turns into amazing meals.

Knight works the front of the house while Howard runs the kitchen, and the team approach ensures that dinner service is as efficient as it is delicious. Breads are baked in-house, and those vegetables that are not used up at the peak of their freshness are preserved and put up to contribute their flavors to dishes in the off-season. During the summer, diners can expect explosive flavor combinations like peaches wrapped in Benton's country ham served with gingered goat cheese, balsamic honey, and spiced pecans.

Fall and winter offer richer dishes like Pork Shoulder Lasagna and Stewed Beef Cheeks to warm up the chilly nights. It does snow in North Carolina, you know! A wood-fired grill provides the palette for pizzas and flatbreads to show off even more local produce in yet another display of elevated comfort food. The Sage Brined Bone-in Pork Chop with sour cherry is recognized as one of the best dishes on the entire dinner menu, and it will certainly leave you with that comfortably full feeling.

That dish isn't the only thing receiving recognition at Chef and the Farmer. Chef Howard has been nominated for a James Beard Award and has been featured often on television, including a series on PBS entitled "A Chef's Life." The region of eastern North Carolina around Kinston and Deep Run has long been a tobacco-growing area, but recently the state has offered support to farmers to convert to raising healthy vegetables instead. The attention that restaurateurs like Howard and Knight have brought to the produce of those farmers has gone a long way to advancing this noble program.

SPECIALTIES: Bourbon-Braised Pork Shoulder with Sweet Potato Lasagna, Creamed Collard Crostini

INSIDER TIP: In addition to offering a deep wine list, Chef and the Farmer has added a wine store next to the restaurant so that diners can pick up a bottle and a pizza to carry home.

Find a recipe from this restaurant on page 218.

CHEF'S MARKET CAFE

900 Conference Drive
Goodlettsville, TN 37072
(615) 851-2433
www.chefsmarket.com

Chef's Market is tucked away in the corner of a strip mall about fifteen miles north of downtown Nashville, so it's easy to overlook unless you know where you're headed. Luckily, you'll know you are close when you see the parking lot full of diners who are huge fans of Chef's Market's brand of down-home cooking and outrageous desserts.

Known primarily for their creative catering services that are consistently voted the best in town, Chef's Market is a favorite place for locals to meet and eat or to do some shopping in their quaint little gift shop. Especially around the winter holidays, the dining room is gaily decorated and divided into several smaller areas for more intimate dining or outdoor seating for your al fresco pleasure.

Don't be fooled by the cafeteria-style steam tables at Chef's Market. The food is worthy of a fine-dining establishment and served fast and hot by a pleasant staff who will be happy to explain any of the dozens of dishes that diners have to choose from. A case of creative salads available for takeaway or dining in stretches almost the length of the dining room and is filled with interesting choices like Old-Fashioned Chicken Salad, Southern Potato Salad, or Crimson Quinoa.

Entrées include what looks like a simple selection of sandwiches and wraps, but closer inspection shows the quality of the ingredients and the talents of the kitchen at work. A Three-Cheese Black Angus Burger with provolone, Swiss, and Cheddar is one of the best burgers in town, and the shaved prime rib sandwich is a run-down-your-chin treat.

The larger entrées rotate often, but you can always expect to find hearty Southern classics like hot chicken salad and roasted pork loin. That second dish is even more amazing when accompanied by Chef's Market's signature Sweet Potato Salad. Other standout dishes include a spicy Snakebite Pasta made with diced grilled chicken breast tossed in a spinach and jalapeño cream sauce served over pasta and grilled Asiago bread.

It's almost cruel that the selection of unbelievable cakes are hidden in a case just inside the front door, but since you don't pay at Chef's Market until you're ready to leave, this offers an opportunity to take a huge slice home since you probably filled up from the buffet anyway. This doesn't make your choice any easier, since you'll have to consider the Strawberry and Cream Cake with fresh strawberries baked inside or two Southern classics, the Chocolate Elvis, a devil's food cake with creamy chocolate icing, and a Hummingbird Cake made with pineapple and bananas. Really, you can't go wrong with any of those dessert choices as long as you don't pass them all by.

SPECIALTIES: Roasted Pork Loin, Snakebite Pasta

INSIDER TIP: If you have trouble making up your mind and have a healthy appetite, visit on Friday or Saturday night for the Chef's Inspired Table where one price will allow you to sample any of Chef's Market's prepared items plus their prime rib and popular treat of a bottomless bowl of tortilla chips and Spinach Con Queso.

Find recipes from this restaurant on pages 197 and 220.

CITY GROCERY

152 Courthouse Square
Oxford, MS 38655
(662) 232-8080
www.citygroceryonline.com

Oxford, Mississippi, is undoubtedly a college town, and on game days The Grove near the football stadium can feel like the center of the universe. Elaborate tailgate parties buzz with excitement as alumni and students dress to the nines to root on their team. The scenery's not bad either, considering Ole Miss is the sort of place where they redshirt Miss Americas so that members of the same sorority can win the prize two years in a row.

But the rest of the year, the gathering point for Oxford residents is Chef John Currence's City Grocery. Located right on the town square, Currence's creative cooking and wicked sense of humor make his restaurant the place to go for a great meal and a good time.

His cheeky attitude shows through on his menu, even in the beverage section, which is divided into Water, Bubbly Water (beer), Kentucky Water (whiskey), and Scotch Water (just like it sounds). Currence also has a real talent for combining traditional Southern ingredients with bold, innovative flavors to create a cuisine that is unique to his restaurants. He was rewarded for this skill with the James Beard Award for Best Chef-South in 2009.

Something as traditional as a luncheon Cobb salad is elevated to a special dish with the addition of molasses-grilled quail, house-smoked ham, minced egg, bacon, avocado, cheese, and a Dijon vinaigrette. Currence channels his experience working in New Orleans with a Fried Pig Ear Po' Boy topped with cayenne mustard, house-made bread-and-butter pickles, and greens for a crunchy delight.

As a member of the Fatback Collective competitive barbecue team, Currence knows his way around a pig and strives to utilize the whole animal whenever possible. A lunch dish of Mississippi Jalapeño Corn Pone served alongside turnip greens with braised pork and hot pepper relish is as Southern as it gets.

Even an international plate like Vegetable and Pork Fried Rice has a Southern flair thanks to the use of slow-braised pork and seasonal local vegetables. Currence's take on the classic shrimp and grits is jazzed up by garlic, mushrooms, scallions, and his Big Bad Bacon that is cured and smoked in-house. Another winner is his Mississippi and Louisiana fusion of Creole Spiced Catfish with marinated cucumbers and tomatoes served with cornbread puree. For a memorable meal in Oxford that features the best of traditional Southern dishes plated with creativity and skill, City Grocery is a clear choice.

SPECIALTIES: Shrimp and Grits, Grilled Pork, Creole Spiced Catfish

INSIDER TIP: The bar upstairs above City Grocery is the gathering spot for both writers who come to Oxford to pay homage to William Faulkner and chefs who seek the wise guidance of Chef Currence. Civilians are certainly welcome as well to bend an arm at the bar.

Find a recipe from this restaurant on page 271.

COMFORT

200 West Broad Street
Richmond, VA 23220
(804) 780-0004
www.comfortrestaurant.com

The Jackson Ward neighborhood of Richmond, Virginia, is undergoing a bit of revitalization, thanks in part to the opening of Comfort, a restaurant whose food fits its name perfectly. Comfort is the sort of place where they serve your sweet tea in a Mason jar to remind you of cooling off on a hot day on a shady front porch. The décor of the dining room is clean and sparsely rustic, which can sometimes lead to a bustling, noisy atmosphere as bar patrons enjoy inventive cocktails and a long list of whiskeys. The energy of the room obviously leaks into the kitchen, where the staff puts out some amazing, hip versions of old-time Southern favorites.

In fact, Comfort emphasizes their side dishes almost as much as the main dishes. Two sets of prices next to every entrée indicate the à la carte prices or plated with two sides. Accompaniments like a light, fluffy squash casserole or buttered cabbage take diners on a culinary trip back to Grandma's kitchen for exemplary versions of these church supper classics. Other favorites are sweet potato puree, fried okra, and a dish of roasted beets that has been known to convert ardent beet-phobics into lovers of the red root vegetable.

Don't miss out on the main dishes just to fill up on vegetables, though. Meatloaf is probably the most popular comfort food on the Comfort menu, but the juicy marinated pork tenderloin with a barbecue glaze is another excellent choice. If you're lucky enough to arrive at the restaurant when they are running the rib special, you'll have the chance to try a rack of perfectly smoked ribs dressed with a unique house-made barbecue sauce made from Cheerwine, the regional favorite cherry soda made in neighboring North Carolina.

Wednesday nights are Fried Chicken Night at Comfort. The special includes both white and dark meat served with "Cat-head" biscuits, hot honey, and the house hot sauce to turn up the heat. No matter what day you visit, be sure to save room for a dish of their Banana Cream Crème Brûlée. This dessert is like banana pudding made by a master pâtissier, with a delicious crunchy crust of caramelized banana slices that cracks satisfyingly under the thunk of a spoon to reveal a rich, creamy custard below. It's the mandatory ending to an enjoyable meal at Comfort.

SPECIALTIES: Meatloaf, Fried Chicken and Catfish, Banana Cream Crème Brûlée

INSIDER TIP: Thanks to the seasonality of the menu, not everything is available every day, but if softshell crabs are in season, ask for the secret "surf 'n' turf" for a remarkable combination of crispy crab and pork tenderloin.

Find recipes from this restaurant on pages 225 and 229.

COTTON CREATIVE SOUTHERN CUISINE

101 North Grand Street
Monroe, LA 71201
(318) 325-0818
www.restaurantcotton.com

Many Louisiana restaurants tend to shape their menus around the traditional Cajun and Creole flavors that mark the state's most famous cuisines. When Chef Cory Bahr decided to open Cotton Creative Southern Cuisine, he knew that he didn't want to necessarily limit himself to the flavors of his native state, preferring to include ingredients and dishes inspired from across the South.

The result is a restaurant that pays attention to every detail of every dish, but that also has its heart based in the recipes that Chef Bahr learned at the elbow of his grandmother as she cooked up traditional meals in a seasoned cast-iron skillet. Bahr showed off his talents in the kitchen as one of the season 12 champions of Food Network's *Chopped* competition series. His North Delta Bouillabaisse also won him the title of Louisiana Seafood King at the prestigious New Orleans Wine and Food Experience. Grandma would be proud!

Diners who come to his swanky restaurant in downtown Monroe may be surprised by how affordable Bahr's upscale Southern cuisine is, especially when they see the elegant dining rooms and the three bars, as well as a balcony that overlooks the Ouachita River. Cotton is a big-city restaurant in a small town with a menu that reflects the best of both.

Perhaps the most popular appetizers are the Duck Wraps, a dish that could be enjoyed at any North Louisiana hunting camp, except those versions probably aren't wrapped in bacon and dressed with a delicious local honey gastrique. The birds that appear in the wraps also contribute to the Duck-Fat Fries that are served with a delightful pig salt to complete the aggressive flavors.

Other down-home classics that are elevated on Cotton's appetizer roster include Black Skillet Cracklin' Cornbread with Sweet Potato Jam and Pimento Cheese Beignets accompanied by roasted poblano pepper aioli and green tomato chow chow.

At lunchtime, diners enjoy the traditional Louisiana classic of Cochon de Lait, the Cajun version of a pulled pork sandwich served up with collards and field peas on the side. More adventurous patrons can try what Chef Bahr calls his Pressed Pig Sammie made with slow-cooked heritage pork shoulder, Gruyere cheese, house pickles, and beer mustard on a house-made ciabatta roll.

Come dinnertime, the portions get bigger, but the prices are still quite affordable. Cotton's North Delta Shrimp and Grits are more Bayou State than Lowcountry, with Louisiana shrimp and andouille sausage taking on starring roles. Pork lovers need to look no further than the Niman Ranch Pork Belly and Cheeks to get their fill. Served with cranberry beans, collard green marmalade, and pepper jelly glaze, either half of this entrée could stand alone, but together they represent the best of the pig.

SPECIALTIES: Duck Wraps, Shrimp and Grits

INSIDER TIP: Cotton is known for their exemplary service, but don't be surprised if a server suggests against substituting any of the side dishes that accompany the entrées. Chef Bahr has designed a menu with very specific combinations of complementary flavors. Trust the man!

Find a recipe from this restaurant on page 275.

CRESCENT PIE AND SAUSAGE COMPANY

4400 Banks Street
New Orleans, LA 70119
(504) 482-2426
www.crescentpieandsausage.com

Chef Bart Bell knows what you need. In a town like New Orleans, sometimes you just want some good spicy sausage or a loaded pizza to soak up the aftereffects of last night's debauchery, and at his Crescent Pie and Sausage Company, he delivers both in spades. The specialty of the house is definitely Bell's revolving array of house-cured sausages.

You can expect at least a few different varieties from a list of Louisiana and international specialty links like Andouille, Chaurice, Boudin, Creole Hot, Bratwurst, Merguez, Mediterranean Lamb, or Chicken Zampina, but the smartest bet is just to put yourself in the chef's able hands. The first item on the appetizer menu is simply called A Link, and diners can expect to be pleasantly surprised by whatever comes out of the kitchen.

For a more extensive sampling, Crescent Pie and Sausage Company offers several different sausage plates. A Cheese and Sausage Platter pairs appropriate cheeses with a selection of links straight from Bell's grinder, while the Deutsche Plate concentrates on German varieties like Bratwurst, served with German potato salad and sauerkraut. For the grand tour, try the Mixed Grill that showcases the chef's Cajun heritage from his upbringing along the Bayou Teche.

Like any self-respecting bayou chef, Bell makes an excellent plate of jambalaya, but Bad Bart's Black Jambalaya is unique in that it uses black-eyed peas along with the usual braised pork, chicken, and sausage to offer a whole new spin on the Cajun classic. There are many who would hold this up against any jambalaya in New Orleans, and that's saying something.

Even the "pie" half of the name of the restaurant revolves around sausage. In addition to excellent small fried meat pies and pot pies that feature a rotating array of fillings, the selection of pizzas at Crescent Pie and Sausage Company takes advantage of Bell's charcuterie skills. The Mid-City Slammer features his spicy Cajun andouille along with an unexpected house-smoked coppa ham. But probably the most popular pie on the menu is the BLT Pizza dressed with bacon, spinach pesto, roasted tomatoes, Cheddar cheese, and a tangy garlic aioli. For many patrons, it's love at first bite.

The fact that the business even exists is a testament to Bell's persistence. His first choice for a location was demolished by Hurricane Gustav before opening. He literally had to build Crescent Pie and Sausage Company from the ground up, and the result is a charming space with both modern flair and homey comfort.

The open kitchen turns the dining area into a performance space as a small kitchen staff prepares sandwiches, pizzas, and sausages. In New Orleans, there's something to entertain you on just about every corner, but the view of the cook line working on your meal can be as much fun as any street performer.

SPECIALTIES: House-Made Sausages, Pan-Fried Mac and Cheese

INSIDER TIP: If you have a craving for great sausage, but can't make it to The Big Easy, Crescent Pie and Sausage Company ships some of their best cured meats. Call them for details.

Find recipes from this restaurant on pages 182 and 261.

DELTA BISTRO

117 Main Street
Greenwood, MS 38930
(662) 455-9575
www.deltabistro.com

Much of the history of the Mississippi Delta revolves around food. From the signature "comeback sauce" on the table of almost every household and restaurant from Jackson to Clarksdale to some of the most amazing tamales you'll ever eat, the food of Northwest Mississippi emphasized the concept of farm-to-table long before it became cool.

At Delta Bistro in downtown Greenwood, Mississippi, Chef Taylor Bowen Ricketts is dedicated to preserving the culture of the region and accurately portraying a sense of place in every aspect of her restaurant. From the funky juke-joint décor to burlap wall hangings and illumination of lamps made from Mason jars, there's no doubt you are in the Delta. Booths are separated by delicate curtains harking back to the private dining areas at some older Greenwood restaurants where cotton merchants took advantage of the privacy to indulge in a little bootleg hooch in their booths.

The signature appetizer dish at Delta Bistro leverages the field peas that grow all over the Delta. The delicious Black-Eyed Pea Cakes are served on baby lettuce with a tangy remoulade sauce, and should be a part of every first-timer's visit. Other excellent starters are inspired by Ricketts's experience cooking with her grandmother in Hammond, Louisiana, near Lake Ponchatrain and feature the seafood of Louisiana. Crab bisque, crab cakes, and a spicy fried alligator dish are all nice ways to take a little culinary trip farther south before returning to the Delta for dinner.

If you have never tried a boiled peanut, Delta Bistro's version of the chewy goobers is a nice way to introduce yourself to this Southern staple.

For smaller appetites, the menu at Delta Bistro offers a nice selection of salads and sandwiches. A trio of Fried Chicken Sliders is served crispy and golden, but the real treat is the bourbon and Coke sauce that tops each sandwich. Another really popular dish is the Fried Green Tomato BLT with pepper bacon and baby greens. Stacked almost too tall to eat, the lovely tomatoes are worth the effort to disassemble the tower.

Heartier fare includes a wild game dish that is rarely seen on menus anywhere, BBQ Elk Brisket. This very lean cut of meat is served with a bourbon molasses barbecue sauce to complement the slight gaminess of the elk. The result is a perfect demonstration of Chef Ricketts's talent at combining the nuances of flavors. The Cook's Rib Eye is a more straightforward dish of a wonderfully cooked steak topped with an herb compound butter and is served with roasted potatoes for a meal that will definitely stick to your ribs.

If you want the full Delta Bistro experience, Ricketts offers a Chef's Table for Two in the kitchen where you can watch her staff at work. Advance reservations are required, but the show is worth planning ahead. Even if you don't leave the dining room, you won't have any trouble recognizing Chef Ricketts's talent just from what she presents on your plate.

SPECIALTIES: Fried Green Tomato BLT, Black-Eyed Pea Cakes, BBQ Elk Brisket

INSIDER TIP: Delta Bistro has no wine list, but they're happy for you to BYOB for an extremely inexpensive corkage fee. They do have an excellent selection of beers, though, including lots of favorite regional brews.

Find recipes from this restaurant on page 184.

DOC CROW'S SOUTHERN SMOKEHOUSE AND RAW BAR

127 West Main Street
Louisville, KY 40202
(502) 587-1626
www.doccrows.com

A hundred years ago, the 100 block of Main Street in Louisville was the center of the bourbon universe. Right smack in the middle of downtown and backed up to the Ohio River, the warehouses along that stretch of Main housed whiskey dealers who shipped their magical brown liquor all over the world via the riverboats that docked behind the warehouses. For this reason, the stretch earned the proud nickname "Whiskey Row."

Fast-forward to the late 1900s and the bourbon manufacturing industry had moved from downtown out to the small towns between Louisville and Lexington, thanks largely to the development of the interstate system that made trucking the easiest and most economical way to transport raw materials to the distilleries and product out to the thirsty public. The warehouses of Whiskey Row had fallen into disrepair and were mostly vacant.

Brett Davis, one of the owners of Doc Crow's, saw the opportunity to restore one of the beautiful old warehouse spaces and rekindle the whiskey heritage of the block with the opening of his new restaurant. He and his partners stabilized the original façade of the building and set to work building an old-school saloon that would quickly become a favorite of visitors to downtown Louisville. It didn't hurt that the YUM Arena is located right next door, providing a steady stream of customers looking for good food and drink before a concert or sporting event.

Davis is a Master Sommelier, so he clearly knows his wine and spirits. He set about curating a selection of whiskeys and bourbons that is unrivaled in the state. (And Kentucky is a state that knows its whiskey!) With over 160 whiskeys and 100 bourbons on the menu, Doc Crow's is the place to find something new or try something different if you are already an aficionado.

The food menu is full of Southern specialties, with a section devoted to seafood dishes labeled "Coastal Critters" as well as plenty of your favorite smoked meat favorites. From pulled pork to a Southern Fried Pork Chop Sandwich, the pig is well represented in the "Between the Buns" category. Both St. Louis and baby back ribs emerge from the restaurant's smoker after a healthy helping of Doc Crow's dry rub and a slow and low cooking over smoldering hickory.

Doc Crow's cares about authenticity, to the point that they import the bread from New Orleans for their impressive roster of po' boy sandwiches. In addition to the expected fried oyster, shrimp, and catfish po' boys, don't overlook the novel Pulled Smoked Rib Tip Sandwich. Topped with tobacco onions, slaw, and a pickle, it really is a unique treat.

For a taste of history or just a nip of whiskey, Doc Crow's Southern Smokehouse and Raw Bar is the place to go in downtown Louisville.

SPECIALTIES: Ribs, Pulled Pork, Po' Boys, and Oysters

INSIDER TIP: Even if you're not a whiskey drinker, don't be afraid to ask for a suggestion to pair with your meal. The staff at Doc Crow's is well trained to match wine, whiskey, or cocktails with their food.

Find a recipe from this restaurant on page 231.

THE SOUTHERN FOODIE'S GUIDE TO THE PIG

DUDLEY'S ON SHORT

259 West Short Street, Suite 125
Lexington, KY 40507
(859) 252-1010
www.dudleysrestaurant.com

Dudley's restaurant has been a fixture in the Lexington dining scene for almost thirty years. Originally located in the historic Dudley Square, the restaurant moved closer to the vibrant downtown scene in 2010 after the owners purchased the Northern Bank Building, a gorgeous edifice constructed in 1889. The building marks the head of Market Street and the entrance to the Gratz Park Residential Historic District on the edge of what was once the main public square and market house of the city.

The neighborhood has been renewed and renovated as Cheapside Park and is the home of Lexington's successful Farmers' Market. It is also just a few blocks away from Rupp Arena where the Kentucky Wildcats play college basketball, making Dudley's a popular pre- or post-game dining destination.

Dinner is served until late on weekends, which is another reason why Dudley's is a popular special occasion destination for diners seeking a casually elegant dining room to enjoy a night out, but the main draw for hungry patrons is the food. Lunch and dinner are served daily, but if you're looking for a taste of what makes Dudley's special without breaking the bank, try their Sunday brunch.

The brunch menu features some of the same dishes that you'll see at lunch: like the popular Pasta Dudley's with angel hair pasta, chicken, vegetables, and Asiago cheese and the Downtown Debbie Brown, an open-faced ham and turkey sandwich smothered in mornay sauce that is decadence on a platter. What makes the brunch menu special is the addition of some really creative egg dishes. Try the Eggs St. Charles for eggs over easy with shrimp, tasso ham, black beans, and

rice and a piquant jalapeño hollandaise sauce or the Quail and Eggs served alongside a candied onion bread pudding and covered with maple sherry gastrique.

If a dinner splurge is in order, then you've come to the right place. A whole section of the menu is dedicated to appetizers for the table that are meant to be shared along with the lively conversation that contributes to the buzzing din of the dining room. Warm Brie served with brioche, Crab Cake Sliders, and Country Ham Gritters (instead of fritters) are great choices for setting the mood for the meal to come.

Entrées are elegantly prepared and dramatically presented, with an emphasis on local ingredients. The French bistro favorite of Steak Frites with crisp fries and truffle garlic butter is one of the less expensive main dishes on the menu, but they taste like a million bucks. If you do happen to have a little extra scratch in your pocket, perhaps after a good day at Keeneland, try the Tournedos Maxwell. This tenderloin dish is heaped with lump crabmeat, served with fresh local vegetables, and covered in a luxurious bearnaise sauce. Even if you weren't lucky at the track, you'll feel like a winner after a meal at Dudley's on Short.

SPECIALTIES: Steak Frites, Pasta Dudley's

INSIDER TIP: When you call to make a reservation, ask for a table on the rooftop patio so you can admire the beautiful old brick buildings of downtown Lexington and the stunning illuminated church steeple of the Christ Church Cathedral.

Find recipes from this restaurant on pages 136 and 163.

RESTAURANT PROFILES

EDLEY'S BAR-B-QUE

2706 12th Avenue South
Nashville, TN 37204
(615) 953-2951
www.edleysbbq.com

While still not as well known as Memphis, its neighbor to the west, Nashville has a growing reputation as a barbecue town. Music City is more recognized for a collection of Southern diners that feature what is locally known as "meat and three," usually a choice of chicken, pork, beef, or fish served as a main dish along with a selection of three vegetables. Of course, in Nashville, mac and cheese or stewed cinnamon apples can count as a vegetable.

When Will Newman decided to open Edley's Bar-B-Que, he wanted to combine the best of both worlds with excellent smoked meats and side dishes that could measure up against the best of Nashville's iconic meat and threes. Using recipes from the mothers and grandmothers of his staff, he has certainly accomplished this goal, much to the delight of the burgeoning hip 12 South neighborhood where he opened his first location.

Together with his chef/partner Bret Tuck, Newman has created a menu of barbecue and sides that should satisfy the palate of any Southerner. The chef is the namesake of the Tuck Special sandwich, a concoction that he put together as an experiment to feed members of the construction crew who were building out the restaurant before opening. This colossal sandwich is piled high with Edley's smoky beef brisket (a rarity in pork-centric Tennessee) that is then topped with a generous smear of pimento cheese, both red and white barbecue sauces, and an over-easy egg to take it right over the top. The work crew was duly impressed, although productivity did flag a bit as the food coma set in.

Hailing from northern Alabama, Newman knew that he wanted to introduce his version of Alabama white barbecue sauce to Nashvillians, and the tangy mayonnaise sauce is a perfect accompaniment to Edley's smoked chicken wings. It also works well with the pulled chicken, turkey, and even the pork that emerges from the smoker at Edley's.

Another excellent way to enjoy that White Oak–smoked pulled pork is as part of Edley's BBQ Nachos plate with shoulder meat and red barbecue sauce served over tortilla chips with creamy nacho cheese, pico de gallo, and sour cream. It's really more of a meal than an appetizer.

True to Newman's plan, the side dishes stand out at Edley's. A zippy vinegar slaw is great on top of the pulled pork sandwich or as an accompaniment if you don't like a little crunch in your bite. In addition to the barbecue staple sides of potato salad, mac and cheese, and baked beans, Edley's offers smoky black-eyed peas that go great with the brisket.

With a new expansion to East Nashville, Edley's has cemented its reputation as the leader in a new category that they have created for themselves, the "smoked meat and three."

SPECIALTIES: Barbecue Nachos, Brisket, Shoulder Sandwiches

INSIDER TIP: Edley's is unique among local barbecue joints in that they have another of Nashville's signature foods on their menu. The Hot Chicken Sandwich is worth trying, but they are not kidding around when they call it "hot." Buyer beware!

Find recipes from this restaurant on pages 164 and 189.

EMPIRE STATE SOUTH

999 Peachtree Street
Atlanta, GA 30309
(404) 541-1105
www.empirestatesouth.com

You might recognize Chef Hugh Acheson as a television celebrity judge on *Top Chef*, or possibly as an award-winning cookbook author, but in Atlanta he is best known as the chef/partner of Empire State South, one of the hottest restaurants in Midtown. For a power breakfast, casual lunch, spectacular dinner, or late-night fun, Empire State South is the first choice for educated diners.

The modern but comfortable dining area is divided into several rooms, with booths ringing the wall around a large bar that is always a popular gathering point. Seating extends outside to a terrace that overlooks a grassy courtyard with a bocce court where games go on late into the night on the fortunate evenings when Atlanta's climate is temperate enough to spend time al fresco.

Tourists and locals alike have learned the wonder of ESS's Breakfast Sandwich that offers a choice of bread between a bagel, biscuit, or nine-grain toast, three meat options of bacon, country ham, or fried chicken, and your choice of toppings between pimento cheese or pepper jelly. Statisticians figure that makes eighteen different possible configurations, but foodies know that fried chicken and pimento cheese on a biscuit is the way to go.

Business lunches are common at Empire State South, but suits or shorts are both welcome. Prices are quite reasonable considering the talent and reputation of the kitchen staff, and you can even take advantage of the "Grab and Go" menu to carry out a first-class bologna or pimento cheese sandwich for not much more than the price of fast food.

If you do dine in, though, that Fried Bologna Sandwich turns even more spectacular with the addition of a fried egg, Dijon, bread-and-butter pickles, and a side of potato chips. The pimento cheese from the sandwich is also available as an appetizer with a luscious smoky bacon marmalade.

At dinner, appetizers are called "Snackies for the Table." In addition to oysters, a charcuterie plate, and cheeses for sharing, another clever starter is the In Jars starter. Small Mason jars are filled with house-made treats like deviled ham, trout mousse, pickles, more of the pimento cheese with bacon marmalade, and a novel boiled peanut hummus. The jars are the perfect size for sharing, or hoarding.

By far the most popular appetizer is a dish that seems simple, but is actually very complex in preparation. The Farm Egg is a perfectly soft-poached egg with a runny yolk that mixes with a bed of oyster mushrooms, crisp Carolina Gold rice, corn puree, scallions, and an ESS hot dog to create a symphony of flavors and textures.

A rotating list of entrées depends on the seasonal availability of ingredients and the whim of the chef, but highlights usually include some sort of crispy pork belly, USDA Prime beef, and Georgia catfish. No matter what you choose, you can bet that your meal will be one to remember.

SPECIALTIES: Farm Egg, Crispy Pork Belly, In Jars appetizer

INSIDER TIP: Sunday Brunch at Empire State South is a great opportunity to sample dishes from the breakfast, lunch, and dinner menus. The meal is served from 10:30 am until 3:00 pm, so there's plenty of time to linger.

Find a recipe from this restaurant on page 151.

FELICIA SUZANNE'S

80 Monroe Avenue
Memphis, TN 38103
(901) 523-0877
www.feliciasuzanne.com

Felicia Suzanne Willett, the owner and executive chef of her eponymous restaurant in downtown Memphis, is quite the trailblazer. Recently she was named as the first female to receive the award as Memphis Restaurateur of the Year in recognition of more than ten years of excellence at the helm of Felicia Suzanne's.

Originally from Arkansas, after graduating from culinary school, Willett moved to New Orleans where she came under the tutelage of the famous Louisiana chef Emeril Lagasse. Emeril took quite a shine to his young protégée, and eventually Willett cowrote two cookbooks with him. After eight years in New Orleans, Willett moved to Memphis to open her own restaurant where she could focus on ingredients from the mid-South region of Tennessee, Arkansas, Missouri, and Mississippi. Felicia Suzanne's is located right in the middle of downtown on the historic Main Street trolley line at the corner of Monroe Street.

The building was the original site of the Peabody Hotel from 1869 to 1925, but was rebuilt as Lowenstein's Department Store in 1926 and operated until the late '70s as such. Part of the dining room still features the ornate cornices and ceilings from the store. The other half of the main dining room is more contemporary, demonstrating Willett's desire to combine elements of classic Southern charm with modern sensibilities. This attitude is quite apparent in the restaurant's menu, where traditional Southern dishes like shrimp and grits are jazzed up with andouille sausage and Creole sauce and served atop a crispy grit cake. Chicken livers benefit from Flo's (a nickname she earned while working for Emeril) pepper jelly, part of Willett's line of preserved products, including tomato jam, bread-and-butter pickles, and chow chow. The shelves of the restaurant are laden with jars of these products, serving as decoration, inventory for her mail order business, and key ingredients to many dishes on the menu.

A Memphis tradition is Friday lunch at Felicia Suzanne's, the only day during the workweek she serves a midday meal. Treats like Natchitoches Meat Pies with creamy horseradish aioli and fresh cilantro or a Braised Short Rib Grilled Cheese Sandwich do tend to make it difficult to go back to work Friday afternoon, but just make an appointment in your calendar for a nap.

The dinner menu is separated into starters, middles, and entrées to help you pace your way through supper. A highlight of the middles section is the BLFGT Salad made with Benton's bacon, fried green tomatos, baby greens, and Tennessee Cheddar spread. A side dish worth seeking out is the BBB Southern Cooked Greens steeped with bacon, Budweiser, and brown sugar. For main dishes at dinner try Willett's preparations of duck and beef.

Whether you go for a more formal experience in the main dining room or a casual evening of drinks and snacks in the bar or on the patio, Felicia Suzanne's has a table waiting for you.

SPECIALTIES: Buttermilk Fried Chicken Livers, BLFGT Salad

INSIDER TIP: Felicia Suzanne's classic New Orleans-style patio is decorated with a trickling fountain and strings of soft lighting. It is a popular gathering spot for locals as soon as it opens at 5:00 p.m. Tuesday–Saturday.

Find recipes from this restaurant on pages 172 and 212.

FIG

232 Meeting Street
Charleston, SC 29401
(843) 805-5900
www.eatatfig.com

Charleston, South Carolina, has emerged as one of the top restaurant cities in the South, if not the entire country. In fact, the James Beard Award winner for Best Chef-Southeast came from "Chucktown" three years in a row, from 2008 to 2010. Chef Mike Lata was recognized in 2009 for his work at FIG, a destination-dining restaurant whose appellation stands simply for "Food Is Good."

That's an understatement at FIG, where Lata has created an honest, straightforward menu that elevates the food of the Lowcountry region while glorifying the seasonal bounty that comes from the nearby sea and farms. The atmosphere at FIG is friendly and casual, and foodies flock to the bistro to experience amazing food in an unpretentious and serene environment. Lata's sense of humor is evident in the quirky décor, and his self-effacing attitude shines through when you see his prestigious James Beard medal hanging on the wall right next to the "Golden Waffle" that he won as the champion of a short-order cooking contest sponsored by Waffle House at a recent Charleston Wine and Food Festival.

Although seafood and meats get the attention on the menu, don't overlook what the talented staff at FIG can do with vegetables. Offerings range from a Nine Vegetable Salad that highlights the freshest farm produce available to skillet-sautéed vegetables that contribute a lovely roasted flavor and that come in portions big enough to share. (Or not, if you're greedy.)

The menu changes frequently according to the seasonality of ingredients, but the level of creativity remains constant. The chicken liver paté is a consistent winner on the list of appetizers, but Ossabaw Pork Head Cheese or beef tartare are exemplary versions of these classic dishes. Lata has a particular talent for Italian cuisine as well, so if the Ricotta Gnocchi with Local Beef Bolognese is on the menu, give it a shot.

Of course, Lowcountry cuisine is always going to emphasize seafood and dishes featuring the pigs that used to roam in the scrub brush around the coastal region. Entrées made with local clams, oysters, and fish are near and dear to the chef's heart who, when pressed, will admit that he grew up in seafood-obsessed New England. However, the South proudly claims him as their own thanks to his talent, particularly when he is working with pork.

His upscale version of the classic Southern barbecue plate lunch of pulled pork with greens and South Carolina mustard sauce is a celebrated Suckling Pig Confit, served with roasted beets, sautéed greens, and a mustard jus. While the dish looks familiar to barbecue fans, the flavors of the incredibly tender pork are intensified by a long, slow cook time in oil at a low temperature. The result is a revelation of what a pig can be.

SPECIALTIES: Tomato Tarte Tatin, Chicken Liver Paté, Suckling Pig Confit

INSIDER TIP: Reservations are tough to get at FIG, but you can order the full menu at the bar or sit at their no-res "community table" where you can make some new friends.

Find a recipe from this restaurant on page 227.

FOX BROTHERS BAR-B-QUE

1238 Dekalb Avenue
Atlanta, GA 30307
(404) 577-4030
www.foxbrosbbq.com

Twin brothers Jonathan and Justin Fox became pit masters pretty much by accident. After moving to Atlanta from Texas, they lamented not being able to find good Lone Star-style barbecue in their new home. Rather than just complain about it, the brothers decided to start cooking their brand of smoked meat at house parties for groups of their friends. Eventually, these barbecue throw-downs became so popular that the Foxes were invited to guest cook at Smith's Olde Bar on Wednesday nights.

Barbecue night at Smith's took off, and they soon added Saturdays and Sundays to the schedule. It evolved into seven days a week with Fox Bros. having their own separate menu from the rest of the bar, which featured a lot of the dishes that would eventually become standards at Fox Bros.

In 2005, Jonathan and Justin made the leap to open their own restaurant, and Fox Brothers Bar-B-Que was born. The building is fun and funky, with smoke pouring from the cooker in the parking lot like a siren song for barbecue aficionados. The casual interior is festooned with beer signs and concert posters and lots of kitschy design elements referencing both their home state of Texas and their adopted home of Georgia.

Thanks to the creativity of Justin and Jonathan, the menu at Fox Brothers is extremely long for a typical barbecue joint. The list of appetizers demonstrates their mad scientist genius status. The smoked baby back ribs at Fox Brothers are already delicious, but the concept of breading them, dropping them in the deep fryer, and serving them with white BBQ sauce is just crazy-smart.

Other great starters are a Half and Half of fried pickle chips and jalapeños served with ranch dressing for dipping and The Lopez, an order of tater tots smothered with smoky brisket chili. That chili also plays a starring role in their Frito pie where it is ladled over corn chips and served in the precious little snack-size bag that originally held the Fritos.

Their version of Brunswick stew is wonderful on its own, but when they combine it with macaroni and cheese to create Fox-a-Roni, it becomes a revelation that might cause you to ponder why you didn't come up with the idea yourself. Like most great barbecue emporiums, Fox Brothers serves until they run out of meat, but with brisket, pulled pork, chicken, and baby back ribs to choose from, you should always be able to find a good option.

Perhaps the most creative plate on the menu is the Fox Bros. "Burger." The kitchen heaps a pile of chopped brisket on a buttered bun spread with jalapeño mayonnaise. The burger is then topped with tomatoes, pickled onions, thick-cut peppery bacon, pickles, and a swath of pimento cheese. The result is a sloppy, juicy, smoky mess of a sandwich that demands that diners roll up their sleeves before digging in. But don't worry about making a mess at Fox Brothers. It's always casual at this wonderful hybrid of Texas and Georgia.

SPECIALTIES: Texas-Style Brisket, Chicken Fried Pork Ribs, Fox Bros. "Burger"
INSIDER TIP: If you get a hankering for Fox Brothers' delicious wing and BBQ sauces, but can't make it to Atlanta soon enough, they are now available in grocery stores around the South or online.

Find recipes from this restaurant on pages 160 and 236.

THE SOUTHERN FOODIE'S GUIDE TO THE PIG

84

THE GREEN ROOM

116 North Main Street
Greenville, SC 29601
(864) 335-8222
www.highstreethospitality.com/
the-green-room

From the street, The Green Room looks like your typical, charming little Southern tearoom. However, once you enter the turn-of-the-century building, you'll immediately be confronted with a differentiating factor that separates the restaurant from the sort of place where you'd expect to find little egg salad sandwiches with the crusts cut off. A long bar runs the length of the exposed brick-lined dining room, and it is normally bustling with patrons enjoying a drink or a beer from the restaurant's lengthy roster of premium brews from around the world as they soak in the hip décor of the room.

The food is surprisingly upscale as well, with fun, unexpected details that elevate the cuisine well above traditional tearoom fare. Take the french fries, for example. These delicious shoestrings are tossed in truffle oil and sprinkled with grated Parmesan and fresh parsley. *Travel + Leisure* deemed them the "Best French Fries in the U.S.," no small honor.

Prices are very affordable at The Green Room, especially when you take the huge portion sizes into account. Seafood is featured in the appetizer section of the menu with Lowcountry Mini Crab Cakes complemented with Chipotle Cilantro Lime Remoulade and Prince Edward Island Mussels on toast points taking top billing.

The lunch menu offers creative salads like the signature Green Room Salad with Gorgonzola cheese, candied walnuts, craisins, and orchard apples or a hearty Angus Steak Salad that are both definitely large enough for a full meal. Burgers and sandwiches offer the option to upgrade your side dish to those truffle fries for a few dollars more, but that shouldn't even be an option. Take the upgrade!

The Farmhouse Burger adds a little crunch with the addition of a fried green tomato on top of a half pound of Black Angus beef. Other sandwich options include an ironically named Lil' Piggy, which is actually piled high with tender pulled pork. Probably the signature dish at The Green Room is their TGR Meatloaf. Regulars plan their whole day around saving room for a couple of slices of this sweet chipotle-glazed comfort food served with three-cheese mac and cheese and creamed peas. Other nice surf and turf entrées range from a garlicky seafood pasta to a pan-seared hand-cut filet mignon. Either is a fine option if for some reason you don't want the meatloaf, but then you'd be missing out.

SPECIALTIES: Truffle Parmesan French Fries, Meatloaf

INSIDER TIP: The Green Room serves the finest Sunday brunch on Main Street with classic French Toast and Eggs Benedict being the most popular choices.

Find recipes from this restaurant on pages 168 and 237.

RESTAURANT PROFILES

HALCYON, FLAVORS FROM THE EARTH

500 South Tryon Street
Charlotte, NC 28202
(704) 910-0865
www.halcyonflavors.com

It's appropriate that Halcyon, Flavors from the Earth is located right next to the front entrance to the Mint Museum in uptown Charlotte. Just as the Mint seeks to curate a collection of great art and design and feature the artists who created these pieces, Halcyon strives to celebrate the artisanal farms, dairies, and even wineries of the Carolinas. With a rigorously seasonal approach to menu creation, the staff at Halcyon truly does showcase the best of the flavors of the earth.

Whether you're a museum patron or a diner looking for a creative lunch, Halcyon provides many excellent choices for a great midday meal. Snack-size "pots" of pimento cheese with barbecued onions or house-made pickles are a clever way to kick off your dining experience, or you can partake of any of several salads designed to highlight the local farmers who are noted right on the menu.

A wonderful variation on the traditional Monte Cristo sandwich features two of North Carolina's neighboring states with barbecue pork from Virginia hogs and Tennessee buttermilk Cheddar cheese. A creamed vinegar slaw adds just the right bite to the dish to make it even more memorable. The Daily Grind Burger is anything but the same old grind with both local chuck and short ribs combined to offer the best of both cuts in a satisfying sandwich.

At dinner, the menu leans toward heavier, but no less creative, fare. Appetizers feature bold combinations of flavors and textures like a dish of unctuous pork belly and scallops served with hen of the woods mushrooms. For the adventurous, crispy pig tails are fried for dipping in a gribiche sauce made from emulsified egg and mustard, like the most wonderful mayonnaise imaginable.

Since the cuisine is so seasonal, a changing array of specials is always worth checking out. Regulars swear by the Pork Belly and Brussels Sprouts when it rotates onto the appetizer list, and a clever Country Calamari dish is actually crispy strips of fried pig ears that are served with a sweet Kentucky bourbon glaze. They're messy, but worth it. Whatever the season, you can be sure that the food coming out of the kitchen at Halcyon, Flavors from the Earth will be a work of art worthy of its neighbors at the Mint next door.

SPECIALTIES: Pulled Pork Monte Cristo, Pork Belly and Brussels Sprouts

INSIDER TIP: The outdoor patio at Halcyon is a delightful place to dine if weather allows. There is a view of an architecturally interesting church as well as of "Firebird," the huge glass statue in front of the nearby Bechtler Museum of Modern Art.

Find recipes from this restaurant on pages 132 and 190.

HAMMERHEADS

921 Swan Street
Louisville, KY 40204
(502) 365-1112
www.louisvillehammerheads.com

The half basement at 921 Swan Street has been some sort of bar or restaurant since the end of Prohibition, and the previous tenant was aptly named Swan Dive to describe the divey atmosphere of the cellar. When the space came open after the demise of Swan Dive, two talented young Louisville chefs seized the opportunity to open their own restaurant where they could serve a creative menu of carnivorous treats at inexpensive prices in a relaxed environment.

You'll smell Hammerheads before you see it, thanks to the large smokers that are in constant use on the sidewalk outside the entrance. Follow your nose to the walk-down front door and sit yourself down at the short bar or at any of the mismatched tables and chairs in this cozy eatery. (Be sure to duck your head so the huge fiberglass shark sticking out of the front of the building doesn't bite you. There's nothing subtle about this joint.)

The menu at Hammerheads emphasizes comfort food that has been raised to the level of gourmet, but is still extremely approachable and affordable. The most popular starters are the Fried Macaroni and Cheese Balls served with a hollandaise sauce and a selection of slider sandwiches available with smoked pork, duck, or brisket. Nontraditional meats and wild game dishes are all over the menu, with a roasted duck sandwich, venison, and elk burgers highlighting a list of favorites among regular diners.

Those smokers out on the sidewalk put out some of the best ribs in the city, but the real specialty of the house is their BBQ lamb ribs that are smoky and fall-off-the-bone tender. Like any great barbecue joint, once they run out of ribs, they are off the menu. You can't rush perfection, so the ribs need time to reach their peak.

Other signature dishes include shrimp and grits and a clever take on chicken and waffles with three chicken wings perched atop a sweet potato waffle and a side of maple syrup. In addition to the burgers and sandwiches, diners can also choose from pork, brisket, duck, or soft-shell crab tacos if they are looking for portable food.

Whatever you order, save room for two things. Hand-cut french fries are available either with sweet and spicy barbecue seasoning or tossed in truffle oil and are the perfect accompaniment for just about anything on the menu. For dessert, you can't go wrong with the Bacon Brownie. Not just superficially topped with a sprinkling of bacon bits, this chocolaty treat contains bacon in every bite distributed throughout the dish. At Hammerheads, they don't ever scrimp on the bacon or cut corners on any of the details.

SPECIALTIES: BBQ Lamb Ribs, Fried Macaroni and Cheese Balls, Truffled Fries

INSIDER TIP: To take the flavor of the truffled fries over the top, order them cooked in duck fat. The option is a buck more, but it will be one of the best dollars you'll ever spend.

Find recipes from this restaurant on pages 168 and 247.

HIGH COTTON

199 East Bay Street
Charleston, SC 29401
(843) 724-3815
www.highcottoncharleston.com

In the South, the phrase "in high cotton" refers to living in a state of prosperity and good fortune. At High Cotton in Charleston, diners indeed feel fortunate to get a reservation at this excellent restaurant that exemplifies Southern genteelness and the best of Lowcountry cuisine.

Entering the elegant dining room feels like being invited into the private parlor of an antebellum mansion, with exposed antique brick walls, ornate columns, and slow-turning palm frond–bladed ceiling fans that ooze with charm. Live music entertains drinkers and diners during happy hour seven days a week, and the entire atmosphere has a very pleasant vibe.

Sunday Brunch at High Cotton is a Charleston tradition, one that encourages diners to linger over creative interpretations of morning meal classics with smooth jazz playing in the background. A particular favorite is the Southern Breakfast Cassoulet, two sunny-side-up eggs over pork belly with shredded duck, butter beans, sweet corn, and baby tomatoes. Their version of chicken and waffles showcases a lovely trussed boneless chicken ballotine served with pecan waffles and is another excellent choice.

Lunch and dinner are also special events at High Cotton and are best kicked off with a delightful sampler they call the High Cotton Picnic Plate. Large enough to share, this platter features fried green tomatoes, La Quercia picante, pimento cheese, toasted baguette, house-pickled vegetables, and BBQ Lowcountry peanuts. A well-crafted charcuterie plate is an interesting alternative with house-cured dry sausages, hams, pâtés, mustards, and pickles to wake up your palate for the meal to come.

Try something you'd never cook at home like the Bacon-Wrapped Stuffed Rabbit Loin served with pimento cheese grits, grilled baby carrots, leeks, and mustard seed jus. Even heartier is the Masami Ranch Bone-In Smoked Pork Chop served with savory Cheddar andouille spoon bread, a bourbon potlikker jus, stewed yellow squash, grilled corn, and strawberry relish.

Another South Carolina tradition that you probably wouldn't be able to recreate easily at home is a Lowcountry Boil, and High Cotton has a standout version of this classic dish. Local shrimp, Blue Hill Bay mussels, and Folly River clams are cooked with fingerling potatoes, tomatoes, corn, and andouille sausage to offer a culinary tour of some of the region's finest products in one bowl.

In fact, the entire menu at High Cotton represents a delightful primer to the native food of the Lowcountry. In a city filled with great restaurants, consider this a place to put high on your to-do list.

SPECIALTIES: Lowcountry Boil, Bone-In Smoked Pork Chop, Shrimp and Grits

INSIDER TIP: There's another outpost of High Cotton in Greenville, South Carolina, with three-story tall windows that offer a stunning view of the Reeder River that flows through the middle of downtown. Check out both locations for the full High Cotton experience.

Find a recipe from this restaurant on page 255.

IVYWILD

36 Ball Park Road
Sewanee, TN 37375
(931) 598-9000
www.ivywildsewanee.com

Sewanee, Tennessee, is a sleepy little mountain town midway between Nashville and Chattanooga. Home to the University of the South, most restaurants in the area cater to students with pizza, sandwiches, and beer as menu staples. So it's surprising to find a fine-dining establishment tucked away in the location of a former dry-cleaner at the edge of campus.

But that's exactly what IvyWild is, a progressive Southern restaurant that emphasizes fresh, local, and seasonal products to create an innovative menu. Even though the food is fancy, it's still affordable, and the atmosphere of the restaurant is laid-back and casual. The lighting is low and the colors are cool, but don't feel the need to dress up for an evening at IvyWild.

The restaurant is BYOB, and you're encouraged to look at the menu online before you call for reservations so that the helpful and knowledgeable staff can offer advice for what wines to bring along to accompany your meal. Since the menu revolves around the availability of humanely raised, sustainable, and local ingredients, the selections rotate frequently according to the season.

Chef Keri Moser is a connoisseur of cheeses, and a selection of Tennessee specialties is always an excellent choice as either a starter or for a savory after-dinner treat. Other great starters include Peaches and Pork Cornbread with pickled peaches, sorghum vinaigrette, and foie gras butter and soups like Caramelized Candied Onion, Chilled Sweet Pea Soup with crème fraiche and marigolds, or Sweet Potato and Applewood Smoked Bacon. There's even a luscious Chocolate Soup on the dessert menu in case one bowl of soup per meal isn't enough for you.

IvyWild serves what might just be the best steak in the area with their Certified Hereford Beef Filet accompanied by pureed potatoes, spinach, leek butter, and horseradish root aioli. Another great meat course is the Heritage Breed Pork served with creamy Gouda grits and a spicy Creole andouille gumbo sauce.

If you decide to skip the Chocolate Soup or cheese plate for dessert, consider any of IvyWild's selection of homemade ice creams for a treat to finish your meal. Fun flavors like Green Tea and Thin Mint Cookie, Key Lime Pie, Bonnie Blue Goat Cheese and Roasted Cherries, or Nutella Gelato can make for a tough decision, but there's not a bad choice in the lot.

For a student taking advantage of a free meal with the parents, a tourist passing through on the way from Atlanta to Nashville, or anyone who is looking for a creative dinner that features the best ingredients of middle Tennessee, IvyWild is the destination of choice in and around Sewanee.

SPECIALTIES: Roast Pork with Andouille Grits, Beef Filet, Ancho-Rubbed Salmon

INSIDER TIP: IvyWild is only open for dinner Thursday through Sunday, so plan a weekend trip to visit Monteagle Mountain and treat yourself to a special meal while you're there.

Find recipes from this restaurant on pages 191 and 233.

LOUIS'S AT SANFORD'S

251 Willbrook Boulevard
Pawleys Island, SC 29585
(843) 237-5400
www.louisatsanfords.com

Chef Louis Osteen has disproved the old maxim "You can't go home again." Born in Charleston, South Carolina, Osteen earned a vaunted reputation for introducing Lowcountry cuisine to the rest of the world with his interpretations of traditional Southern dishes at his restaurant Louis's at Sanford's, located on what locals call "The Strand," the vacation paradise of Pawleys Island between Charleston and Myrtle Beach.

He is known for elevating the dish of shrimp and grits from its humble soul food origins to a ubiquitous menu item throughout the South. His definitive version is more of a bacon-laden stew with rich African and Caribbean flavors interplaying with creamy grits. After earning the James Beard Award for Best Chef-Southeast in 2004, Osteen decided to take his show on the road in 2007 and open a restaurant in Las Vegas. Unfortunately, the economy was not kind to his move, and he chose to return to his native South, consulting and cooking in new restaurants in Florida, Georgia, and Tennessee.

In 2012, Osteen knew that it was the right time to return to Pawleys Island, so he partnered with the owners of Sanford's Restaurant to reinvent their establishment as Louis's at Sanford's. The result is a wonderfully casual spot to enjoy some truly inspired food cooked by one of the masters. The dining room is comfortable and laid-back, with views of a placid lake through the open garage doors of the bar area.

Some of the best food on the entire menu is served as snacks in that bar. What Osteen cheekily calls "Pâté of the South" is simply a crock of pimento cheese served with flatbread or crackers. What makes this particular pimento cheese remarkable is the substitution of rich cream cheese for some of the obligatory Duke's mayonnaise in the recipe. Other great bar snacks include Crispy Black-Eyed Peas, Praline Candied Bacon, Smoked Salmon Deviled Eggs, Bacon-Scallion Hush Puppies with Buttermilk Ranch Dipping Sauce, and Roast Pig Tacos.

A short list of sandwiches is also worth your attention with burgers, po' boys, pulled BBQ pork, and a very popular Fried Grouper Sandwich leading the list. The smoker at Louis's pumps out dish after dish of pulled pork, brisket, and St. Louis ribs to the delight of visiting barbecue fans.

Entrée highlights include the Grilled Berkshire Pork Chop with onion gravy, collard greens, and Carolina Gold rice as well as what Osteen calls a Proper Southern Vegetable Plate. His definition of *proper* is difficult to question when it includes beer-braised collards, mac and cheese, squash casserole, and slow-cooked green beans. In fact, there is very little to debate at Louis's at Sanford's. With Osteen's experience in the kitchen, diners recognize the authenticity of his creations.

SPECIALTIES: Shrimp and Grits, Barbecue Pork, Fried Grouper Sandwich

INSIDER TIP: When there's some extra space in the smoker, sometimes Osteen will smoke lamb ribs as a special. If this dish is on the menu, it is a unique treat.

Find recipes from this restaurant on pages 213 and 238.

THE MACINTOSH

479B King Street
Charleston, SC 29403
(843) 789-4299
www.themacintoshcharleston.com

Blessed with an ideal name to be a chef, Jeremiah Bacon, a native of St. John's Island, worked in some of the most highly regarded kitchens in Manhattan including Per Se and Le Bernadin for over a decade before returning to Charleston to be near his hometown. After working in several local restaurants, Bacon decided to open The Macintosh in 2011. The establishment was immediately recognized as one of the best new restaurants in town, and, in fact, the whole country by *Esquire* and *Bon Appétit* magazines.

From the very beginning, Bacon knew that he wanted to create a comfortable neighborhood hangout, so the location beneath a popular lounge called The Cocktail Club assured a built-in audience of regulars. The long shotgun-style brick-lined dining room of "The Mac," as it is affectionately known by Charlestonians, encourages a convivial atmosphere. An open-air patio at the back is a popular gathering spot before or after dinner.

Bacon is fond of homegrown cuisine and has developed a style of focusing on a particular main ingredient on a plate that he then accompanies with sauces and other ingredients that add intense flavors. For example, the crispy pork belly appetizer offsets the fattiness of the pork with the sweetness of grilled peaches and a tangy peach vinaigrette and then completes the dish with earthy oyster mushrooms. Another novel vinaigrette, featuring guanciale, the unsmoked Italian bacon made from hog jowls, dresses a simple salad of Bibb lettuce, potatoes, and onions to great effect.

Other starters also pay homage to the hog with a Crispy Head Terrine, Sausage Plate, and Hot and Sour Pork Belly Soup, making for bold, flavorful appetizer choices. For a lighter option, consider the Watermelon Panzanella Salad made with heirloom tomatoes, red onions, cucumbers, basil, and a tart raspberry dressing.

In addition to inventive fish dishes, the dinner menu features some excellent meat plates. "The Mac" 8 oz. House-Ground Burger is always available whenever the kitchen is open and features aged Cheddar, Nueske's bacon, and addictive Pecorino truffle frites. Perhaps the most substantial item on the entire menu is a grilled 10-ounce bone-in pork chop served with broiled okra, peppers, heirloom tomatoes, arugula, and a piquant pepper jus.

True to its role as a neighborhood hang, The Macintosh features late-night dining until 1:00 a.m. on the weekends so that night owls can grab a bite or a drink after an evening out on the town. A popular Sunday brunch also draws crowds to the dining room for clever items like the "Mac Attack," an incredibly rich dish of pork belly, bone marrow bread pudding, and a poached egg to remind you that it's breakfast.

SPECIALTIES: "The Mac" Burger, Ricotta Gnudi, Pan-Roasted Duck Breast

INSIDER TIP: How can you not love a place that has a daily "Bacon Happy Hour" Monday–Friday from 5:00 until 7:00? The special is named after the chef, not the food, but it is usually a small pig-centric treat for just $5.00 that will make you squeal with delight.

Find a recipe from this restaurant on page 211.

MAMA J'S KITCHEN

415 North 1st Street
Richmond, VA 23219
(804) 225-7449
www.mamajskitchen.com

Sometimes when a restaurant seeks to attract a new clientele, the tendency is to take traditional Southern recipes and introduce some sort of fancy fusion elements to impress upscale diners. At Mama J's Kitchen in Richmond, Virginia, owner Velma Johnson instead chose to simply respect the ingredients and down-home dishes that she learned in her own mother's kitchen and cook the best Southern food she knows how to make.

Fans have taken the bait and keep the tables at Mama J's turning over. Located in the revitalizing Jackson Ward neighborhood about a mile from the state capitol, Mama J's Kitchen features a brightly colored dining room and an energetic ambiance. A long bar is usually filled with regulars, and the sound of their conversations bounces off the high ceilings to create a pleasant din like a great dinner party where everyone is excited to make new friends.

The family-style atmosphere shines through on the menu as well. Homey appetizers like Chicken Wingettes, Fried Catfish Nuggets, and Pork Shanks are designed for sharing and are great for passing around the table, if maybe a little messy. Not quite as sharable, but still excellent as a starter, is a bowl of spicy Creole Crab Soup.

Richmond's proximity to the Atlantic Ocean and Chesapeake Bay ensures a steady supply of great seafood, which Mama J's Kitchen uses to their advantage. Two specialties are the Famous Seafood Salad and crab cakes that are full of real crab instead of breading or filler.

Mama J herself makes most of the best side dishes, like candied yams, macaroni and cheese, cabbage, and collard greens, and then turns the kitchen over to her talented staff. The busiest folks in the kitchen work the fryer, from which emerge some fantastic examples of fried catfish, fried chicken, and country-fried steak. Fried pork chops with onions and peppers somehow manage to arrive on the plate perfectly crispy and golden brown on the outside, yet still juicy and tender when cut into.

The same can be said for Mama J's Baked Chicken, which rivals any baked bird at the finer dining establishments of the region. The crispy skin holds up to the topping of homemade chicken gravy and still delivers a satisfying crunch at first bite.

Diners might be intimidated by the variety of freshly baked cakes available for dessert, but if you seize up when it's time to decide, go for the Pineapple Coconut Cake, and you'll be glad you did.

SPECIALTIES: Seafood Salad, Fried Pork Chops, Baked Chicken

INSIDER TIP: Hungry people line up in advance to be the first in the door when Mama J's opens at noon on Sunday. Don't be intimidated if you're twentieth in line, because they seat everybody at once until they're full.

Find recipes from this restaurant on pages 161 and 241.

MEMPHIS BARBECUE COMPANY

709 Desoto Cove
Horn Lake, MS 38637
(662) 536-3763
www.memphisbbqco.com

Considering the quality and volume of smoked pork that is available in the Bluff City, it takes a lot of guts to name your restaurant Memphis Barbecue Company. Especially if your restaurant isn't located in Memphis, or even in Tennessee. However, when you've won as many competition barbecue awards as Memphis BBQ Company owners Melissa Cookston and John Wheeler, it's not too difficult to convince fans to cross the state line a few miles into Mississippi for some great 'que.

At the annual Memphis in May World Championship BBQ Cooking Contest, Cookston took home the top prize in whole hog, the pinnacle of competitive cooking, an unprecedented three years in a row from 2010 to 2012, and then again in 2014, with her Yazoo's Delta Q team, and is the only female BBQ World Champion ever. Wheeler's competition specialty is ribs, and his Natural Born Grillers cooking team has also won the Grand Champion title at Memphis in May.

After years of friendly competition against each other, Cookston and Wheeler decided to join forces to bring championship-quality barbecue to the masses. Since it is difficult, if not impossible, to taste a competitive pit masters food unless you are a certified barbecue judge, aficionados have jumped at the opportunity to make their own judgment of Memphis Barbecue Company's wares.

It's difficult not to fill up on the addictive cheese fritters made with four different cheeses and served with honey-dijon dressing as an appetizer. Be strong! Another starter worth noting is the chicken wings that are smoked and then fried before finally being tossed with your choice of barbecue or wing sauce. The most popular appetizer is a Memphis tradition that is rarely found outside of the area, BBQ Nachos. A pile of fried tortilla chips, smothered in pulled pork shoulder, queso dip, lettuce, tomatoes, sour cream, and jalapeños. You can even substitute smoky beef brisket for a Texas touch.

For your entree, try some World Championship ribs! Baby backs are smoked for five hours over pecan wood and served dry or wet. The Memphis version of dry ribs are the real deal, meaning that they are smoked with only a seasoning rub made with ingredients like paprika, salt, onion salt, celery powder, black pepper, and cayenne pepper to flavor the meat. Dry ribs are served without sauce and may be mopped a few times with a thin mixture of the rub and water. It takes a special talent to create meaty, smoky ribs that aren't too dry: a special talent like John Wheeler.

Cookston's influence shines through with the tender hand-pulled pork that is available in a sandwich or as a part of one of the restaurant's many platters. These samplers are the best way to experience the breadth of the best of Memphis with escalating titles and sizes from the Pitmaster Sampler all the way to the World Champion Platter, a massive helping of spare and baby back ribs, smoked chicken legs and thighs, sausage, pulled pork, brisket, cornbread, and three family-size side dishes. Come hungry!

SPECIALTIES: World Championship Smoked Pork Shoulder and Ribs

INSIDER TIP: If you're not in the mood for barbecue (well, what's wrong with you?!), the Memphis Barbecue Company also serves an excellent selection of what they call "Jukeburgers." Picture two fresh beef patties served on top of a donut bun. Even better, don't picture it. Eat it.

Find recipes from this restaurant on pages 192 and 248.

NEELY'S SANDWICH SHOP

1404 East Grand Avenue
Marshall, TX 75670
(903) 935-9040

When it comes to barbecue, Marshall in East Texas is square in the middle of smoked beef territory, but at Neely's Sandwich Shop they've been making a unique version of pork barbecue for almost a hundred years. The restaurant was started in 1927, but the Neely family recipe for their famous "Brown Pig" has been around for generations before then.

Of course, the exact formulation is a well-guarded secret, but it starts with whole pork butts cooked over indirect heat from a hickory wood fire. After a long and low exposure to the sweet smoke of the hickory, the pork is removed from the steel cylinder pit and the large shoulder bone is removed. Actually, the bone just about falls out of the tender meat.

One of the special secrets to the Brown Pig is the way the meat is separated. Instead of being traditionally chopped or pulled, the kitchen runs the shoulder through an ancient grinder to produce a texture that is unique to their restaurant. The grinding further distributes the sweet notes of the wood throughout the pork to create a distinctive flavor in every bite.

After scooping a hearty helping of the sloppy joe–consistency meat onto a bun, a thin red sauce (also a secret, don't ask!) is squirted on top and the pork is dressed with mayo and shredded lettuce. Some locals customize their Brown Pig with jalapeños or pickles to add some bite to the sandwich, but try the original first. A century of Neely family tradition needs to be experienced as they originally designed it.

Not totally averse to change, the Neely family has expanded their repertoire over the years. You can now order a Brown Ham or a Brown Beef to experience their talents with the smoker in slightly different configurations. If you're not in the mood for a sandwich, the Brown Pig meat is also available served on top of a mixed salad with your choice of a long list of toppings and your favorite dressing.

Another novel way to enjoy the secret sauce and meat combo is as part of a Brown Pig Pie, their take on the traditional chili Frito pie. The sauced pork is ladled over corn chips, and then beans, a spoonful of chili, and a rich coating of shredded cheese are added on top. It's your choice whether to mix up the meal or eat your way through, one delicious layer at a time, but asking for jalapeños as an add-on is a good way to jazz up the dish.

With its strip-mall exterior and down-home décor, you don't come to Neely's for the atmosphere. It's the friendly service and a hundred years of East Texas history on a bun that will keep bringing you back for another Brown Pig.

SPECIALTIES: The Brown Pig in many various forms
INSIDER TIP: Willie Nelson counts Neely's among his favorites, so you know that the Red-Headed Stranger would never steer you wrong!

Find a recipe from this restaurant on page 174.

NOFO @ THE PIG

2014 Fairview Road
Raleigh, NC 27608
(919) 821-1240
www.nofo.com

To understand the appeal of NoFo @ the Pig, first you need some background information. NoFo stands for the North Fourth Street District of Wilmington, North Carolina, the eclectic neighborhood where this fun little kitschy gift shop and café started out. In 2001, NoFo opened a second outpost in the Five Points section of Raleigh in an old Piggly Wiggly grocery store. Many Southerners who grew up shopping at this chain have long affectionately referred to it simply as "The Pig," and so the name was born.

In its new incarnation as NoFo, The Pig still maintains the character of the original store, with a bar created from old Piggly Wiggly food cans and a hand-blown glass chandelier adorned with precious little piglets. The final "o" in "NoFo" on the sign out front even has a little curly tail in case there's any confusion as to where you are.

Inside there is a large eclectic selection of gifts, specialty foods, and furnishing for your purchasing pleasure while you wait for a table in the café. All that shopping can work up a terrible thirst and hunger, so fortunately there is a full bar and a talented kitchen staff to serve lunch, dinner, and brunch on the weekends to keep visitors fueled for more commerce.

Pigs show up as often on the menu as they do in the design scheme at NoFo, and to good use. Bacon or pork shoulder is an ingredient in about half the dishes, even more if you add them as an option to the roster of burgers. (Bacon on a spinach burger? Why not?) The most popular appetizer at lunch and dinner is the Hot Pimento Cheese Dip served with vegetables and crackers and garnished with two slices of crisp country-style bacon crossed like a pair of skis planted in the snow.

A clever avocado BLT dresses up the standard sandwich with bacon, lettuce, tomato, avocado, Brie, and pepper jelly served on grilled Hawaiian bread and is exactly as rich as it sounds. For a more traditional lunch or dinner option, try the shrimp and grits that are made in the style of the late Bill Neal's iconic recipe from Crook's Corner in nearby Chapel Hill. This particular version includes shrimp sautéed with bacon, sliced mushrooms, garlic, Tabasco, lemon, and scallions served over cheese grits. Chef Neal would be proud.

Probably the most substantial entrée on the entire menu, and also one of the favorites, is the pork loin stuffed with spinach, goat cheese, and sun-dried tomatoes. The moist and tender loin is served with caramelized onions, roasted vegetables, and a balsamic demi-glacé that demonstrates a subtlety of flavors that is a nice contrast to the bold décor that surrounds the diners.

Whether you're there to shop or to eat, a trip to NoFo @ the Pig is guaranteed to be a rewarding experience. Really, no other place in town better exemplifies the fun and funky attitude that Raleigh is so proud of.

SPECIALTIES: Shrimp and Grits, Hot Pimento Cheese Dip

INSIDER TIP: Locals take advantage of NoFo's "The Joy of NOT Cooking!" carryout service to enjoy their food at home and share it with others.

Find recipes from this restaurant on pages 193 and 197.

NOSE DIVE

116 South Main Street
Greenville, SC 29601
(864) 373-7300
www.thenosedive.com

At Nose Dive, a casual gastropub in Greenville, they embrace both parts of their name. "Nose" refers to the aroma of a beer or wine, or in this case, the heady aromas of smoke emanating from the burgers and ribs that emerge from the kitchen. Another clever explanation of the name comes from the fact that the space used to house a much more formal restaurant named O, so Nose could be an acronym for "Not O. Something Else." "Dive" is probably too harsh a term for the atmosphere of the bar, but they claim the title proudly.

In actuality, the dining area at Nose Dive is not especially divey at all. The bar is a popular gathering area for locals who take advantage of a long list of craft brews and a wine menu that emphasizes interesting, affordable selections. A small stage in the corner of the dining room features live entertainment after the dinner hour to keep the party going after the plates are cleared.

Like most gastropubs, Nose Dive places more emphasis on their food than an average bar, much to the delight of regular diners. A large part of the menu revolves around elevated bar snacks that are easy to eat while standing up or leaning on the bar. An outstanding Scotch egg is made with homemade sausage and is served with fiery hot sauce. You'd better sit down for the Oxtail Cheese Fries, though. Potato wedges are fried in duck fat and then piled high with braised oxtail, white Cheddar cheese, and pickled scallions. They're worth the mess. Nose Dive's decadent version of mac and cheese is made with confit duck leg and aged Cheddar and then topped with crumbled Cheez-Its for a clever way to add some crunch.

For supper, regulars recommend the Butcher's Steak served with more of those duck fat potatoes or any of the Nose Dive's excellent burgers. Seafood lovers lean toward the Fried Shrimp and Clam Basket or the Lobster Roll made with plenty of sweet Maine lobster meat. But the signature dish at Nose Dive is saved for the end of the meal. A Dark Chocolate Candied Bacon Brownie is the perfect ending to any meal for bacon lovers and chocoholics alike. Chewy chunks of sweet bacon are distributed throughout the gooey brownie, which is served with American Honey Bourbon ice cream to finish off this crazy concoction.

If you don't leave Nose Dive with a smile on your face, then perhaps you need to return for a few more happy hours.

SPECIALTIES: Bacon Brownie, Skillet Broccoli, Butcher's Steak

INSIDER TIP: Happy Hour at Nose Dive is a Greenville institution, thanks to incredible drink specials and a regular crowd of handsome and winsome locals gathering around the bar.

Find a recipe from this restaurant on page 286.

OLD HICKORY BAR-B-QUE

338 Washington Avenue
Owensboro, KY 42301
(270) 926-9000
www.oldhickorybar-b-q.com

Owensboro, Kentucky, is known for great barbecue, but probably not the kind you would expect. Mutton is king in this northwestern Kentucky town. During the first part of the nineteenth century, the region was settled by Scotch-Irish immigrants who brought their skills as sheep farmers and textile processors. The wool-producing span of a sheep is shorter than its lifespan, so at a certain point the animal becomes better to eat than shear. Unfortunately, older sheep, known as mutton, are not nearly as tender as the lamb that most diners prefer.

Kentucky pit masters figured out that by cooking the mutton slowly over a low fire and mopping it with a salt water, vinegar, and pepper solution that they call "mutton dip," they could produce barbecue that is palatable. In fact, it is pretty danged delicious, and folks travel from all over the area to enjoy the sweet, slightly gamey meat.

At Old Hickory Bar-B-Que, six generations of the Foreman family have been smoking meats over hickory wood since 1918. Their dedication to maintaining the old methods of Charles "Pappy" Foreman results in a fiercely loyal following. Although sliced or chopped mutton is the specialty of the house, there are also many other excellent options on the menu.

Another unique Owensboro product is a meaty vegetable stew called burgoo. Kentuckians prefer a variety of meats in their burgoo, and you're liable to find everything from mutton to pork to squirrel stewing in giant pots at church picnics in the region. Fortunately, you don't have to worry about any strange meats in Old Hickory's burgoo; it's mutton, pork butt, and chicken based.

The smokers work overtime to pump out rack after rack of mutton and pork ribs, smoked beef, chickens, turkeys, hams, and delicious pork butts that are served chopped or pulled. The combination plate of any three meats is always a popular choice for the diners who crowd into the cozy dining rooms at Old Hickory.

Side dishes are fairly traditional for a barbecue joint, and if you decide not to try the burgoo, there is a great bean soup with cornbread to warm you up. Pies and fruit cobblers highlight the dessert menu, especially during the heat of the summer when the blackberries are at their ripest.

Even though most first-time visitors come for the mutton, the rest of the meats at Old Hickory Bar-B-Que keep them coming back.

SPECIALTIES: Mutton, Smoked Pork Butts, Ribs

INSIDER TIP: Regulars know to order their meals "off the pit" for a small upcharge. It's definitely worth it to have your meat carved fresh to order with the sauce on the side.

Find a recipe from this restaurant on page 171.

PARLOR MARKET

115 West Capitol Street
Jackson, MS 39201
(601) 360-0090
www.parlormarket.com

The building that houses the Parlor Market in downtown Jackson was built way back in 1898 and has undergone many incarnations in more than a century as a commercial space. The current owners maintain a reverential attitude about the building's history and have sought to incorporate the spirits of years past in many elements of their popular restaurant that focuses on locally grown products and house-cured meats.

The name of the establishment harks back to an earlier Parlor Market, which was a grocery store that served as a farmers' market for local food producers. A lumber company was located above the grocery, so the newest owners of the building made sure to include recovered cypress beams from a nineteenth-century Louisiana plantation and repurposed wooden planks as flooring. Fine details also help tell the story of the building with leather-backed chairs and menus that refer to a stint as Continental Leather and marble bar tops that hint of another past resident, Dixie Marble.

The cuisine choices at Parlor Market also have historical precedents. The location, 115 West Capitol Street, once served as the only oyster bar in the city, Al's Half-Shell, so modern patrons can belly up to the raw bar in the back of the restaurant to slurp down a half dozen. The erstwhile Jackson Smokehouse and Capital Meat Market businesses are certainly present as inspiration for the many house-cured meats on the menu, and the purse hooks under the bar even look like little meat hooks.

An attentive, knowledgeable staff will be happy to answer any questions diners might have about the restaurant or the menu, including the specific farm or supplier of individual ingredients. Start your meal with a delightful Country Ham Salad made with peppery arugula and a sweet hint of mint to play off the salt of the house-smoked ham. Another popular small plate is Parlor Market's Duck Sausage, a sweet and smoky delight served with grits, kale, and duck cracklins. Braised pork cheeks are also a very flavorful way to get your dining experience rolling.

The dinner menu features creative and unexpected preparations of proteins including Rabbit Confit with coppa ham and a carrot puree as well as Duck Carbonara served over house-made pappardelle pasta. Even heartier options for the hungry diner range from Chicken Fried Quail with chili molasses sauce to a massive Duroc pork chop served alongside a candied pecan salad. These bold combinations of flavors are notable, especially since the kitchen maintains such a laser focus on using local ingredients to create them.

Prices at the Parlor Market are higher than at most Jackson restaurants, but for the premier dining experience in the city, local foodies know where to go.

SPECIALTIES: Duck Sausage, Smoked Catfish Paté

INSIDER TIP: There is a daily Blue Plate Special that includes a glass of the ubiquitous house wine of the South, sweet tea. If you happen to see that the deal of the day is the Smoked Cheddar-Crusted Pork Chop, you can just close up the menu, because that's the winner!

Find a recipe from this restaurant on page 163.

PASTURE

416 East Grace Street
Richmond, VA 23219
(804) 780-0416
www.pastureva.com

When Chef Jason Alley thinks of Southern food, the tenets that come to mind are fresh, local, seasonal ingredients and sharing food and conversation around a table with friends and family. At Pasture, he has designed a restaurant and menu to feature the best of his beliefs.

The décor is sparse but comfortable, with tall ceilings and dark rough-hewn recovered wood planks covering the walls from floor to ceiling. The effect is like dining in a warm, cozy barn with a particularly talented camp cook manning the chuck wagon.

To encourage sharing and interactive dining, the menu at Pasture moves away from the traditional sequence of appetizer, main course, then dessert. Instead, it is divided into sections labeled Snacks, Cold, Hot, and Desserts, all of which are appropriately scaled for building a meal for the entire table by ordering one to two items per person, like a Southern version of tapas dining.

Alley believes in featuring the best of Virginia's farmers and producers whenever possible, and diners can check out the sources of the ingredients that make up their meal on a large farmers' board that is featured prominently in the dining room. Local hams, cheeses, fish, produce, and other meats are all important components of the Pasture's seasonal menu of comfort food with a hint of Lowcountry influences.

The pimento cheese at Pasture is a real treat, so a starter of at least one order of the creamy delight served with Ritz crackers is well-nigh mandatory. Other fun snacks include Black-Eyed Pea Falafel, fried peanuts, and pork rinds with jalapeño, lime, and guacamole for a Virginia version of chicharrón.

Other heartier plates are still good for passing around, like a vegetarian Frito pie with meatless chili, Cheddar cheese, and onions. Decidedly nonvegetarian is the house-smoked chicken sausage that is served with barbecue sauce, pickles, onions, and crackers. A rich Mexican pozole broth teems with house-made Pork and Chorizo Meatballs and an order of Chili Grits that will warm you on a chilly Virginia night and cure whatever ails you.

The Lowcountry classic of Country Captain contains half of a roasted chicken with a rich tomato and curry gravy over rice and green beans. Perhaps the most difficult dish on the menu to share is the Pan-Roasted Pork Chop with herb spoon bread and pickled corn chow chow.

But be nice to your fellow diners and give them a bite or they might not let you have any of the can't-miss dessert, the Homemade Candy Bar, a rich chocolate ganache with hazelnut crunch and Nutella. If you went home without trying that one, your visit to Pasture would be incomplete.

SPECIALTIES: Pimento Cheese, Pork Belly, Homemade Candy Bar

INSIDER TIP: Brussels sprouts are often much maligned, but Pasture's version of these buttery sprouts tossed with squash and preserved lemon rinds will make a convert out of almost any Brussel-phobe.

Find a recipe from this restaurant on page 222.

POOLE'S DOWNTOWN DINER

426 South McDowell Street
Raleigh, NC 27601
(919) 832-4477
www.ac-restaurants.com/pooles

Ashley Christensen is quietly building a restaurant empire in Raleigh, North Carolina. In the past few years, the James Beard Award–winning chef has opened four restaurants, including Beasley's Chicken + Honey; Chuck's, a burger bar; and Fox Liquor Bar, a fine cocktail emporium. But her flagship location is her original restaurant located around the corner from those three, Poole's Downtown Diner.

The décor and the name of Poole's come from the original resident of the building, one of downtown Raleigh's first restaurants, but the cuisine is much more inspired than your typical diner fare. The original Poole's was known for their Hot Plate specials and amazing pies, and Christensen still pays homage to the past with a constantly changing menu of upscale classics that are posted nightly on large chalkboard menus spread around the dining room.

Although predicting the specific menu can be difficult, there are a couple of options that you can depend on. Christensen's decadent mac and cheese (which is named Macaroni au Gratin to indicate its upgraded status) is a real favorite of Poole's patrons. Incredibly rich and savory, this golden brown bowl of goodness features three different cheeses, each contributing to the unexpected layers of flavors in this dish.

Another stalwart is the Royale, a nod to the "Royale with Cheese" burger from the movie *Pulp Fiction*. This tasty burger is made with 100 percent ground chuck that is rolled in toasted tellicherry pepper and cooked in duck fat. The Royale is served open faced on a toasted brioche and topped with the chef's choice of cheese, depending on Christensen's latest favorite. A small ramekin of red wine and shallot jus on the side is a perfect accompaniment to this juicy classic.

The buttermilk fried chicken at Poole's is so exemplary that Christensen opened Beasley's to feature the dish by itself. From its original appearances on the Poole's menu, Raleigh diners learned the wonders of combining the flavors of crispy chicken and local honey. Try that trick at home sometime, and you'll learn what they are raving about.

Christensen is a member of the Fatback Collective competitive barbecue team, an assemblage of renowned chefs who band together to glorify heritage hogs by entering major barbecue contests and combining their culinary knowledge to create some amazing pork dishes. She demonstrates those talents with several pork dishes on the menu at Poole's, so when you enjoy the fried pork shoulder steak and gravy or pulled pork with fried onions, collards, and red beans, you can be assured that you are in the presence of a master. As if the rest of the menu hadn't already convinced you . . .

SPECIALTIES: Fried Chicken, The Royale Burger, Macaroni au Gratin

INSIDER TIP: Like all good diners, Poole's doesn't take reservations. If you have a big party, get there at the 5:30 opening time or plan to enjoy some well-crafted cocktails at the bustling bar.

Find a recipe from this restaurant on page 248.

PURPLE PARROT CAFÉ

3810 Hardy Street
Hattiesburg, MS 39404
(601) 264-0657
www.purpleparrotcafe.net

It's easy to accidentally drive by the Purple Parrot Café, located just off the interstate in Hattiesburg, Mississippi. After all, who expects to find a white tablecloth fine-dining establishment tucked among the strip malls and gas stations and just down the street from an Applebee's? But there it is in a nondescript gray building with a simple black awning marking the entrance. Once you step inside, however, you'll discover some of the finest cuisine in the state.

The brains and talent behind the operation is Chef Robert St. John, an acclaimed culinarian who has published several cookbooks and coffee-table books dedicated to the cuisine of his native South. Obviously a talented writer as well as a chef, St. John shares much of his philosophy toward food as part of an essay he titled "My South."

"In *my* South, soul food and country cooking are the same thing. My South is full of fig preserves, cornbread, butter beans, fried chicken, grits, and catfish. In my South we eat foie gras, caviar, and truffles."

That pretty much sums up the cuisine at the Purple Parrot Café, where Southern ingredients are served with an international flair. Take the pork and egg dish that highlights the list of appetizers. A spin on the traditional bacon and eggs, this version features Niman Ranch pork belly topped with tomato marmalade and served on a brioche with a slow-poached egg yolk and what St. John calls "foiellendaise," a buttery egg sauce made even more rich through the addition of foie gras.

In an homage to New Orleans, which lies just a little more than one hundred miles down the road from Hattiesburg, the Purple Parrot Café offers a bowl of Gumbo Ya Ya made with a classic dark roux overflowing with chunks of chicken, andouille sausage, and duck. The Big Easy should be proud.

Much of the dinner menu revolves around the freshest Gulf Coast seafood available, so look for dishes listing items like redfish and striped marlin when they are in season. Landlubbers should scan down the *carte du jour* directly to the Hickory Nut Gap Farms Pork Shank, a country classic made with redeye gravy, Benton's country ham, braised collard greens, and stone-ground grits. Possibly the best way to truly experience Chef St. John's vision is to give yourself over to his Chef's Tasting Menu, an ever-changing culinary sojourn that also features matching wine pairings from the restaurant's voluminous wine cellar. Each course of the tasting menu is specifically crafted to showcase the best seasonal ingredients that the kitchen can source, and the result is truly a magnificent journey.

SPECIALTIES: Pork and Egg, Andouille Crusted Redfish

INSIDER TIP: Chef St. John has started a charity called "The Extra Table," which helps provide food to families in need in Mississippi through a partnership with other restaurants and food suppliers. By eating at the Purple Parrot, you'll be helping feed someone else too.

Find recipes from this restaurant on pages 250 and 253.

THE RAVENOUS PIG

1234 North Orange Avenue
Winter Park, FL 32789
(407) 628-2333
www.theravenouspig.com

Chefs James and Julie Petrakis are Orlando natives who spent their formative years working in some of the finest kitchens on the East Coast. In the back of their minds, they always intended to return home to open their own restaurant, and The Ravenous Pig is the proud result of their dreams. In a few short years, it has quickly evolved into one of the favorite foodie destinations in the Orlando area.

The couple first encountered a gastropub in New York City, but the concept originated in Europe where cozy neighborhood restaurants serve traditional pub fare, but elevate the cuisine to a more upscale level without sacrificing the comfortable, warm atmosphere of a local corner tavern.

At The Ravenous Pig, the Petrakises add unique Southern touches to the gastropub experience. Pub grub includes an excellent Pub Burger with truffle fries, a raw bar of Southern seafood, and some seriously addictive Gruyere Biscuits that require great willpower to save room for dinner.

More substantial are starters like a house-made charcuterie platter featuring regional meats and cheeses and a bourbon-glazed pork belly appetizer served with an intriguing combination of pistachio butter and cherry-vanilla jam. The Farmer Salad is another fine first dish thanks to the flavor combination of bitter greens, house-made bacon, a soft-boiled egg, and creamy Caesar vinaigrette.

A wonderful choice for lunch is the Fried Chicken BLT made with chicken thighs that are first smoked, then fried and topped with a bacon aioli and tomato jam before being served atop a salt and pepper challah bun baked in-house. The jam and aioli impart the expected flavors of a traditional BLT while allowing the crispy chicken to remain the star of the dish.

Pork chops are available in a few different presentations depending on the mood of the kitchen, but it seems like the Petrakises are always in a good mood. During the heat of summer, you might encounter a Pork Porterhouse accompanied by cool compressed watermelon and a concentrated barbecue gastrique. As the temperatures drop (as low as they ever do in the World of Disney), the pork chop comes with more substantial sides like polenta, buttermilk ricotta, pickled shallots, and a dense, sweet wine sauce.

Once a month at lunch on the first Saturday, The Ravenous Pig puts on a roast where one affordable price gets you a heaping plate of roasted meat, a special side dish, and a pint of microbrew beer. These entertaining afternoons feature dishes like house-smoked pork ribs, pulled pork, bacon-braised collard greens, black-eyed peas, and jalapeño cornbread. As comfortable as the ambiance is at The Ravenous Pig, it might not be as cozy and relaxing as your own couch at home after a meal like that.

SPECIALTIES: Pork Porterhouse, Gruyere Biscuits, Fried Chicken BLT

INSIDER TIP: If you do make it to one of the monthly special roasts, the restaurant offers a discount if you come in wearing your Ravenous Pig T-shirt or hat.

Find a recipe from this restaurant on page 257.

RESTAURANT EUGENE

2277 Peachtree Road
Atlanta, GA 30309
(404) 355-0321
www.restauranteugene.com

Chef/owner Linton Hopkins has a very firm and clear idea of what sort of food he wants to come out of the kitchen at Restaurant Eugene, his sophisticated, intimate Midtown bistro that is renowned for serving some of the most consistently delicious food in Atlanta. In addition to showcasing the freshest of seasonal regional ingredients on his menu, Hopkins strives to make as many elements of these dishes from scratch as possible, down to the hot sauce, ketchup, mustard, and mayo served as condiments.

The menu changes constantly depending on which ingredients from the local purveyors on the menu Hopkins deems most appropriate and interesting. Don't expect to find fried green tomatoes in February, but in their place you might experience the most marvelous greens cooked outside of your mamaw's kitchen. The descriptions of the dishes might sound high-tone, but the food at Restaurant Eugene is steeped in the foodways and traditions of the South.

If you're indecisive, or you just want to place your evening's experience in the very capable hands of Chef Hopkins, consider trying the nightly tasting menu. Following along in the menu as dish after dish is delivered to your table is like taking a tour of some of the finest farms in the region, with the bonus of never having to leave your seat. Portions are small but appropriate considering that you certainly wouldn't want to be full before the dessert course.

Restaurant Eugene is also known for its superb service and intimate atmosphere, so it's an excellent place for date night. The restaurant's creativity reaches to the offerings from the bar with clever cocktails and bar snacks available to kick off your special evening. An excellent wine list and knowledgeable staff also ensure a perfect accompaniment to whatever you order with dinner.

Dining at Restaurant Eugene may make you forget that you are in the middle of a major Southern city; you might feel like you are splurging in Manhattan, San Francisco, or even Europe. But Chef Hopkins has a very definite sense of place that shines through in the form of hospitality, seasonal locavore cuisine, and lovely little touches to remind you that this is, after all, a consummately Southern establishment.

For example, there might be foie gras on the menu, but it is seared in a cast-iron skillet. Dishes with French-sounding names that might tangle your tongue are actually roasted vegetables served with cornbread and sorghum butter. Make a reservation, order a cocktail or a glass of wine, and sit back for a sophisticated culinary tour of the South.

SPECIALTIES: Pork Belly, Soft-shell Crab

INSIDER TIP: This is the kind of restaurant that you could visit on every trip to Atlanta, especially since the menu changes nightly. Order the tasting menu for the complete experience.

Find recipes from this restaurant on pages 193 and 226.

RUFFINO'S

18811 Highland Road
Baton Rouge, LA 70809
(225) 753-3458
www.ruffinosbatonrouge.com

During the 1990s, Gerry Dinardo was the coach of the LSU Tigers football team, a position that is probably more revered than the governor in the state capitol in Baton Rouge. During the height of his career as coach, Dinardo capitalized on his popularity by opening an Italian restaurant, which he named after himself.

Unfortunately, as often happens, Dinardo's career as coach came to a sudden halt before the end of the 1999 football season, and he moved out of town, leaving an opening at his eponymous restaurant. In a stroke of kismet, Ruffin Rodrigue, a former LSU lineman, was looking to get into the business and took over the location. Rodrigue teamed up with Peter Scalfani, an Italian/Creole chef out of New Orleans, to open Ruffino's.

Together they created one of Baton Rouge's most beloved dining destinations thanks to a menu that features excellent seafood and both Italian and Creole classics. The cuisine revolves around the freshest available ingredients used in recipes that emphasize the flavor profiles of Italy and the spicy cuisine of Louisiana.

A peppery New Orleans-style BBQ shrimp makes an excellent, albeit messy, starter to your meal. Don't be afraid to ask for extra napkins if you order that one. It's worth the trouble thanks to the creamy butter sauce that accompanies the dish. A sweet and savory bacon jam made from Benton's bacon tops a starter of braised pork cheeks, which are slow-cooked in a pork jus for two days to render them tender and then served with a butternut squash puree.

Not necessarily Southern, but delicious nonetheless, is an incredibly rich lobster mac and cheese made with Maine lobster and two different creamy cheeses. Almost too much for an appetizer, this cheesy dish could be a meal by itself. Plus, you have to love a restaurant that lists bacon as an appetizer. The kitchen at Ruffino's braises cured Niman Ranch bacon for four days before serving it with a creamy mascarpone polenta.

If there's any room left in your belly after these appetizers, look for the Pork Tchopitoulas. Besides being a great pun (pronounced "CHOP-i-too-lus"), this center-cut pork chop weighs three-quarters of a pound and is broiled to perfect doneness before being topped with a helping of those spicy BBQ shrimp and served with garlic mashed potatoes. The combination of the meaty chop and the piquant shrimp nicely reflects the multiple influences that drive the cuisine at Ruffino's.

Some Tiger fans arrive in town days before Saturday kick-off, so for them Ruffino's offers a special Friday lunch that can extend all the way to dinner. There's also a nice Sunday brunch to fuel up your tank on your way out of town after the game. Whether LSU wins or loses, you can be sure at least your stomach will be happy after a meal at Ruffino's.

SPECIALTIES: New Orleans-Style BBQ Shrimp, Pork Tchopitoulas

INSIDER TIP: The atmosphere is classy, but feel free to visit wearing casual clothes. Especially when the Tigers are playing, LSU garb is always welcome.

Find a recipe from this restaurant on page 269.

RUKA'S TABLE

163 Main Street
Highlands, NC 28741
(828) 526-3636
www.rukastable.com

Chef Justin Burdett came to the cozy North Carolina community of Highlands in 2012 after stints working in the kitchen of some of the South's best restaurants. Burdett also added to his reputation by winning Food Network's *Chopped* cooking competition show during season 7, so he was greeted with great anticipation when he stepped in as the head chef at Ruka's Table, an elegant restaurant that features locally grown produce to create an inventive upscale Southern menu.

Burdett brought his wife, Brooke, along to run the beverage program at Ruka's, and her copper-topped bar is quite popular thanks to her innovative take on classic cocktails. The ambiance of the restaurant is classy but not pretentious, with vaulted ceilings and a huge stone fireplace serving as a centerpiece of the dining room.

The menu showcases regional specialties and many preserved products, thanks to Chef Burdett's talent for pickling. An excellent starter is the Peach and Tomato Salad with sweet onion, cucumber, basil, and a vinaigrette made from ramps, the strong-flavored relative of garlic and onion that grows wild in the forests of North Carolina and is eagerly foraged every spring. Another nice opening dish is the House-Made Pimento Cheese Toast served with a poached egg. Even more substantial is the Sorghum-Glazed Pork Belly with spicy okra and rice grits.

Wild game like venison and duck are popular entrées, but the dry-aged local beef is probably the highlight of the list of entrées. Both the rib eye and NY strip are excellent choices, especially with intriguing Southern accompaniments like Blackberries and Beets or Stewed Heirloom Hominy. A lean cut of Niman Ranch pork loin is drizzled with mustard jus and served with fragrant fennel, poached radishes, kale, and farro.

All desserts are made in-house, including a delightful version of s'mores with chocolate, graham crackers, and homemade marshmallows. The Southern Pecan Tart served with peach ice cream is another excellent choice, but perhaps the best of the batch is Ruka's Blackberry and Buttermilk Buckle Cake. Although the name of this dish is a mouthful to say, this cobbler-like dessert is certainly a delicious mouthful to eat.

Ruka's Table stays open late for a romantic place to grab a nightcap at the bar or maybe a slice of pie after a show. For residents of Highlands, Ruka's is definitely the table to pull up to any time of the evening.

SPECIALTIES: Pork Belly, Brasstown Rib Eye, Niman Ranch Pork Loin

INSIDER TIP: For more down-home fare, visit Ruka's sister restaurant just about a half mile down the road. Highlands Smokehouse is a super spot to pick up some ribs or pulled pork.

Find a recipe from this restaurant on page 254.

THE SHED BBQ AND BLUES JOINT

7501 Highway 57
Ocean Springs, MS 39565
(228) 875-9590
www.theshedbbq.com

Brad Orrison is not afraid to admit that he's trashy. In fact, he's an old dumpster diver from way back, hoarding just about anything found that he could possibly repurpose. When he scavenged an old barbecue smoker from the debris of a storm that ravaged the Mississippi Gulf Coast, Orrison realized that he had the makings of a great barbecue joint in his junkyard.

He returned to his hometown of Ocean Springs, Mississippi, where he convinced his brother, Brett, and sister, Brooke, to join him in the venture and then recruited his parents to come aboard in charge of marketing and sauce manufacturing. Together this family affair has grown into a small empire that emphasizes a frantic, fun atmosphere where the barbecue and blues attract diners who usually stretch in a line out the door to "Get fed at The Shed."

Even a 2012 fire that burned the original Shed to the ground couldn't slow the Orrisons for long, and they continued to operate out of a tiny mobile kitchen to keep the masses happy and fed while they built a new/old Shed from the ground up with scraps from their carefully curated pile of junk across the street. Fans, called "ShedHeds," contributed license plates and tacky memorabilia from around the country to help decorate the new joint that reopened within months of the fire.

The Shed also operates as a competitive barbecue team, cooking whole hogs in a unique smoker constructed out of a 1952 Willys Jeep. Like you would expect from the mad scientist/scavenger mind of Brad Orrison, the cook team smokes over pecan wood, with their hog positioned upright on a complicated armature they built from scrap to create what they call a "flying pig." More than just a novelty, The Shed BBQ team won first place at the prestigious 36th Annual Memphis in May World Championship Barbecue Cooking Contest in 2013. As a bonus, the team entered the Poultry category in the Memphis in May competition that year and also took home the top prize, so you know The Shed puts out some great smoked meats.

The menu at The Shed revolves around the pig, with both spare ribs and baby back ribs recognized as specialties of the house. But don't skimp on the pulled pork or what they call "Serious Sausage." Available as a plate or on a sandwich, either piggy preparation is worthy of inclusion on a combo plate with the ribs.

Sides are simple and down-home. Named after the patriarch of the family, Daddy-O's Cole Slaw is creamy and tangy. Momma Mia's Mac Salad is a nice change of pace from the traditional mac and cheese that shows up on most barbecue menus. Save room for a bowl of Nanner Puddin' made fresh daily at The Shed for the proper ending to a fantastic fun meal.

SPECIALTIES: Baby Back Ribs, Spare Ribs, Macho Nachos

INSIDER TIP: The whole Orrison family and some of their colorful coworkers were the subject of their own reality show on Food Network. If you drop by the original Ocean Springs location, you're likely to meet the stars of the show on any given day and realize that they weren't acting. It really is that crazy every day at The Shed.

Find recipes from this restaurant on pages 173 and 186.

SLIGHTLY NORTH OF BROAD

192 East Bay Street
Charleston, SC 29401
(843) 723-3424
www.slightlynorthofbroad.net

On the surface, it would seem easy for Chef Frank Lee to be pretentious. Classically trained as a chef in French restaurants, Lee is one of the preeminent chefs in a town full of great chefs. In fact, many of Charleston's finest kitchens are run by former employees of Lee who learned how to run a kitchen from the man himself. Heck, even the affectionate nickname of his restaurant, Slightly North of Broad, is SNOB.

But the executive chef at SNOB is anything but high falutin'. (In truth, the blueblood side of Broad Street is actually the south side, but we won't spend much time thinking about what you might call people who live South of Broad.) Lee is the kind of chef who prefers to wear a baseball cap while working instead of a chef's toque to indicate his station in the kitchen. With SNOB, Lee has created a restaurant where people who really care about good food can enjoy it in a relaxed atmosphere of a rehabbed warehouse from the 1700s. His goal is to cook "real food for real people."

From his travels in France and his experience working in French kitchens, Lee learned the value of creating food from the best local products using classic techniques. The open kitchen at SNOB allows diners to watch the staff at work and see the ingredients that are being employed to make their meals.

A longtime supporter of local farmers, Lee encourages his fellow Charlestonian restaurateurs to share his suppliers rather than hoarding the best for himself. He believes that demand will help create more supply and raise the quality of ingredients in other restaurants. Although, looking at the menu, it's sometimes difficult to believe that SNOB isn't getting first pick of some of the produce. The entrée-size vegetable plate is clearly described as "a variety of the best local vegetables we can find."

Like many coastal Carolina restaurants, the shrimp and grits at SNOB are a signature dish. This particular edition of the Lowcountry classic features sautéed shrimp, sausage, country ham, fresh tomatoes, green onions, garlic, and Geechie Boy yellow grits, and fans just never seem to tire of the dish. Another really popular entrée is the BBQ Tuna, which is ingeniously topped with succulent fried oysters and served with country ham, greens, and a brush of mustard-based barbecue sauce. Like much of the menu at SNOB, it is a dish that you won't find anywhere else, north or south of Broad.

SPECIALTIES: Shrimp and Grits, Stuffed Carolina Quail Breast, BBQ Tuna

INSIDER TIP: Lunchtime is very popular at Slightly North of Broad, both for business folks seeking a great power lunch and frugal diners who take advantage of a very affordable Express Lunch Special, which consists of the entrée of the day served with soup or salad, coffee or tea.

Find a recipe from this restaurant on page 158.

SOBY'S NEW SOUTH CUISINE

207 South Main Street
Greenville, SC 29601
(864) 232-7007
www.sobys.com

Soby's New South Cuisine is a member of a Greenville, South Carolina, restaurant group that owner/partner Carl Sobocinski named "Table 301." The table from the name is actually a special spot in the mezzanine of Soby's that looks directly down into the open kitchen, and Sobocinski wants the employees at all of his restaurants to behave as if their customers are always watching them. This leads to dedication to quality and service that drives every decision and action at Soby's New South Cusine.

Even with the high ceilings of the dining room and the balcony level hanging over the kitchen, the environment of Soby's is still very warm and comfortable. The restaurant is located in a hundred-plus-year-old building that through the years has housed a cotton exchange, a grocery store, a bicycle shop, and a shoe store. Sobocinski and his partners refurbished the building to expose the charming original brick and the hardwood floors that creaked under the feet of cotton merchants and farmers in the late 1800s.

A different sort of farmer takes center stage today at Soby's, where the kitchen features fresh, seasonal ingredients to create new Southern classics. Chef Shaun Garcia even swaps his apron for overalls as the head farmer at the ten-acre Soby's Farm at Dark Hollow where he and a staff of volunteers raise heirloom fruits and vegetables to augment the produce that Soby's purchases from local farmers. You can't get much more "farm to table" than that. The vibrant bar area of Soby's is a popular place to meet for a drink and a snack in Greenville, with spicy pimento cheese and a rich lobster mac and cheese being the favorite small plates for the bar crowd. Both dishes make a fine start to a full meal at Soby's as well. The BLT wedge salad is redolent with smoke thanks to the addition of Benton's bacon to accompany the creamy blue cheese dressing.

For dinner, take a look at the pork tenderloin with applewood-smoked bacon wrapped around roasted slices of loin served atop a habanero butter sauce. Another interesting sauce at Soby's is their Cheerwine BBQ Sauce made from the regional favorite cherry soft drink. Soby's serves this sauce over braised short ribs for a sweet and fruity finish to the beef. With horseradish mashed potatoes on the side to add some zing to the plate, the short ribs make for a very hearty and flavorful dinner.

But hopefully that plate isn't so filling that you'll pass on dessert, because then you might miss out on a slice of Soby's famous White Chocolate Banana Cream Pie, and that would just be wrong.

SPECIALTIES: Barbecue Shrimp and Grits, Bacon-Wrapped Pork Tenderloin, Crab Cakes Remoulade

INSIDER TIP: Soby's New South Cuisine is open for dinner only except on Sundays when they serve a popular brunch. For breakfast or lunch during the week, check out Soby's on the Side, a sister restaurant that serves deli/bistro food right around the corner from the front door of Soby's.

Find a recipe from this restaurant on page 242.

SOMETHING DIFFERENT

213 Old Virginia Street
Urbanna, VA 23175
(804) 758-8000
www.pine3.info

Dan Gill is a real character, in the absolute best sense of the word. Most people appreciate how hard a job it is to run a country store and restaurant, but Gill knows all about hard work. He grew up on a family farm in eastern Virginia and then attended Virginia Tech where he earned both his bachelor's and master's degrees in poultry science with the intention of continuing the family turkey business.

However, he learned just enough in college to realize that there was no way to compete with the huge factory farms that were beginning to dominate the industry in the 1970s, so he moved to diversify the farm into hogs, cattle, and soybeans. Even this strategy proved to be a losing proposition, so Gill decided to buy a small convenience store.

Knowing that he needed to stand out, Gill expanded the store to include a small dining area and named it Something Different. Apparently the region was looking for something different because his little store has become a popular destination for diners looking for great food, especially barbecue. Gill's talent for smoked meat is the result of his innate curiosity and knowledge of the scientific process of cooking meat over wood.

Gill considers himself an "Ethno-Gastronomist," which he describes as a student of "the food of the people." He contributes his musings on culture and cuisine to a regional magazine and publishes them on the restaurant's website. Cooking methods, preserving techniques, and family recipes are all popular topics for Gill's studies, and diners at Something Different delight in his ongoing commentary while they enjoy their meals.

Gill's dining room/classroom is a quaint, comfortable space with just a few butcher-block tables and a bar that stretches the length of the dining room. Burlap sacks ring the top of the room like rustic crown molding dividing the walls from the tin-paneled ceilings.

Every dish on Something Different's menu has a story behind it. The famous Virginia Sandwich was created to tell Virginia's culinary heritage between two slices of bread, with Virginia country ham and smoked turkey salad so tasty that it was featured in a book of great American sandwiches.

There is always something cooking on the smoker at Something Different, from Piedmont-style pulled pork to smoked turkey, roast beef, salmon, and pork ribs. A unique treat is a dry-rubbed Angus sirloin tri-tip that is smoked to medium-rare and sold either by the pound or as the star of a super sandwich.

Pies, cakes, and cobblers are all popular desserts, but the real treat is Gill's selection of super-premium homemade ice creams. The best flavor of the bunch is the Hot Chocolate Ice Cream, which is not hot like cocoa in a mug, but rather fired up with chili peppers to create a unique sweet and spicy, hot and cold treat that demonstrates the genius results of Gill's ethno-gastronomic studies. Class is in session!

SPECIALTIES: Smoked Tri-Tip, Virginia Sandwich, dense all-natural ice creams

INSIDER TIP: Something Different's Applechain is a crazy take on the traditional hot dog. The wiener is sliced and assembled crossways on a bun like links in a chain. The Applechain is topped with local apple butter and prepared mustard to create a sandwich so popular that it has its own fan club on Facebook.

Find recipes from this restaurant on pages 260 and 282.

THE SOUTHERN FOODIE'S GUIDE TO THE PIG

114

SOUTH ON MAIN

1304 South Main Street
Little Rock, AR 72202
(501) 244-9660
www.southonmain.com

Oxford American magazine is well-known as an authoritative documenter of "the complexity and vitality of the American South." The magazine studies many aspects of Southern society including literature, music, film, and food. So when they acquired new offices in downtown Little Rock, it was logical for them to consider some use for the rest of the building complex that might highlight the best of Southern culture.

The result is South on Main, an innovative space that is both restaurant and performing venue where Chef Matt Bell can concentrate on the region's cuisine and patrons can enjoy musical and theatre performances in the space after dinner service. As part of *OA*'s educational mission, South on Main seeks to explore the culinary traditions of the region and glorify the resourcefulness of Southern cooks.

Chef Bell describes the food at South on Main as "Refined Southern," focusing on showcasing the sort of cooking that folks do at home, but served in a fine-dining environment that manages to avoid being overly formal. The dining area is very comfortable with huge windows, bright walls, and tile floors. Tea and water are poured out of ceramic pitchers into blue Mason jars that would look at home on your grandmother's table.

In a nod to their landlords at *Oxford American*, an old-style typewriter appears both as a room decoration and as part of the restaurant's logo. A low wall divides the dining room from the bar and stage area, and a prominent sign identifies the farmers, bakers, and other purveyors who are crucial to the success of South on Main.

The menu kicks off with a selection of snacks that include Southern specialties like boiled peanuts, creamed greens, and an updated version of chicken liver mousse with fig mustard and pickles. Livers appear again on the popular Hot Chicken Liver Salad with blue cheese and bacon to intensify the flavors of this rich dish. Soup options include white bean and tomato soups as well as a rabbit and vegetable stew with cornbread croutons that could easily grace the dining table of any hunting camp in Arkansas.

Main dishes feature more meaty pleasures like a grilled rib eye served with potato mash and onion rings and a big plate of pork chops atop a bed of bacon-studded creamed greens garnished with fried hominy. Another cross-regional treat is a catfish Hoppin' John with pickled tomatoes and fried okra.

The desserts at South on Main are cleverly labeled "Pies, Bars, and Jars." The "Pie" section is self-explanatory, but remarkable, particularly when the selection of the day is the Chocolate-Peanut Butter Pie. "Bars" refers to the homemade candy bars like the Buttery Finger made by the talented pastry chefs at South on Main. "Jars" can be filled with just about anything, as long as it's gooey and delicious. Combinations like Oatmeal Cream Pie and Loblolly Ice Cream will have you asking for a longer spoon to scoop out every last bite.

SPECIALTIES: Rabbit and Vegetable Stew, Catfish Hoppin' John, Pork Chops with Fried Hominy

INSIDER TIP: South on Main invites guests to submit their favorite Southern recipes, which Chef Bell might just add his own flair to and feature the dish and the family's name on the menu.

Find a recipe from this restaurant on page 175.

RESTAURANT PROFILES

SOUTHERN SOUL BARBECUE

2020 Demere Road
St. Simons, GA 31522
(912) 638-7685
www.southernsoulbbq.com

Legend has it that the first Brunswick stew was made in 1898 on St. Simons Island near Brunswick, Georgia, so when folks say that Southern Soul Barbecue makes the prototypical version of this thick, smoky, meaty concoction, history is on their side. But while the historians fight over whether Georgia or Virginia is the true home of Brunswick stew, pit masters Griffin Bufkin and Harrison Sapp continue to put out bowl after bowl of this hearty delicacy in addition to some of the best smoked meats in the entire South.

Their smokehouse is located in a converted gas station that was once known for keeping chimpanzees to attract tourists in to buy fuel. Now it's the smell of smoky oak that encourages folks to detour off of Interstate 95 on the way to or from Florida. It's always a good rule of thumb that if you don't see a stack of wood somewhere near the building when you pull into the parking lot of a barbecue joint, you're better off to just keep on moving down the road. At Southern Soul, ricks of wood are positioned all over to help feed those hungry smokers, since just about everything on the menu spends some time cooking over wood.

A long list of sandwiches features the products of those smokers with the Southern Soul Jumbo Pork Sandwich leading the pack. Topped with your choice of four sauces—their signature tomato-based Sweet Georgia Soul Sauce, a mustardy Low Southern Soul Sauce, a vinegar-based Red Swine Wine Sauce, or the cayenne and Sriracha Hot Southern Soul Sauce—the sandwich can take on decidedly different characters based on your decision. Or try all four!

Other unique sandwiches include the Knuckle Sammich, which is two small barbecue pork sliders, an excellent Burnt Ends Sandwich that features chopped and sauced beef brisket on a toasted bun, and the cleverly named and constructed Barbecuban with pork, pickles, Swiss cheese, and prepared mustard. Even the normally ho-hum pimento cheese sandwich can be kicked up a notch by asking the kitchen to grill it on top of the flat-top so that it picks up extra flavors from the griddle.

Other meats can be ordered by the plate or by the pound. Smoked sausage and St. Louis-Cut Smoked Pork Dry Rub Ribs are particular specialties of the house, but you really can't go wrong with any of the choices, including smoked turkey, brisket, chicken, pork butt, and some really interesting smoked chicken salad.

Southern Soul Barbecue offers a much longer list of side dishes than at a typical barbecue restaurant, and all the options are very Southern (and soulful). Choose between Soul Slaw, fried okra, that famous Brunswick stew, Lowcountry specialty Hoppin' John, and collard greens as a side or by the pint. Some truly addictive fried green beans are a real treat, and Southern Soul sells them by the sack if you want some for the ride home. Though it's hard to imagine having any room left for extra beans after a meal at Southern Soul Barbecue.

SPECIALTIES : Smoked Sausage, St. Louis-Cut Smoked Pork Dry Rub Ribs, Brunswick Stew, Pulled Pork

INSIDER TIP : All of Southern Soul's sauces and their secret St. Simon's Soul Dust rub are available for sale at the restaurant and online. Bufkin and Sapp suggest you "rub it on anything and everywhere."

Find recipes from this restaurant on pages 162 and 194.

ST. JOHN'S RESTAURANT

1278 Market Street
Chattanooga, TN 37402
(423) 266-4400
www.stjohnsrestaurant.com

Chef Daniel Lindley took a long path to get back to his hometown of Chattanooga to become the chef at St. John's Restaurant. His first big gig after college was cooking for a crew of 350 people on the *Anastasis*, a hospital ship that ran between Europe and West Africa. After a job like that, working in the kitchen of a Manhattan restaurant was a piece of cake, even if his boss at Gramercy Tavern was Tom Collichio, the tough head judge of television's *Top Chef*.

Eventually home and family called, and Lindley returned to Chattanooga to cook at his brother's new restaurant, St. John's. Recognized as the top fine-dining establishment in the city, St. John's is located in the St. John's Hotel building, a flatiron construction that had fallen into disrepair and been abandoned over the years.

Rescued from condemnation, the building has been restored into a dramatic example of urban renewal and has become a centerpiece of the Southside neighborhood near the famed Chattanooga Choo Choo. The interior of the two-story restaurant is romantically lit and has a very contemporary décor. Downstairs is the more vibrant area, with servers rushing in and out of the kitchen between tables of animated diners enjoying their meals. For a quieter, more intimate experience, request a table upstairs where you can watch the action from above.

The very professional waitstaff offers excellent service without ever appearing too stuffy. While many patrons do dress up for a meal at St. John's before an evening out, casual diners are not made to feel uncomfortable. Servers are well-informed about the dishes, which is fortunate since the menu changes often according to the season, and the ingredients utilized by the kitchen can shift depending on what are the freshest vegetables brought to the kitchen daily by local farmers.

Even apparently simple dishes like house-made potato chips are made novel thanks to the addition of eighteen different Indian-inspired spices to create a truly unique bar snack. St. John's version of bacon and eggs is actually a crispy pork belly served with a perfectly poached egg and a delightful cornbread pudding.

More traditional sliced bacon is wrapped around a quail and served on top of a nest of creamy grits to create a luxurious dish. The Pork Tasting offers a triptych of loin, sausage, and pork ribs accompanied with a sweet potato puree and jalapeño and smoked onion relish for a delightful tour of the pig.

You must save room for the perfect ending to a memorable evening at St. John's with their Chocolate Molten Cake made with graham crackers and espresso-chocolate granache and s'mores ice cream. It sure is a far cry from hospital ship food.

SPECIALTIES: Bacon-Wrapped Quail, Chocolate Molten Cake

INSIDER TIP: For a different experience of Chef Lindley's cuisine, try the more casual St. John's Meeting Place right next door or his Italian restaurant, Alleia, just around the corner.

Find recipes from this restaurant on pages 198 and 252.

STELLA'S KENTUCKY DELI

143 Jefferson Street
Lexington, KY 40508
(859) 255-3354
www.stellaskentuckydeli.com

Stella's calls itself a deli, but there aren't many delis around where you can get a properly made Sazerac cocktail along with your meal. At Stella's Kentucky Deli in Lexington, this famous New Orleans libation is just one example of the delightful surprises you'll encounter on their menu.

Open for brunch, lunch, and dinner, any hour is the right time to visit if you're in search of creative soups, salads, or sandwiches that demonstrate the restaurant's dedication to simple, high-quality foods that represent the best of Kentucky's local farmers and ingredients. The basis for many of the top lunch options is the Kentucky Burger, a local bluegrass-finished Black Angus burger served with lettuce, tomato, and crisp onions. This burger is the launching pad for several incredible variations. The Griff Burger adds bacon, blue cheese, Dijon, and apples for a delightfully crunchy and funky change of pace. The Revro tops the Kentucky Burger with more bacon, an expertly fried green tomato, and herbaceous basil mayo to add a gourmet touch to a down-home treat.

The dinner hour offers an even more extensive menu with an interesting array of appetizers, salads, and entrées to accompany the sandwiches and burgers. Start your meal with a platter of local sausage bites featuring chorizo, bratwurst, or double-smoked andouille from nearby Stone Cross Farms. Delightful Deviled Eggs or a Pimento Cheese Plate are also quintessentially Southern ways to kick off the evening meal. Stella's takes advantage of the availability of excellent Kentucky country ham to top one of their best dinner salads along with apple slices and blue cheese. Vegetarians can feel at home in the deli too, thanks to some excellent meat-free options like a Hummus Plate and a popular Lentil Burger. There's even a vegetarian version of the famous Kentucky stalwart, the Hot Brown, that substitutes grilled seasonal local veggies for the turkey and bacon on the traditional sandwich, but without skimping on the ridiculously cheesy mornay sauce.

Speaking of cheese, the Truffled Mac and Cheese made with Kenny's Farmhouse Asiago, Swiss, Jack, and Cheddar cheeses finished with white truffle oil and garlic croutons is a meal in and of itself and a "can't miss" experience at Stella's. If you still have any room after that, try the delicious pork loin finished with a sweet pan sauce made from apples and two Bluegrass favorites, bourbon and Ale-8-one soda.

For a high-end meal at affordable prices served in the casual atmosphere of a cozy deli, Stella's is a wonderful choice if you're dining out any time of day in Lexington.

SPECIALTIES: Kentucky Burger, Truffled Mac and Cheese
INSIDER TIP: Lots of folks visit just to try that decadent Truffled Mac and Cheese, but be warned that it's only served after 4:00.

Find recipes from this restaurant on pages 130 and 224.

SWINE SOUTHERN TABLE AND BAR

2415 Ponce De Leon Boulevard
Coral Gables, FL 33134
(786) 360-6433
www.runpigrun.com

After the success of Yardbird, a sister restaurant dedicated to the glorification of the chicken, there was little doubt that the Miami area would accept Swine Southern Table and Bar. This casual shrine to the pig hit the ground trotting when it opened in early 2013 to almost universal acclaim from diners.

The atmosphere is decidedly laid-back at Swine, where they'll text you when your table is ready, which is good since they don't take reservations and waits can be long. The interior is rustic, faced with barn wood to offer a hip vibe. A popular bar extends the piggy motif with cocktails like a bacon-infused Old Fashioned and the spicy Ready, Fire, Aim, a drink that features mezcal, pink peppercorns, and Hellfire bitters.

Any of these libations should get your juices flowing for the upcoming pork feast, because at Swine, they use bacon as a condiment. The salty smoked belly meat appears on the menu as an ingredient in several small dishes and sides, including the Fried Green Tomato BLT (naturally), cornbread, mac and cheese, several salads, and even as part of the vinaigrette drizzled over delicious, crispy Brussels sprouts.

High-end barbecue dishes like 1855 Black Angus Burnt Ends, Wood-Grilled Pork Cheeks, BBQ Bone Marrow, Heritage Pork 'N' Beans, and a 14-Hour House Smoked Brisket demonstrate an homage to the pit masters of old but with a decidedly modern twist on the traditions. After all, you can't get much farther south than the Miami area, so it's only appropriate for Swine to develop as a caretaker for Southern food culture in South Florida.

More exotic versions of Southern classics like Hoppin' John and chicken and waffles receive unique Swine treatment thanks to the substitution of new proteins. The Hoppin' Jack adds lusciously rich confit rabbit leg to the Lowcountry staple, and the result is delightfully toothsome. Country fried bacon replaces the expected chicken in the waffle dish, and the addition of bourbon maple syrup takes this savory dish right over the top!

In true barbecue tradition, the Memphis-style spare ribs are available "till we run out," so get there early if your heart is set on a half-rack of these smoky treats. Fortunately, unlike getting shut out at a barbecue shack in the middle of nowhere, when the "out of meat" sign goes up in the window, at Swine Southern Table there are always plenty of other excellent options on the menu for fans of the Miami meat.

SPECIALTIES: Hoppin' Jack, Spare Ribs
INSIDER TIP: A huge sign in the main dining room offers sage advice: "What bacon and whiskey don't cure, there ain't no cure for."

Find a recipe from this restaurant on page 264.

THE SOUTHERN FOODIE'S GUIDE TO THE PIG

TABLE 100

100 Ridge Way
Flowood, MS 39232
(601) 420-4202
www.tableonehundred.com

Thanks to a cozy atmosphere, an affordable menu filled with big flavors, and a popular piano bar, Table 100 is one of the Jackson area's favorite spots for a night out. The restaurant's namesake table has a special story behind it. It was built by a local craftsman who used salvaged bodock wood, discovered in a Mississippi woodpile stacked with detritus from the aftermath of Hurricane Katrina. Another chunk of this gorgeous wood was used to craft a chair for former president George W. Bush, so you can be seated next to a piece of history while you dine. The legs of the chairs at the table are hewn from walnut, also salvaged from Katrina.

This sort of reverence for history and locale comes through in the culinary options presented by Chef Mike Romhold. Born in Germany, Chef Romhold traveled the world picking up international influences in the many kitchens where he worked. Finally, in 2010, he settled in Flowood, Mississippi, where he gained U.S. citizenship and began to share his fusion cuisine with the residents of his new home.

International techniques meet down-home ingredients in the kitchen of Table 100, and the result is a lovely melding of the old and new worlds. Instead of using garbanzo beans to make a traditional hummus for an opening dish, Romhold employs local farmers' field peas to introduce pure Mississippi brilliance to the plate. His fried blue crab claws are served with his version of Jackson's famous comeback sauce, a proprietary remoulade that is found everywhere in the region, but that maintains distinct nuances of flavor from recipe to recipe.

Table 100's shrimp and grits are notable in that the shrimp are wrapped in bacon and served with a delicious ham jus that is also the flavor base for some amazing turnip greens on the side. This wonderful combination of pork and greens also appears in a slightly different form as part of another dinner menu highlight, the thick-cut pork chop. This pork porterhouse is served with a spoon bread casserole, wilted kale in place of the turnip greens, and a sweet and tangy cider mop jus to amplify the flavors.

Also acclaimed is the Aspen Ridge Short Rib entrée, which is braised to perfection in a bath of merlot and pomegranate jus. Fall-off-the-bone tender, this dish absolutely melts in your mouth. Local beef takes center stage in Table 100's gourmet hamburger, with Two Run Farms artisanal beef topped with house-smoked tomatoes, white Cheddar, applewood smoked bacon, lettuce, and mustard aioli served on a brioche bun. For just two dollars extra, you can add a sunny-side-up farm egg on top. And you should.

For lunch or dinner, Table 100 is tough to beat for a classy meal in the Flowood area. Whether it's for a business lunch or a special occasion, the atmosphere and the food will ensure a memorable experience.

SPECIALTIES: Shrimp and Grits, Short Ribs

INSIDER TIP: The Sunday Jazz Brunch at Table 100 is a wonderful way to wind down your weekend. Try the Signature Eggs Benedict on an old-fashioned buttermilk biscuit with hickory smoked pulled pork, poached eggs, and smoked tomato BBQ hollandaise sauce.

Find recipes from this restaurant on pages 166 and 235.

RESTAURANT PROFILES

TANGLEWOOD ORDINARY COUNTRY RESTAURANT

2210 River Road West
Maidens, VA 23102
(804) 556-3284
www.ordinary.com

Tanglewood Ordinary Country Restaurant is located basically in the middle of nowhere about thirty miles west of Richmond, Virginia, but the fact that it is anything but "ordinary" makes it a dining destination for locals and visitors from all over the region. Originally constructed as a log cabin for about eighty dollars in the 1920s, the building has served as a restaurant and dance hall for almost a century with seven different additions cobbled onto the building through the years.

The result of all of this refurbishing is a charming brunch and dinner spot that retains its original character and is believed to be one of the largest log structures still in commercial use in America. The building is now listed on the National Register of Historic Places, but it's the wonderful atmosphere, friendly staff, and great food that keep folks coming back.

Anne and Jim Hardwick have operated the business since they purchased it in 1986. Their model of serving Southern comfort food family style around large communal tables is reminiscent of boarding house meals of days gone by. The Hardwicks use recipes from friends and family to ensure that their food is authentic and delicious.

Open Thursday through Saturday for supper and Sunday for brunch and "Grandma's Sunday Dinner," Tanglewood Ordinary is the sort of place that encourages you to skip a meal before visiting. For a set price, diners are served platters of fried chicken and a choice of one other meat from a rotating list that can include roast beef, country ham, pulled pork, pot roast, meatloaf, shrimp, catfish, turkey, and many others, so every meal at Tanglewood can be different from your last visit.

After choosing your meat and beverage, a dizzying array of delicious side dishes begin their march from the kitchen to the table. Mashed potatoes and gravy are made from scratch along with cornbread and biscuits, stewed tomatoes, black-eyed peas, green beans, creamed corn, pinto beans, cole slaw, squash, or sweet potatoes. Diners pass the dishes around the table, but don't worry about running out because seconds are on the house.

If there's room on the table or in your tummy for dessert, even more options confront you. The specialty of the house is Sly Fox Pie, a delectable chocolate, buttermilk, and pecan concoction that weighs about a pound per slice. Other great desserts include chocolate chess pie, pecan pie, homemade apple cobbler with ice cream, and a fudgy brownie sundae.

It's probably a good thing that the tables are topped with old-fashioned checkerboard tablecloths at Tanglewood Ordinary Country Restaurant. That grid pattern might just help you lay out your food in the most efficient manner possible for maximum usage of the limited real estate.

SPECIALTIES: Fried Chicken, Country Ham, Sly Fox Pie

INSIDER TIP: If you're not hungry enough for the family-style deal, Tanglewood offers a single-plate option with your choice of one meat and two sides. Of course, you might get jealous watching the servers load up all the adjacent tables.

Find recipes from this restaurant on pages 192 and 195.

TOUPS' MEATERY

845 North Carrolton Avenue
New Orleans, LA 70119
(504) 252-4999
www.toupsmeatery.com

Chef Isaac Toups' family has roots reaching back over three centuries in Louisiana. The chef was born and raised in Rayne, Louisiana, and he cut his culinary teeth working in some of Emeril Lagasse's kitchens around the Big Easy. So it was no surprise that when Toups and his wife, Amanda, decided to open their own place in the Mid-City neighborhood of New Orleans that the restaurant would be steeped in Louisiana traditions. Specifically, at Toups' Meatery, the focus is on house-made sausages and meats cured by Toups himself in the kitchen.

At this shrine to four-legged fare, the absolute must-order appetizer is the Meatery Board, a selection of the chef's latest charcuterie creations. Individual items change on the whim of the kitchen, but you can expect some incredible combination of cured meats, sausages, boudin balls, pickled vegetables, and mustards. The meatballs with ginger-lemongrass BBQ sauce and Gruyere are also an excellent choice to kick off a meal at the Meatery.

The menu encourages mixing and matching plates to create your own experience thanks to a long roster of á la carte options designed for the adventurous eater. Toups' crispy Pork Cracklins are seriously addictive and pair nicely with other innovative small dishes like Fried Green Beans, Curry Roasted Cauliflower, Chicken Liver Mousse, and Hog's Head Cheese.

Many of the small plates could also serve as appropriate side dishes for the impressive entrées. Even the more straightforward dishes like a huge double-cut pork chop benefit from Toups' creative touch. The chops are glazed with a cane syrup gastrique that harks back to the sugar cane plantations of Louisiana. Another sweet glaze, this time made from root beer, adds a depth of flavor to the short ribs that are another excellent large plate choice.

This being a Meatery, after all, it's not surprising that the Roasted Pork Shoulder Grillade is wonderfully over-the-top. Perfectly cooked shoulder is formed into a brick of meat, drizzled in delicious gravy, and served atop a grit cake and garlic flan as a foundation. For something even more unusual, try the lamb neck that is braised for hours until it is so tender that it falls off the bone. An accent of mint creates a traditional flavor pairing for lamb presented in a wholly unexpected way.

Toups' Meatery outsources their desserts to a local bakery named Debbie Does Doberge. A doberge is a traditional New Orleans dessert with many thin layers of cake alternating with pudding, and Debbie does it extremely well! The doberge flavors change periodically but are uniformly great.

The casual atmosphere of the restaurant fits perfectly in the funky Mid-City neighborhood and makes Toups' Meatery an ideal place to stop in for a creative cocktail and a few small plates or a full-on meatfest.

SPECIALTIES: Meatery Board, Pork Cracklins
INSIDER TIP: Toups' Meatery offers a short lunch menu, the highlight of which is pure New Orleans. The Chef's Lunch consists of boudin, a burger, and a beer. Take the afternoon off!

Find recipes from this restaurant on pages 196 and 239.

PART 3

···

RECIPES

DRINKS

Pig on the Porch from American Grocery

Watermelon Strawberry Lemonade

Jalapeño Soda from Stella's Kentucky Deli

Southern Fruit Tea

Mint Iced Tea

Some Pig Cocktail from Halcyon

PIG ON THE PORCH FROM AMERICAN GROCERY

Ice
2 ½ ounces Bacon-Infused Bourbon (recipe
follows)

Ginger ale*
Pork rinds for serving

Fill a Collins glass with ice. Add the Bacon-
Infused Bourbon. Top the glass with ginger
ale. Garnish with the pork rinds or a strip of
cooked bacon.

>> MAKES 1 SERVING.

* American Grocery uses Blenheim's.

BACON-INFUSED BOURBON

1 liter good bourbon

8 strips thick-cut high-quality bacon

Pour the bourbon into a nonreactive container, preferably glass. Save the bourbon bottle to serve the finished bacon-infused bourbon. Fry the bacon in a skillet over medium-high heat. Remove the bacon to a plate lined with paper towels and reserve ½ cup of the rendered bacon fat. Allow to cool but not congeal. Use the bacon for a garnish or for another use . . . perhaps for snacking while you complete the process.

Once the rendered fat has congealed slightly, pour it into the bourbon. Cover and store in a cool, dark place for 3 to 5 days, then refrigerate for 2 more, allowing the bacon fat to congeal on the surface. Skim off the bacon fat and discard. Strain the infused bourbon through a cheesecloth-lined strainer to remove any smaller bits of fat. Using a funnel, pour the bacon-infused bourbon back into the original bottles and store in a cool, dark place.

>> MAKES 1 LITER OF BOURBON.

WATERMELON STRAWBERRY LEMONADE

photo on page 126

1 cup water
1 cup sugar
4 cups seedless watermelon, chopped
1 ½ cups strawberries, caps removed and coarsely chopped

Juice of 4 large lemons
Ice
Mint leaves to garnish, optional

Bring the water and sugar to a boil in a medium saucepan over medium to medium-high heat. Set aside to cool. Place the watermelon, strawberries, and the juice of the lemons in a blender. Add the cooled sugar water. Blend on high speed until the fruit is pureed. Pour into a pitcher and place, covered, in the refrigerator. When ready to serve pour over ice-filled glasses. Garnish with mint leaves.

>> MAKES 8 SERVINGS.

JALAPEÑO SODA FROM STELLA'S KENTUCKY DELI

2 ounces Jalapeño Simple Syrup (recipe follows)

12 ounces club soda
Ice

Place the syrup, soda, and ice in a tall glass and stir. Serve immediately.

>> MAKES 1 SERVING.

JALAPEÑO SIMPLE SYRUP

1 cup sugar
1 cup water

2 to 3 medium jalapeño peppers, sliced and stem discarded (do not seed)

Mix the water and sugar in a medium saucepan and bring to a boil over high heat. Once boiling, add the jalapeños and turn off the heat. Let steep for 10 minutes and strain.

>> MAKES 2 CUPS.

SOUTHERN FRUIT TEA

Tea bags to make 1 gallon tea
3 cups boiling water
1 cup sugar
1 (6-ounce) can frozen lemonade

1 (6-ounce) can frozen orange juice
24 ounces pineapple juice
Ice

Place the tea bags in a 1-gallon pitcher and pour the boiling water over them. Add the sugar, stirring to dissolve. Let the tea bags steep in sugar water for several hours or overnight. Discard the tea bags. Add the lemonade, orange juice, and pineapple juice, stirring well. Refrigerate. Shake well before serving. Serve over ice.

>> MAKES 8 SERVINGS.

MINT ICED TEA

4 cups water
4 family-size tea bags
2 cups sugar

1 lemon, sliced for garnish
1 bunch mint leaves for garnish

Bring the water to a boil in a medium saucepan over high heat. Remove the pan from the heat, add the tea bags, and allow to steep for 20 minutes. Pour the sugar into a 1-gallon pitcher and cover with some hot tap water. Stir the sugar around to dissolve while the tea is steeping. Once the tea has steeped, remove the tea bags and pour the tea into the pitcher with the sugar and stir. Stir the tea well, making sure the sugar dissolves. Fill the pitcher with cold water to yield 1 gallon. To serve, pour each glass of tea and garnish with a slice of lemon and mint leaves.

>> MAKES 8 SERVINGS.

SOME PIG COCKTAIL FROM HALCYON

2 ounces Fat-Washed Bourbon (recipe follows)
Dash of orange bitters
Pinch of kosher salt

1 teaspoon maple syrup
Ice
1 strip cooked bacon

Pour the bourbon into a cocktail shaker. Add the orange bitters, salt, and maple syrup. Fill with ice. Cover and shake vigorously until the ice starts to break apart. Pour the contents into a rocks glass and serve garnished with a strip of cooked bacon.

>> MAKES 1 SERVING.

FAT-WASHED BOURBON

6 ounces bacon fat (rendered from high-quality bacon, such as Benton's)

1 (750 ml) bottle bourbon (a standard fifth)

Heat the bacon fat in a pan until it just starts to sizzle. Pour into a large glass container. Pour the bourbon over the fat and stir to mix well. Let the mixture sit for 48 hours covered at room temperature. Place the container in the freezer for 60 minutes and remove the frozen fat from the top. Run the remaining mixture through a very fine filter (disposable coffee filters work best) two times to remove any remaining fat solids. Pour the strained bourbon into a bottle and store indefinitely.

>> MAKES 750 ml.

BREAKFAST

Breakfast Pizza

Pork Sausage and Milk Gravy

Sausage Cups

Country Ham Gritters from Dudley's on Short

Caramel-Sour Cream Coffee Cake with Pecan Filling

Country Ham and Redeye Gravy

Sausage, Egg, and Cheese Casserole

San Diegan Omelet from Brother Juniper's

Bacon and Potato Breakfast Casserole

Maple Bacon Muffins

Bacon Tomato Gravy

Sausage Pancakes

BREAKFAST PIZZA

1 (6-ounce) package pizza dough mix

1 pound bulk pork sausage

1 cup frozen hash brown potatoes, thawed

1 ½ cups Cheddar cheese, shredded

4 large eggs

3 tablespoons milk

½ teaspoon salt

¼ teaspoon black pepper

¼ cup grated Parmesan cheese

1 large tomato, diced, optional

Preheat the oven to 375 degrees. Lightly grease a 14-inch, deep-dish pizza pan.

Prepare the pizza dough according to package directions. Pat the dough over the bottom and up the sides of the prepared pan. Bake for 3 to 4 minutes.

Brown the sausage in a large skillet over medium-high heat, stirring until crumbly. Remove to a plate lined with paper towels to drain. Sprinkle the sausage over the baked dough. Top with the thawed hash browns and Cheddar cheese. Whisk together the eggs, milk, salt, and black pepper in a small bowl until blended. Pour over the hash browns and Cheddar. Sprinkle with the Parmesan cheese. Bake for 30 minutes or until golden brown and bubbly. Garnish with diced tomatoes, cut into wedges, and serve.

>> MAKES 8 TO 10 SERVINGS.

PORK SAUSAGE AND MILK GRAVY

1 tablespoon vegetable oil
¼ cup minced yellow onion
1 teaspoon garlic, chopped
1 pound pork sausage
⅓ cup all-purpose flour

1 ⅓ cups whole or 2% milk
1 ⅓ cups heavy cream
1 teaspoon sea salt
Pinch of freshly ground black pepper
Biscuits for serving

Pour the vegetable oil into a sauté pan over medium-high heat. Add the yellow onions and garlic and sauté until wilted, 5 to 7 minutes. Add the pork sausage and break up while browning. Add the flour and stir to begin building a roux. Cook about 7 minutes, toasting the flour and stirring constantly.

Reduce the heat to medium and add the milk and cream, whisking constantly. Reduce the heat to medium-low and stir until thickened. Season with sea salt and pepper. Serve over biscuits.

≫ MAKES 5 CUPS.

SAUSAGE CUPS

½ pound sausage
1 ½ cups shredded Cheddar Jack cheese

½ cup ranch salad dressing
36 small (2-inch) phyllo cups

Preheat the oven to 350 degrees.
Cook the sausage in a small skillet over medium heat, breaking up into small pieces. Remove to a plate lined with paper towels to drain. Cool completely. Place sausage in a medium bowl, add the cheese and ranch

dressing, and mix. Place the phyllo cups on a large baking sheet. Put 1 tablespoon of the sausage mixture in each cup. Bake for 15 minutes or until bubbly. Serve immediately.

≫ MAKES 12 TO 14 SERVINGS.

COUNTRY HAM GRITTERS FROM DUDLEY'S ON SHORT

Gritters

8 to 12 (12-ounce) center-cut slices of country ham

12 cups (3 quarts) chicken stock

4 cups (1 quart) heavy cream

1 tablespoon kosher salt

5 cups white stone-ground grits*

3 cups grated white Cheddar cheese

Salt and freshly ground pepper to taste

Vegetable oil for frying

Seasoned Flour

2 cups all-purpose flour

2 tablespoons salt

1 tablespoon black pepper

4 tablespoons paprika

2 tablespoons garlic powder

TO MAKE THE GRITTERS: Line 2 loaf pans with parchment paper. Chop up the country ham slices into small cubes and place in a skillet over medium heat. Cook for 3 to 4 minutes until cooked through. Drain on a plate lined with paper towels and set aside. Combine the chicken stock, cream, and salt in a 6-quart pot and bring to a boil over medium heat. Whisk in the grits and reduce to low heat. Simmer, stirring occasionally so as not to scorch the grits, for about 30 minutes or until soft and thick. Add the chopped country ham and white Cheddar and stir to incorporate the cheese. Check and adjust seasoning. Pour into the loaf pans and allow to cool in the refrigerator overnight uncovered.

When you are ready to serve, gently remove the grits from the pans and slice into ¾-inch slices (as you would a loaf of bread), then into sticks (as you would French toast).

Preheat vegetable oil in a deep fryer to 350 degrees.

TO MAKE THE SEASONED FLOUR: In a shallow bowl combine the flour, salt, pepper, paprika, and garlic powder. Dredge the gritter sticks through the seasoned flour and place in the deep fryer in small batches. Don't overcrowd the fryer or the temperature will drop. Cook until crisp and golden, 4 to 5 minutes. Drain on a paper towel before serving.

≫ MAKES 14 SERVINGS.

* Dudley's uses Kentucky's Weisenberger brand.

NOTE: Dudley's serves the gritters with Kentucky ale beer cheese and celery slaw (see recipes on page 190 and 163).

CARAMEL-SOUR CREAM COFFEE CAKE WITH PECAN FILLING

Cake

1 ½ cups sugar

1 cup (2 sticks) butter, softened

2 large eggs, beaten

1 teaspoon vanilla extract

2 cups all-purpose flour

½ teaspoon baking soda

1 teaspoon baking powder

1 cup sour cream

½ cup firmly packed brown sugar

1 ½ teaspoons ground cinnamon

1 cup pecans, finely chopped

Topping

½ cup (1 stick) butter

½ cup light cream

1 cup firmly packed brown sugar

1 cup pecans, finely chopped

Preheat the oven to 350 degrees. Grease and flour a 9 x 13-inch baking dish.

TO MAKE THE CAKE: Place the sugar and butter in the bowl of an electric mixer (or use a hand mixer and a large bowl) and cream the sugar and butter together. Add the eggs and vanilla. In a medium bowl combine the flour, baking soda, and baking powder together. Alternating with the sour cream, add the flour mixture to the butter mixture. Beat until fluffy or about 2 minutes.

Combine the brown sugar, cinnamon, and pecans in a small bowl. Pour half of the batter in the baking dish. Sprinkle half of the pecan mixture on top of the batter. Spread the remaining batter on top and sprinkle with the remaining pecan mixture. Bake for 30 to 35 minutes or until a toothpick inserted comes out clean.

TO MAKE THE TOPPING: Prepare the topping while the cake bakes. Melt the butter in a medium saucepan over medium heat. Add the cream, brown sugar, and pecans and stir for 4 minutes.

When the cake is done, remove from the oven and set the oven to broil at the low setting. Pour the caramel topping over the cake, spreading evenly. Place the cake under the broiler for 2 minutes or until the topping begins to bubble. Watch carefully. Let the cake cool. Store leftovers covered in the refrigerator.

>> MAKES 24 SERVINGS.

NOTE: You can make this a day ahead.

COUNTRY HAM AND REDEYE GRAVY

8 country ham slices
2 cups water

2 teaspoons instant coffee for every 2 slices
fried ham
Hot biscuits for serving

Preheat a large cast-iron skillet over medium-high heat. Fry the ham slices. Remove the country ham from the skillet, leaving the drippings. Add the water and stir until it comes to a boil. Add the coffee and boil a little longer. Serve with hot split biscuits and a spoonful of gravy.

>> MAKES 4 SERVINGS.

SAUSAGE, EGG, AND CHEESE CASSEROLE

1 pound breakfast sausage
9 large eggs
9 slices white bread, crusts removed, cubed
¾ cup shredded Swiss cheese

¾ cup shredded Cheddar cheese
¾ cup milk
1 ½ teaspoons salt

Place the sausage in a skillet over medium heat and crumble while cooking until no longer pink. Drain on a plate lined with paper towels. In a large bowl whisk the eggs until combined. Mix in the bread, Swiss and Cheddar cheeses, milk, and salt, and then fold in the sausage. Pour the mixture into a greased 9 x 13-inch baking pan. Cover and refrigerate overnight.

Preheat the oven to 350 degrees. Bake uncovered for 45 minutes. Let sit for 10 minutes before serving.

>> MAKES 8 SERVINGS.

SAN DIEGAN OMELET FROM BROTHER JUNIPER'S

2 small red potatoes

1 tablespoon margarine, plus more to grease the omelet pan

1 tablespoon butter

3 slices bacon

Large pinch of granulated garlic

¼ cup diced yellow onion

Salt and freshly ground black pepper to taste

½ cup diced portobello mushroom

3 large eggs

2 ½ tablespoons sour cream

½ cup tomatoes, diced

3 tablespoons crumbled feta cheese

Fill a small saucepan with enough water to cover the potatoes and bring to a boil over high heat. Boil until the potatoes are almost cooked through, 6 to 8 minutes. Drain and cool the potatoes in the refrigerator until cold. When the potatoes are cold, cut into ½-inch chunks.

In a large skillet cook the cold potato chunks with the margarine and butter for 5 to 7 minutes. In a separate skillet cook the bacon until crisp; drain on a plate lined with paper towels, then cut into small pieces. Just before the potatoes become browned, add the garlic, onions, salt, and pepper. Stir to combine. Drain off the excess oil. Remove the potatoes and set aside. In the same skillet cook the mushrooms for about 5 minutes. Remove mushrooms and set aside.

In a small bowl whisk the eggs together. Grease a 10-inch omelet pan or nonstick skillet with margarine and place the pan over medium heat. Make sure that all other ingredients are ready to assemble quickly after the eggs are cooked. Pour the eggs into the pan and cook slowly over medium heat. With a spatula, push the eggs to the center of the pan. As the eggs cook and begin to stick to the bottom of the pan, keep folding the loose eggs under the cooked portion. When almost all the egg has cooked, flip the eggs over with a spatula and cook on low for 30 seconds longer. Lay the cooked eggs on a flat plate. Spread with sour cream and then place potatoes on top, followed by the mushrooms, tomatoes, and bacon. Top with feta cheese.

>> MAKES 1 SERVING.

Cook the bacon in a skillet over medium-high heat or in a 400-degree oven (see page 13 for tips). While the bacon is cooking, put the potatoes in a 9 x 13-inch baking dish. Mix the pepper Jack and Cheddar cheeses together and sprinkle on top of the potatoes. When the bacon is done cooking, drain it on a plate lined with paper towels. Crumble the bacon and sprinkle it over the cheese and potato mixture.

In a small bowl whisk together the eggs, milk, salt, and pepper until completely combined. Pour the egg mixture evenly over the potato mixture. Cover and refrigerate overnight or for 7 to 8 hours.

When ready to bake, preheat the oven to 350 degrees. Bake uncovered for 40 to 45 minutes or until the cheese is bubbly but not brown. Allow to stand for 15 minutes before cutting.

>> MAKES 8 SERVINGS.

BACON AND POTATO BREAKFAST CASSEROLE

12 ounces bacon

4 cups hash brown potatoes, completely thawed

1 ½ cups pepper Jack cheese

1 ½ cups Cheddar cheese

3 large eggs

1 cup milk

½ teaspoon salt

½ teaspoon black pepper

Preheat the oven to 400 degrees. Grease or spray 12 regular-size muffin cups.

In a large bowl mix the flour, brown sugar, baking soda, and salt. In a small bowl stir the milk, syrup, butter, and egg until blended. Add the milk mixture to flour mixture and stir just until the dry ingredients are moistened. Stir in the bacon. Fill the muffin cups ¾ full. Bake for 16 to 18 minutes or until a toothpick inserted in the center comes out clean. Immediately remove the muffins from the pan. Serve warm.

>> MAKES 12 MUFFINS.

MAPLE BACON MUFFINS

1 ²/₃ cups all-purpose flour

¹/₃ cup firmly packed brown sugar

2 teaspoons baking soda

¹/₈ teaspoon salt

¹/₂ cup whole or 2% milk

¹/₂ cup real maple syrup

¹/₃ cup butter, melted

1 large egg

¹/₂ cup bacon, cooked and crumbled (about 6 slices)

BACON TOMATO GRAVY

½ pound sliced bacon, diced
1 small onion, chopped
2 tablespoons all-purpose flour
¼ teaspoon salt

¼ teaspoon black pepper
1 (14.5-ounce) can diced tomatoes, undrained
3 cups tomato juice
Hot biscuits for serving

In a skillet over medium heat, cook the bacon until crisp. Reserve 2 tablespoons of the drippings and drain the bacon on a plate lined with paper towels. Add the onion to the drippings and cook until tender. Reduce the heat to low and stir in the flour, salt, and pepper. Stir until the mixture is golden brown. Add the tomatoes and juice slowly and stir well. Increase the heat to medium and bring to a boil, cooking and stirring for 3 more minutes. Reduce the heat back to low and simmer uncovered for 10 or 15 minutes or until thickened, stirring occasionally. Stir in the bacon and serve over biscuits.

>> MAKES 8 SERVINGS.

SAUSAGE PANCAKES

1 pound breakfast sausage
2 cups self-rising flour
3 tablespoons sugar
¼ teaspoon salt
¼ teaspoon baking powder

1 ¾ cups buttermilk
2 large eggs, separated
¼ cup (½ stick) butter, melted
Maple syrup

Place the sausage in a large skillet over medium heat. Break it apart as it begins to brown. Remove the sausage from the pan to drain on a plate lined with paper towels. Discard the excess grease or keep 2 tablespoons for frying the pancakes.

In a large bowl combine the flour, sugar, salt, and baking powder. In a small bowl whisk together the buttermilk and egg yolks until smooth and velvety. In another small bowl place the egg whites. Add the buttermilk mixture to the flour mixture. Stir with a spoon until well incorporated. Add the melted butter and stir until well incorporated. Using a hand mixer, beat the egg whites until stiff peaks are formed, 2 to 3 minutes. Fold the egg whites into the batter using a rubber spatula. The batter should be fluffy.

In a large nonstick skillet over medium heat, add the 2 tablespoons of the reserved sausage fat (you can also use 2 tablespoons of butter if you wish). Working in batches, ladle the batter into the pan to form 4-inch pancakes. Sprinkle a heaping tablespoon of cooked sausage onto each pancake. The batter should puff up around sausage. Cook each pancake for 2 to 3 minutes, then flip, cooking for an additional 2 to 3 minutes until nicely browned and cooked through. Repeat with the remaining batter and sausage. Once finished, remove the pancakes from the pan onto a platter. Serve with syrup.

>> MAKES 4 SERVINGS.

BREAD

Sweet Potato Biscuits with Pecans

Spicy Pecan Cheese Wafers

Southern Buttermilk Biscuits

Bacon Cheddar Hush Puppies

Maple Bacon and Cheddar Biscuits

Bacon Cinnamon Pull-Apart Bread from Empire State South

Sweet Potato Hush Puppies

BBQ Cornbread

Bacon-Crusted Cornbread

Sausage Cornbread

SWEET POTATO BISCUITS WITH PECANS

1 small sweet potato*
2 ¼ cups all-purpose flour
1 tablespoon baking powder
½ teaspoon salt
½ cup vegetable shortening
½ cup pecans, chopped

½ cup sour cream
2 tablespoons brown sugar
½ teaspoon ground cinnamon
Deli-sliced country ham, optional
Peach preserves, optional

Preheat the oven to 350 degrees. Wrap the sweet potato in aluminum foil. Bake for 45 minutes or until tender. Cool, scoop out the pulp into a small bowl, and mash. (You will need ¾ cup.)

Increase the oven to 425 degrees. Lightly grease a baking sheet.

In a large bowl combine the flour, baking powder, and salt. Add the shortening and mix with pastry blender or your fingers until it becomes crumbly. Stir in the pecans. Add the sour cream, brown sugar, and cinnamon to the sweet potato. Add the sweet potato mixture to the flour mixture and stir until just moistened. Turn out on a lightly floured surface and knead 6 or 7 times. Roll the dough to a ¾-inch thickness. Cut with a 2-inch biscuit cutter. Place on the baking sheet. Bake for 12 to 15 minutes or until golden brown. If desired, split in half and top with country ham and peach preserves.

>> MAKES 20 BISCUITS.

* You can use ³/4 cup canned sweet potatoes. Just add to the sour cream, brown sugar, and cinnamon.

SPICY PECAN CHEESE WAFERS

1 cup sharp Cheddar cheese, room temperature
½ cup (1 stick) butter, softened
1 ¼ cups all-purpose flour

¼ teaspoon salt
¼ teaspoon cayenne pepper
1 cup pecans, chopped

Combine the cheese and butter in the bowl of an electric mixer and beat at low speed until smooth. Combine the flour, salt, and cayenne pepper in a small bowl. Add the flour mixture to the cheese mixture and beat until blended. Stir in the pecans. Shape the dough into a log. Wrap in plastic wrap and refrigerate overnight.

Preheat the oven to 325 degrees. Lightly grease a large baking sheet. Slice the dough in ¼-inch thick wafers. Place on baking sheet. Bake for 10 to 12 minutes or until lightly brown.

>> MAKES 2 DOZEN.

SOUTHERN BUTTERMILK BISCUITS

4 cups all-purpose flour, plus more for dusting the work surface

1 tablespoon plus 1 teaspoon baking powder

1 teaspoon baking soda

1 teaspoon salt

1 teaspoon sugar

1 cup (2 sticks) butter, cold and cut into small pieces

1 ¾ cups buttermilk

Preheat the oven to 375 degrees.

In a large bowl mix together the flour, baking powder, baking soda, salt, and sugar. Use a pastry blender or your fingers to cut the butter into the flour until it resembles coarse crumbs with a few large clumps remaining. Pour in the buttermilk and fold it into the dough, working in all directions and incorporating crumbs at the bottom of the bowl, until the dough just comes together. The dough will be slightly sticky. Do not overmix.

Turn out the dough onto a lightly floured work surface. With floured fingers, gently pat the dough into a 1-inch thick round, pressing in any loose bits. Do not overwork the dough. Use a floured biscuit cutter to cut out the biscuits (if you use a 2 ¼-inch cutter, you should get about 12 biscuits) as close together as possible. Place the biscuits about 1 ½ inches apart on an unlined baking sheet. Brush the tops with butter or buttermilk if desired. Bake for 18 to 20 minutes.

≫ MAKES 12 BISCUITS.

BACON CHEDDAR HUSH PUPPIES

Vegetable oil for deep frying

2 cups cornmeal mix

1 cup buttermilk

1 large egg

¼ teaspoon salt

¼ teaspoon freshly ground pepper

1 cup (4 ounces) shredded Cheddar cheese

6 slices bacon, crisply cooked, crumbled

In a deep fryer or large saucepan, heat the oil to 360 degrees. In a large bowl add the cornmeal mix, buttermilk, egg, salt, and pepper. Stir in the cheese and bacon. Drop batter by the tablespoon into the hot oil. Fry for 2 to 3 minutes, turning several times, until golden brown. Drain on paper towels. Serve warm.

≫ MAKES 12 SERVINGS.

MAPLE BACON AND CHEDDAR BISCUITS

6 slices bacon

3 tablespoons maple syrup

3 cups all-purpose flour

4 teaspoons baking powder

1 teaspoon baking soda

3 tablespoons sugar

¼ teaspoon kosher salt

¾ cup (1 ½ sticks) butter, cold and cut into small cubes

1 ½ cups shredded Cheddar cheese

1 ½ cups buttermilk

Preheat the oven to 425 degrees. Line a baking sheet with aluminum foil and place the bacon slices flat on the baking sheet. Cook in the oven for 7 to 8 minutes. When the bacon is brown and crispy, remove the pan from oven and use a pastry brush to glaze with the maple syrup. When cool, finely chop up the bacon into small pieces.

Place the flour, baking powder, baking soda, sugar, and salt in a large bowl. Add the cold butter cubes and use your fingers or a pastry blender to create a crumbly mixture. Add the cheese and bacon and stir to combine. Add the buttermilk to moisten the dough and fold together. Drop by ½ cupful onto a parchment-lined baking sheet, spacing them about 1 ½ inches apart. Bake for 15 to 17 minutes, until golden brown.

>> MAKES 18 BISCUITS.

In a large skillet over medium heat, cook the bacon until it is crispy. Remove the bacon from the pan to a plate lined with paper towels to drain and strain the pan grease into a small heat-proof bowl. Set aside and keep warm. Chop the bacon.

Grease a 10-inch Bundt pan with butter. In a small saucepan over medium heat, bring the milk to 110 degrees. Add the yeast.

In the bowl of an electric mixer with a paddle attachment, mix the flour, sugar, salt, and chopped bacon. On low speed, slowly add the beaten egg, the milk mixture, and melted butter. Mix until the dough comes together. Switch to the hook attachment and mix another 5 minutes. The dough should be slightly tacky, but should not stick to the bottom of the bowl. If it is too sticky, add a small amount of flour until it comes together. Place the dough in a large greased bowl, cover with plastic wrap, and allow to rest until it has doubled in size, about 1 hour.

After the dough has rested, punch it down in the bowl. Pinch the dough off in golf ball–size pieces and place on a baking sheet covered with plastic wrap.

Mix the brown sugar and cinnamon in a small bowl. Place the warm bacon fat in another small bowl, taking care that the fat is not hot enough to burn but not cold enough to congeal. Unwrap the dough and use a slotted spoon to dip 1 to 3 balls at a time into the bacon fat. Drain the excess and roll the balls in the sugar mixture. Remove and place in the Bundt pan. Repeat. If the fat becomes too cold and congeals, warm on the stovetop and keep going. When you are finished you should have a few layers with the dough placed in random order. Wrap the Bundt pan in plastic and let it rest until the dough doubles in size again, 45 to 60 minutes.

Preheat the oven to 350 degrees. Once the dough has doubled, remove the plastic wrap and cook for 30 minutes. Cool for 5 minutes.

>> MAKES 12 SERVINGS.

BACON CINNAMON PULL-APART BREAD FROM EMPIRE STATE SOUTH

1 pound bacon

2 tablespoons butter (or reserved bacon fat), melted, plus extra for greasing the pan

1 ⅓ cups whole or 2% milk

2 ¼ teaspoons instant yeast

3 ½ cups all-purpose flour

¼ cup sugar

2 teaspoons salt

1 large egg, lightly beaten

1 cup firmly packed dark brown sugar

2 teaspoons freshly ground cinnamon

SWEET POTATO HUSH PUPPIES

Vegetable shortening for frying

½ cup cooked sweet potato puree

2 large eggs

¼ cup cornmeal

¼ cup all-purpose flour

½ teaspoon salt

¼ teaspoon ground cinnamon

Freshly ground black pepper to taste

Heat the shortening to 360 degrees in a deep skillet or deep fryer. In a large bowl mix the sweet potato puree, eggs, cornmeal, flour, salt, cinnamon, and pepper together. Drop by the tablespoon into the hot grease. Fry 2 to 3 minutes until golden brown. Drain on paper towels and serve warm.

>> **MAKES 8 SERVINGS.**

Preheat the oven to 325 degrees. Lightly grease a deep 9 x 13-inch baking dish with butter.

Shred the pork into fine pieces. In a large bowl stir together the remaining 1 ½ cups butter, milk, and sugar. Beat in the eggs, one at a time, until well incorporated. Add the creamed corn, chilies, cheese, and shredded pork and stir until well incorporated.

In a large bowl stir together flour, cornmeal, baking powder, and salt. Add the flour mixture to the corn mixture and stir until smooth. Pour the batter into the prepared pan. Bake for 1 hour 10 minutes, or until golden brown and a toothpick inserted into the center of the pan comes out clean.

» MAKES 12 SERVINGS.

BBQ CORNBREAD

1 ½ cups butter, melted, plus more for greasing the dish

¾ pound cooked barbecue pulled pork

¼ cup plus 2 tablespoons milk

1 ½ cups sugar

6 large eggs

1 ½ (15-ounce) cans creamed corn

1 (4.5-ounce) can chopped green chilies, drained

1 ½ cups shredded Cheddar cheese

1 ½ cups all-purpose flour

1 ½ cups yellow cornmeal

2 tablespoons baking powder

Pinch of salt

BACON-CRUSTED CORNBREAD

10 thick-cut slices bacon

1 ½ cups cornmeal

1 ½ cups all-purpose flour

3 tablespoons light brown sugar

1 tablespoon baking powder

½ teaspoon salt

1 ⅔ cups whole or 2% milk

3 large eggs

3 tablespoons honey

2 tablespoons butter, melted

2 cups frozen corn kernels (unthawed)

Cook the bacon in a large skillet over medium heat until crisp. Drain on a plate lined with paper towels and reserve 2 tablespoons of drippings from the skillet. Crumble the bacon into small pieces.

Preheat the oven to 375 degrees. Coat a 12-inch ovenproof skillet with bacon drippings. Place the skillet in the oven until very hot, about 10 minutes.

Whisk the cornmeal, flour, brown sugar, baking powder, and salt in a large bowl. In another large bowl whisk the milk, eggs, honey, and butter. Stir the milk mixture into the flour mixture. Mix in the corn.

Pour the batter into the skillet. Sprinkle the bacon over the top. Bake the cornbread until golden brown, about 50 minutes. Cool in the skillet at least 30 minutes.

>> MAKES 12 SERVINGS.

SAUSAGE CORNBREAD

1 pound pork sausage

1 ½ cups cornmeal

¼ cup all-purpose flour

2 ¼ teaspoons baking powder

½ teaspoon salt

1 (15-ounce) can creamed corn

¾ cup milk

2 large eggs

¼ cup vegetable oil

2 cups (8 ounces) shredded sharp Cheddar cheese

Preheat the oven to 425 degrees. Grease a 10-inch cast-iron skillet.

In a skillet over medium heat, cook the sausage, crumbling into small pieces, and then drain. In a large bowl combine the cornmeal, flour, baking powder, and salt. Add the corn, milk, eggs, and oil. Pour half into the prepared skillet. Sprinkle with the sausage and cheese. Spread the remaining cornmeal mixture on top. Bake for 45 to 50 minutes or until a toothpick inserted in the cornbread comes out clean.

>> MAKES 8 TO 10 SERVINGS.

SOUPS AND SALADS

Smoked Pork and Okra Soup from Slightly North of Broad

Bar-B-Q Brisket Chili from Fox Brothers BBQ

Bacon, Onion, and Red Potato Soup from Mama J's Kitchen

Southern Soul Brunswick Stew from Southern Soul Barbecue

Celery Slaw from Dudley's on Short

Warm Bacon Vinaigrette from Parlor Market

Edley's Bean Salad from Edley's

Mike's Cole Slaw from Table 100

Sour Apple Jalapeño Slaw from Hammerheads

Cauliflower Gorgonzola Soup from The Green Room

Ham and Corn Chowder

Old Hickory Burgoo from Old Hickory Bar-B-Que

Applewood Bacon Salad with Fried Green Tomatoes from Felicia Suzanne's

Momma Mia's Mac Salad from The Shed

Layered Spinach Salad

Brown Pig Salad from Neely's Sandwich Shop

Bacon Salad with "Deviled" Egg from South on Main

Broccoli, Bacon, and Apple Salad

Wilted Brussels Sprouts Salad from Dudley's on Short

Green Tomato Soup with Country Ham

Bacon, Cheese, and Baked Potato Soup

SMOKED PORK AND OKRA SOUP FROM SLIGHTLY NORTH OF BROAD

1 ham hock

1 smoked pig tail

1 smoked pig neck bone

1 tablespoon butter

1 medium onion, chopped

1 bell pepper, chopped

4 celery stalks, chopped

1 carrot, sliced

1 teaspoon salt

1 cup chopped tomatoes, fresh or canned

1 pound fresh okra, chopped

2 bay leaves

1 bunch fresh thyme

Hot sauce to taste

1 tablespoon sugar

1 teaspoon black pepper

Place the ham hock, pig tail, and neck bone in a large pot over medium-low heat and cover with water. Cover and cook until falling apart, about 2 hours. Strain, saving the broth. Skim the fat from the broth. Pick the meat off the bones and save. The bones can be used again to enrich greens or butterbeans.

Add the butter, onion, pepper, celery, and carrot to the pot and cook over low heat for 5 to 10 minutes. Season with the salt. Add the hock stock and meat back to the pot and raise heat to medium-high. Add the tomatoes and okra. Season with the bay leaves, thyme, hot sauce, sugar, and pepper. Add more water if too thick. Bring to a gentle boil and then remove from the heat, discard the bay leaves, and serve.

>> MAKES 10 SERVINGS.

BAR-B-Q BRISKET CHILI FROM FOX BROTHERS BBQ

¾ cup seeded and chopped jalapeño peppers (leave seeds in for more heat)

2 pounds smoked beef brisket, chopped into 1-inch cubes

1 (28-ounce) can high-quality crushed tomatoes

1 (32-ounce) container homemade or high-quality beef stock

2 tablespoons adobo sauce (from can of chipotles in adobo)

2 tablespoons masa (corn flour)

1 cup warm water

In a heavy-bottom large pot over medium heat, add the jalapeños and sweat until tender. Add the brisket, crushed tomatoes, beef stock, and adobo sauce, turn up the heat to medium-high, and bring to a boil. Reduce the heat to low and simmer for 20 minutes. In a small bowl whisk the masa into the water, making a slurry. Add the slurry to the pot to thicken the chili. Let simmer for 5 to 10 minutes, stirring often so the meat won't settle on the bottom.

» MAKES 12 SERVINGS.

VARIATION: To make single-serving Frito pies, open 1-ounce bags of Fritos and ladle 2 tablespoons of chili over the Fritos, sprinkle with 1 tablespoon shredded Cheddar cheese, 1 tablespoon diced red onion, and 1 tablespoon fresh sliced jalapeño peppers for more heat, and maybe even a dollop of sour cream! Mix it up and eat!

Wash and slice or dice the red potatoes. Place the water, potatoes, and salt in large saucepan and bring to a boil over high heat. Reduce the heat to low and simmer for 15 minutes.

Cook the bacon in a skillet over medium-high heat until crisp. Remove to a plate lined with paper towels to drain.

Place the butter, 5 cups milk, parsley, and white pepper into the saucepan with the potatoes and bring to boil over high heat. Reduce the heat to low.

In a small bowl whisk the cornstarch into the remaining ⅛ cup milk. Pour into the saucepan and gently stir so as not to break up the potatoes. Simmer for 5 minutes on low heat. Add the onions and cook for 5 more minutes while stirring gently. Remove from the heat. Ladle into a warm soup bowl and top with slices of bacon and some shredded cheese. Serve while hot.

>> MAKES 10 TO 12 SERVINGS.

BACON, ONION, AND RED POTATO SOUP FROM MAMA J'S KITCHEN

12 medium red potatoes

8 cups water

¼ teaspoon salt

½ pound bacon

½ cup (1 stick) salted butter

5 ⅛ cups milk, divided

¼ cup fresh parsley

¼ teaspoon white pepper

½ cup cornstarch

1 large red onion, chopped

Shredded Cheddar cheese for garnish

SOUTHERN SOUL BRUNSWICK STEW FROM SOUTHERN SOUL BARBECUE

1 cup (2 sticks) salted butter

3 cups finely diced sweet onions (2 large)

2 tablespoons minced garlic

2 teaspoons cayenne pepper

1 tablespoon freshly ground black pepper

1 tablespoon sea salt

¼ cup high-quality Worcestershire sauce

½ cup North Carolina vinegar barbecue sauce (see page 42 for recipe)

1 cup sweet mustard-based barbecue sauce (try the South Carolina Sauce on page 39)

3 pounds meat (preferably smoked): pulled pork shoulder, pulled chicken, turkey, and/or chopped beef brisket in any combination

8 cups (2 quarts) crushed fresh tomatoes or high-quality canned tomatoes

2 cups coarsely chopped fresh tomatoes

4 cups fresh shucked sweet yellow or white corn kernels (or frozen, thawed)

4 cups fresh baby butter beans (or frozen, thawed)

8 cups (2 quarts) homemade or canned chicken stock

10 shakes of your favorite cayenne pepper sauce

Saltines or buttermilk cornbread for serving

In a good-size cast-iron Dutch oven or pot, melt the butter over medium-high heat. Add the onions and garlic and sweat until translucent, about 15 minutes. Stir in the cayenne pepper, black pepper, salt, and Worcestershire. Simmer for 6 to 8 minutes, then add the vinegar and mustard barbecue sauces and the meat to the pot (you want to completely cover the meat with the sauces), and cook for another 10 minutes. Add the crushed and chopped tomatoes, corn, and beans, and stir in the chicken stock and cayenne pepper sauce. Bring the mixture to a boil and reduce the heat to medium. Simmer for at least 2 hours, adding more stock to thin if needed. Plate up with saltines or warm buttermilk cornbread.

>> MAKES 18 SERVINGS.

CELERY SLAW FROM DUDLEY'S ON SHORT

4 cups celery, julienned (about 8 stalks)
4 cups carrots, julienned (about 6 carrots)
1 red bell pepper, julienned

1 cup green onions, julienned (1 to 2 bunches)
Kosher salt to taste

Combine the celery, carrots, red pepper, and green onions in a large bowl. Season lightly with salt. Toss to combine.

>> MAKES 12 SERVINGS.

WARM BACON VINAIGRETTE FROM PARLOR MARKET

4 slices bacon
4 tablespoons minced shallot (4 medium)
2 tablespoons minced garlic (2 cloves)
3 tablespoons brown sugar
6 tablespoons orange juice

5 tablespoons balsamic vinegar
3 tablespoons coarse-grain mustard
⅓ cup olive oil
½ teaspoon salt

Cook the bacon in a large skillet over medium-high heat for 8 to 10 minutes or until crisp. Remove and drain on a plate lined with paper towels. Reserve 2 tablespoons of drippings in the skillet. Crumble the bacon, and reserve for another use or to sprinkle over your salad. Or just eat it while you're making the salad! Add the shallots and garlic to the bacon drippings and cook over medium heat, stirring occasionally, 3 minutes or until tender. Add the brown sugar and cook, stirring constantly, 1 minute or until the sugar is dissolved. Add the garlic mixture, orange juice, balsamic vinegar, mustard, olive oil, and salt to a blender and process until combined.

Drizzle over a salad or store in a sealed container in the refrigerator for up to a week.

>> MAKES ENOUGH FOR 8 SERVINGS OF SALAD.

EDLEY'S BEAN SALAD FROM EDLEY'S

1 (12-ounce) can field (black-eyed) peas, rinsed

2 cups shoepeg corn

1 (15-ounce) can black beans, rinsed

1 cup finely diced red onion

1 cup finely diced red bell pepper

8 green onions, chopped

¼ cup fresh cilantro, chopped

½ cup sugar

½ cup white vinegar

3 tablespoons canola oil

2 tablespoons your favorite medium-hot pepper sauce

In a large bowl mix the peas, corn, black beans, red onions, red peppers, green onions, cilantro, sugar, vinegar, oil, and hot sauce together. Cover and refrigerate for 3 hours to allow the flavors to meld. Serve cold.

≫ MAKES 8 SERVINGS.

MIKE'S COLE SLAW FROM TABLE 100

This slaw is excellent on top of a pulled pork sandwich to add a little crunch.

2 pounds white cabbage
2 ½ teaspoons salt, divided
2 tablespoons sugar, divided
1 cup julienned onion
¼ cup sliced green onion

3 cups julienned carrots
1 tablespoon coarse black pepper
⅓ cup white vinegar
½ cup vegetable oil

Remove the leaves from the outside of the cabbage and cut in half. Remove the heart from the cabbage. Cut each half into 3 equal wedges. Slice the first 3 wedges in fine julienne and place in a large bowl. Add 1 ¼ teaspoons salt and 1 tablespoon sugar. Slice the remaining cabbage and add to the bowl along with the onion, green onion, and carrots. In a small bowl combine the remaining 1 ¼ teaspoons salt and 1 tablespoon sugar, pepper, and vinegar. Whisk in the oil. Pour the mixture on the vegetables and use both hands to knead the salad for at least 5 minutes. Check the seasoning and adjust if needed. Cover and refrigerate for at least 2 hours to marinate.

>> MAKES 8 SERVINGS.

SOUR APPLE JALAPEÑO SLAW FROM HAMMERHEADS

This slaw is great on top of any pork sandwich or on fish tacos.

½ head red cabbage, julienned
2 sour apples, fine julienne
¼ large jalapeño pepper, finely diced
¼ cup dried Italian seasoning

⅓ cup sugar
1 cup sweet chili sauce
3 cups red wine vinegar

In a large metal bowl combine the cabbage, apples, jalapeño, Italian seasoning, sugar, chili sauce, and red wine vinegar and toss with salad tongs.

» MAKES 4 SERVINGS.

CAULIFLOWER GORGONZOLA SOUP FROM THE GREEN ROOM

1 medium onion, diced
1 medium head of cauliflower, trimmed into florets
4 cups (1 quart) vegetable stock

1 cup Gorgonzola cheese, crumbled
1 cup heavy cream
Salt and black pepper to taste

In a large pot over low heat sweat the onions until translucent, 10 to 12 minutes. Add the cauliflower and vegetable stock, cover, and bring to a boil. Turn down to a simmer and let cook for 20 minutes. Strain and keep the liquid the cauliflower has cooked in.

In a blender place some of the cooked cauliflower, some of the Gorgonzola cheese, and some of the heavy cream. Then add about 2 to 4 ounces of the cauliflower liquid in order for the vegetables and cheese to emulsify. Repeat until all ingredients are pureed into the soup. Season to taste.

» MAKES 4 SERVINGS.

Sauté the onion in the butter in a large saucepan over medium heat until tender. Whisk in the flour and cook for 2 minutes, stirring constantly. Continue to stir and add the chicken broth, potatoes, and black pepper. Simmer for 30 minutes or until the potatoes are tender, stirring occasionally. Add the ham, whole kernel corn, and creamed corn. Simmer for 10 minutes.

Stir in the evaporated milk and salt. Heat but do not let boil. Serve immediately.

>> MAKES 10 TO 12 SERVINGS.

HAM AND CORN CHOWDER

1 cup finely chopped onion

¼ cup (½ stick) butter

¼ cup all-purpose flour

8 cups canned chicken broth

3 medium red potatoes, peeled and diced

1 teaspoon black pepper

3 cups cubed, cooked ham

4 cups frozen whole kernel corn, thawed

2 (14.75-ounce) cans creamed corn

1 (12-ounce) can evaporated milk

½ teaspoon salt

Heat the vegetable oil in a large soup pot (at least 8 quarts) on medium-high heat. Salt and pepper the pork shoulder, chuck roast, and chicken legs well and brown them on all sides. You may need to do this in batches.

After the meats are well seared, remove them to a separate bowl. Add the onions, carrots, celery, and green pepper to the pot and sauté for 5 minutes until browned, adding more oil if necessary. Salt the vegetables halfway through the cooking. Add the garlic to the pot and cook for 30 seconds, until fragrant.

Return the meats to the pot and add the chicken and beef stocks and the tomatoes. Stir to combine. Bring to a boil, then reduce the heat to low and simmer covered for 2 hours. After 2 hours, remove the meats from the pot using a slotted spoon. Allow to cool slightly until safe to handle and strip the meat from the bones of the chicken and use a fork to break the tender beef into smaller pieces. Remove the chicken skin, if desired, and return the meats to the pot to continue to simmer uncovered.

Peel the potato and cut into 2- to 3-inch chunks and add to the pot. Raise the heat to medium and cook until the potato is done, about 45 minutes. When the potato is cooked, add the Worcestershire, mix well, and taste for salt. Add more Worcestershire to taste if needed. Add the frozen corn and lima beans and mix well. Cook for at least 20 minutes for brighter colored, crunchier vegetables or as long as an hour more if you prefer a traditional mushier burgoo with better blending of flavors. The final consistency should be as thick as a good pot of chili.

Before serving, taste again for salt and add either Worcestershire or more salt if desired. Serve with crusty bread or cornbread and a bottle of hot sauce for punching up the heat.

» MAKES 8 TO 12 SERVINGS.

OLD HICKORY BURGOO FROM OLD HICKORY BAR-B-QUE

3 tablespoons vegetable oil

Salt and black pepper to taste

2 pounds pork shoulder or country ribs, cut into 3- or 4-inch-wide chunks

1 pound chuck roast, cut into 3- or 4-inch-wide chunks

3 bone-in chicken legs or thighs

1 medium onion, chopped

1 carrot, chopped

1 celery stalk, chopped

1 green bell pepper, chopped

3 garlic cloves, chopped

2 cups chicken stock

2 cups beef stock

1 (14-ounce) can crushed tomatoes

1 large russet potato

4 to 8 tablespoons Worcestershire sauce

1 (1-pound) bag frozen corn

1 (1-pound) bag frozen lima beans

Crusty bread or cornbread for serving

Hot sauce, optional

APPLEWOOD BACON SALAD WITH FRIED GREEN TOMATOES FROM FELICIA SUZANNE'S

2 cups vegetable oil

2 large green tomatoes

Salt to taste

Freshly ground black pepper to taste

1 cup all-purpose flour

2 large eggs, beaten with 2 tablespoons water

1 cup fine dry bread crumbs

4 cups baby mixed greens

8 tablespoons remoulade dressing or creamy French dressing, divided

4 (½-inch) slices fresh mozzarella cheese

8 slices applewood smoked bacon or any other smoked bacon, cooked and crispy

Parsley for garnish

Heat the oil in a large frying pan over medium-high heat. Slice each tomato into 1-inch slices. Season both sides of the tomatoes with salt and pepper. Let the tomatoes sit for 15 minutes. Place the flour in a shallow bowl, the egg wash in another shallow bowl, and the bread crumbs in a third shallow bowl. Season each bowl with salt and pepper. Dredge the tomatoes in the flour, coating completely. Then dip them in the egg wash, letting the excess drip off. Then dredge the tomatoes in the bread crumbs, coating completely. Fry the tomatoes in batches until golden brown, about 2 minutes on each side. Remove the tomatoes from the pan and drain on a plate lined with paper towels. Season with salt.

In a large bowl toss the mixed greens with 4 tablespoons of the dressing. Season with salt and pepper. Mix well.

Evenly spoon the remaining 4 tablespoons of dressing in the center of four plates. Place a tomato on top of the dressing. Layer each tomato with a slice of the cheese, crisscross 2 slices of the bacon, and top with ⅛ of the mixed greens. Place the remaining tomatoes and mixed greens on top of each salad. Secure each salad by placing a toothpick through the center of the salad. Garnish with parsley.

>> MAKES 4 SALADS.

MOMMA MIA'S MAC SALAD FROM THE SHED

Make the Mac Juice early so it can rest and absorb the flavors. When chopping
the bell peppers, make sure to clean out all the seeds. Use fresh seasonings,
especially the black pepper and a good-quality, finely shredded cheese.

Mac Juice

2 ¼ cups mayonnaise
1 ¾ cups sour cream
1 tablespoon Dijon mustard
½ tablespoon black pepper
1 teaspoon kosher salt
¾ cup sugar
⅓ cup cider vinegar
1 ½ teaspoons onion powder
2 teaspoons garlic salt

Mac Salad

Salt
5 cups large pasta shell noodles
1 tablespoon oil
2 large purple onions, diced
2 large green bell peppers, diced
3 cups shredded sharp Cheddar cheese

TO MAKE THE MAC JUICE: In a large container
with a lid mix the mayonnaise, sour cream,
mustard, pepper, kosher salt, sugar, cider
vinegar, onion powder, and garlic salt.
Refrigerate and let rest for a couple hours.

TO MAKE THE SALAD: Bring a large pot of
water to a boil over high heat. Generously
season the water with salt and add the noodles
and the oil to keep the noodles from sticking
together. Boil according to the package
directions. Strain the noodles and move to

large bowl. Add the onions, green peppers,
cheese, and Mac Juice and stir to combine.
Serve immediately or refrigerate up to 4 hours.

>> MAKES 8 SERVINGS.

NOTE: Make a double batch of Mac Juice and use
it to refresh the next day's leftovers or to add a
little goodness to anything. This is a great base for
recipes.

LAYERED SPINACH SALAD

1 (8-ounce) package fresh spinach, torn into pieces and divided

1 cup button mushrooms, sliced

1 bunch green onions, sliced

1 (10-ounce) package frozen green peas, thawed but uncooked

1 cup thinly sliced celery

2 cups grated Cheddar cheese, divided

1 ½ cups mayonnaise

1 ½ cups sour cream

1 tablespoon sugar, divided

½ teaspoon salt, divided

½ teaspoon black pepper, divided

4 large hard-boiled eggs, grated

1 red bell pepper, chopped

1 medium cucumber, peeled and thinly sliced

2 cups cauliflower, chopped

1 cup shredded Monterey Jack cheese

You will need a very large bowl for this salad, about 10 inches in diameter. Layer half of the spinach, all the mushrooms, green onions, peas, and celery, and half the Cheddar cheese into the bottom of the bowl. In a small bowl combine the mayonnaise and sour cream and spread ½ over the top of the cheese. Sprinkle with half of the sugar, salt, and pepper.

For the next layer, use the remaining spinach, all the eggs, red peppers, cucumbers, and cauliflower, and the remaining Cheddar cheese. Spread the remaining mayonnaise mixture on top. Sprinkle with the remaining sugar, salt, and pepper. Top with the Monterey Jack cheese. Cover with plastic wrap and refrigerate overnight.

≫ MAKES 14 TO 16 SERVINGS.

BROWN PIG SALAD FROM NEELY'S SANDWICH SHOP

16 ounces smoked pork shoulder, cut into 2-inch cubes

8 tablespoons Eastern Carolina red pepper and vinegar sauce (see page 42 for recipe)

½ pound mixed salad greens

1 large tomato, sliced

Olives and pickles for garnish, optional

¼ cup buttermilk ranch dressing

To make what Neely's calls the "Brown Pig Meat," place the smoked pork shoulder and the vinegar sauce in the bowl of a food processor. Pulse quickly until it reaches the consistency of sloppy joe meat. Place ¼ of the mixed salad greens on each plate. Add the fresh tomato slices. Top with the Brown Pig Meat. Place the olives and pickles around the edge of the plate if desired. Drizzle the dressing on top and serve immediately.

≫ MAKES 4 SALADS.

Trim the frisée of its green ends and then cut it in half. Submerge it in ice-cold water to clean it and crisp it. Remove the frisée and lay it out on paper towels to dry. Place the eggs in a small saucepan and cover with water. Add salt and bring to a boil over medium-high heat. Soft-boil the eggs for 5 minutes.

While the eggs are cooking, heat a skillet over medium heat and add the cubed bacon. Cook until the bacon bits are crisp. Remove the bacon to a plate lined with paper towels and reserve the grease. Remove the eggs from the water and place in a bowl of ice water to cool.

In a medium jar with a tight-fitting lid, mix 6 tablespoons of the reserved bacon grease with the sherry vinegar, tarragon, salt, and smoked paprika. Screw the lid on the jar and shake vigorously to combine. Drizzle the frisée with a few tablespoons of vinaigrette.

Preheat a grill to medium and place the frisée cut side down until charred, about 3 to 4 minutes, then flip and cook until charred on the other side. In a medium bowl toss the frisée, red onion, reserved bacon, and the remaining vinaigrette. Portion the tossed salad onto four plates. Gently crack and peel each soft cooked egg into a bowl. Using a slotted spoon, add one egg to each salad and serve immediately.

>> MAKES 4 SERVINGS.

BACON SALAD WITH "DEVILED" EGG FROM SOUTH ON MAIN

2 pounds frisée, trimmed and washed

4 large eggs

6 ounces slab bacon, cut into ½-inch cubes

2 tablespoons sherry vinegar

1 tablespoon fresh minced tarragon leaves

Salt to taste

Smoked paprika to taste

2 ½ tablespoons shaved red onion

Combine the mayonnaise, vinegar, and sugar in a small bowl. In a large bowl combine the broccoli, red onions, raisins, and apple. Add the mayonnaise dressing and toss until well mixed. Chill for 2 hours or until ready to serve. Add the bacon and mandarin oranges to the salad just before serving.

>> MAKES 8 TO 10 SERVINGS.

BROCCOLI, BACON, AND APPLE SALAD

1 cup mayonnaise

2 tablespoons white vinegar

1 tablespoon sugar

6 cups broccoli, chopped

½ cup chopped red onion

1 cup raisins

1 large red apple, chopped

10 slices (¾ pound) bacon, cooked and crumbled

1 (11-ounce) can mandarin oranges, drained

WILTED BRUSSELS SPROUTS SALAD FROM DUDLEY'S ON SHORT

This has quickly become one of our signature dishes at Dudley's. It is such a simple dish that will make almost anyone love Brussels sprouts.

2 tablespoons soybean oil
2 pounds Brussels sprouts, cut into a chiffonade
Kosher salt and black pepper to taste

5 ounces pine nuts
8 ounces Manchego cheese, diced
2 tablespoons aged balsamic vinegar

Heat a sauté pan over medium-high heat. Add the soybean oil, then the chiffonade of Brussels sprouts. Season with kosher salt and black pepper. Toss a few times and then add the pine nuts. Cook for about 30 seconds, just long enough to wilt the Brussels sprouts and toast the nuts. Get your plate ready. Then add the Manchego cheese, tossing a few times to incorporate, and immediately transfer to the plate. You don't want the cheese to melt in the pan; the residual heat will take care of that. Drizzle the aged balsamic vinegar over the salad and serve. The aged vinegar is more mellow and sweet and can be used more liberally than regular balsamic vinegar.

>> MAKES 6 SERVINGS.

Heat the butter in a medium saucepan over medium-low heat. Add the ham, onion, and garlic and sauté, stirring until the onion is tender. Add the chicken broth, green and red tomatoes, and jalapeño. Bring to a boil over high heat. Reduce the heat to medium-low and simmer for about 30 minutes.

Working in batches, add the soup to a blender or food processor and pulse until almost smooth. Pour the soup back into the saucepan and bring to a boil over high heat, reduce heat to low, and simmer for 5 minutes. Taste and add salt and pepper and hot sauce as desired.

>> MAKES 4 TO 6 SERVINGS.

GREEN TOMATO SOUP WITH COUNTRY HAM

2 tablespoons butter

6 ounces country ham, diced

1 small onion, diced

2 cloves garlic, minced

4 cups chicken broth

8 medium green tomatoes, peeled and chopped

2 medium red tomatoes, peeled and chopped

1 jalapeño pepper, seeds and stem removed, minced

Salt and black pepper to taste

Dash of hot sauce, optional

BACON, CHEESE, AND BAKED POTATO SOUP

1 cup (2 sticks) butter

1 cup all-purpose flour

8 cups whole milk

5 large potatoes, baked and cubed (you can peel them if you prefer)

2 pounds bacon, cooked and crumbled (about 2 cups)

3 cups shredded Cheddar cheese

2 cups sour cream

1 tablespoon kosher salt

1 tablespoon ground black pepper

1 clove garlic, minced

¼ cup grated Parmesan cheese

Melt the butter in the bottom of a large pot over medium-high heat. Add flour and whisk to combine until thickened. Whisking continuously, slowly pour in the milk and whisk until the mixture is smooth. Be sure to get the corners of the pan. Add the baked potatoes, bacon, Cheddar cheese, sour cream, kosher salt, black pepper, garlic, and Parmesan and lower the heat to medium. Stir occasionally until the cheese is melted and the soup is warmed through. Be careful not to burn.

>> MAKES 10 TO 12 SERVINGS.

SIDE DISHES

Pan-Fried Mac and Cheese with Kale and Chorizo from Crescent Pie and Sausage Company
Fried Deviled Eggs from American Grocery
Pimento Cheese Hash Browns from Delta Bistro
Cheese and Bacon Grits from The Shed BBQ and Blues Joint
Buffalo-Style Crispy Fried Okra from Delta Bistro
Tuck's Sweet Potato Hash from Edley's Bar-B-Que
KY Ale Beer Cheese Spread from Dudley's on Short
Grandmother's Baked Beans from Halcyon, Flavors from the Earth
Smoked Gouda Grits from IvyWild
Skillet Green Beans from IvyWild
Potato Salad from Memphis BBQ Company
Black-Eyed Peas from Tanglewood Ordinary Country Restaurant
3 Cheese Baked Macaroni from NoFo @ The Pig
Lady Peas, Rice, and Tomatoes from Restaurant Eugene
Hoppin' John (Peas and Rice) from Southern Soul BBQ
Stewed Tomatoes from Tanglewood Ordinary Country Restaurant
Louisiana Hot Sauce Deviled Eggs from Toups' Meatery
Collard Greens from NoFo @ The Pig
Sweet Potato Casserole from Chef's Market
Peaches and Cream Corn Salad from St. John's Restaurant
Lima Bean Casserole
Central BBQ Baked Beans from Central BBQ
Squash Pickles
Creamy Corn Dip
Fresh Green Peas with New Potatoes
Mac 'n' Cheese from The Cask and Larder
Fried Dill Pickles
Fried Apples
Bacon Cheddar Corn Pudding

PAN-FRIED MAC AND CHEESE WITH KALE AND CHORIZO FROM CRESCENT PIE AND SAUSAGE COMPANY

¼ cup olive oil

3 cloves garlic, chopped

1 cup white wine

2 pounds kale, trimmed and rinsed

Salt and freshly ground black pepper to taste

1 ½ pounds chorizo sausage

1 pound elbow macaroni

1 teaspoon Dijon mustard

16 ounces Cheddar cheese, grated

2 tablespoons all-purpose flour

¼ cup (½ stick) butter

1 ½ cups heavy cream

In a large pot heat the olive oil over medium heat. Add the garlic and stir for 30 seconds until it becomes fragrant. Add the white wine, then the kale in handfuls. Allow each handful to wilt slightly before adding the next. Season with salt and pepper, cover, and cook over medium heat for 10 minutes.

While the kale is cooking, place the chorizo in a skillet over medium heat and cook for 6 to 9 minutes, turning frequently, until cooked through. Cut the sausage into 4-inch pieces and set aside for plating. Remove the lid from the kale and cook until the liquid has evaporated, about 5 minutes longer. Drain and set aside for plating.

Bring a large pot of salted water to a boil over high heat. Cook the macaroni until it is al dente, about 6 minutes. Drain the pasta in a colander, run it under cold water to stop the cooking, and place in a large nonstick skillet over low heat and sauté for 4 minutes. Add the mustard and grated cheese and toss the macaroni in the pan to distribute the cheese evenly. Stir in the flour and stir constantly for 1 minute. Increase the heat to medium, and slowly whisk in the butter and cream. Bring to a boil, whisking frequently. Reduce the heat to low and cook for another 5 minutes until the cheese is melted completely and the cream has been distributed throughout the noodles. Season to taste with salt and pepper.

Increase the heat to medium-high and cook the macaroni for another 3 to 4 minutes until a golden brown crust begins to form on the bottom. Flip the macaroni like a pancake and remove the pan from the heat. Plate individual portions with a scoop of cooked kale and a piece of chorizo on top.

>> MAKES 8 SERVINGS.

Slice the hard-boiled eggs in half lengthwise and scoop out the yolks into a medium bowl and mash with a fork. Mix in the mayonnaise, Dijon, vinegar, salt, pepper, cayenne, and hot sauce. Whisk well until everything is incorporated. Check seasoning and adjust if needed. Fill the egg halves with the yolk mixture, leveling to the top of the egg white as it would look if you had simply sliced it in half. Take 2 stuffed halves and marry them as if you were "gluing" the egg back together. Secure the egg with 2 wooden skewers through each half so it holds together. Reserve leftover yolk mixture.

Place the flour in a shallow bowl. In another bowl crack the two eggs, add water, and whisk to combine. Place the bread crumbs and pork rinds in a third shallow bowl. Roll each hard-boiled egg carefully in the flour, then dip it into the egg wash, and roll it in the bread crumb mixture. Place on a baking sheet or cutting board.

Fill a large Dutch oven with oil and bring to 375 degrees over high heat. Carefully lower a few eggs at a time into the oil. Fry until golden brown, 5 to 7 minutes. Remove, drain on paper towels, and finish with additional salt and a sprinkling of bacon or pancetta bits on top. Carefully remove the skewers. Sometimes a slight twisting motion with your fingers will ease the skewer from the hardened breading. The eggs are fragile, so handle carefully. Use a serrated knife to slice the eggs across the hemisphere of the egg (opposite of the way they were originally cut). Spread 2 small dollops of the leftover yolk mixture on a small plate and "stick" the egg halves down on top of the dollops to serve or serve in a deviled egg plate.

>> MAKES 24 SERVINGS.

FRIED DEVILED EGGS FROM AMERICAN GROCERY

12 hard-boiled large eggs

½ cup mayonnaise

1 ½ teaspoons Dijon mustard

2 tablespoons cider vinegar

Kosher salt to taste

Freshly ground black pepper to taste

Dash of cayenne pepper
(or 2, if you like it spicy)

Splash of hot sauce

1 cup all-purpose flour

2 large eggs

1 teaspoon water

½ cup panko bread crumbs

½ cup (1.5-ounce bag) ground
pork rinds

Canola oil for frying

4 ounces bacon or pancetta, cooked
and minced for garnish

PIMENTO CHEESE HASH BROWNS FROM DELTA BISTRO

2 tablespoons bacon grease
3 pounds Yukon gold potatoes, diced and parboiled

2 cups (1 pound) Delta Bistro Pimento Cheese (recipe follows)

Lightly cover the bottom of a frying pan or cast-iron skillet with bacon grease and heat over medium-high heat. Place the potatoes in the pan and sauté for 7 to 8 minutes, until almost crispy. Then spoon the pimento cheese on top and lightly toss till melted and gooey.

>> MAKES 8 SERVINGS.

DELTA BISTRO PIMENTO CHEESE

1 (7-ounce) jar diced pimentos
½ cup mayonnaise
1 ½ tablespoons Worcestershire sauce
¾ teaspoon salt
¾ teaspoon black pepper
½ tablespoon hot sauce

¾ teaspoon white wine vinegar
1 tablespoon Dijon mustard
¾ teaspoon celery seeds
¼ cup chopped green onion
24 ounces white Cheddar cheese, grated

In a large bowl mix the pimientos, mayonnaise, Worcestershire, salt, black pepper, hot sauce, vinegar, Dijon, celery seeds, and green onions until well combined. Stir in the cheese, cover, and refrigerate.

>> MAKES 8 CUPS.

CHEESE AND BACON GRITS FROM THE SHED BBQ AND BLUES JOINT

24 ounces processed cheese spread, cut into 1- to 1 ½-inch cubes

1 pound sharp white Cheddar cheese, shredded

½ cup (1 stick) butter, sliced

1 tablespoon minced garlic

1 teaspoon onion powder

1 teaspoon cayenne pepper

½ teaspoon black pepper

4 tablespoons finely chopped pickled jalapeño peppers

2 large eggs

½ cup heavy whipping cream

2 cups quick-cooking grits (cooked according to package directions*)

8 slices bacon, cooked and chopped

1 cup shredded sharp yellow Cheddar cheese

Preheat the oven to 350 degrees.

Place the processed cheese and white Cheddar cheese in a deep-sided 9 x 13-inch casserole dish. Add the butter, garlic, onion powder, cayenne pepper, black pepper, and jalapeños to the casserole dish. Pour a teaspoon or two of the pickled jalapeño juice to the dish if you like it spicy. Stir the ingredients in the dish with a large spoon.

Place the eggs in a small bowl and whisk. Add the heavy whipping cream and whisk to combine. Pour the egg mixture into the casserole dish and mix thoroughly. Pour the hot grits over all the ingredients and stir until the cheeses and butter have melted. Gently fold in the chopped bacon.

Bake for 45 minutes. Cover with the yellow sharp Cheddar and return the pan to the oven for another 15 minutes. Let this dish cool for an hour prior to serving so it will set up.

>> MAKES 8 SERVINGS.

* Eight servings of grits should fill the 9 x 13-inch casserole pan 2 inches deep with grits.

Pour the oil into a large skillet to at least 1 inch deep and bring to 350 degrees over medium heat.

Combine the flour and salt in a shallow dish. Dredge the okra in the flour mixture. Add to the oil and fry for 5 to 6 minutes, until the bottom is golden brown. Flip the okra and continue cooking until it is golden on all sides, about 5 to 6 minutes more.

While the okra is cooking, make the sauce. In a large bowl combine the chili sauce, Sriracha, canola oil, ginger, garlic, curry, parsley, and green onions. Remove the okra from the pan, drain on paper towels, and toss in the sauce. Add the crumbled bacon and serve.

>> MAKES 6 SERVINGS.

* Delta Bistro uses Wondra flour.

BUFFALO-STYLE CRISPY FRIED OKRA FROM DELTA BISTRO

Vegetable oil for frying

4 cups all-purpose flour*

2 teaspoons salt

1 pound fresh okra, cut lengthwise into quarters

½ cup chili sauce

¼ cup Sriracha

1 tablespoon canola oil

1 teaspoon ground ginger

1 teaspoon garlic puree

¼ teaspoon curry powder

½ tablespoon dried parsley

½ cup sliced green onions

1 pound high-quality bacon, cooked, crumbled (see pages 12–14 for bacon cooking techniques)

In a large skillet over medium-low heat cook the bacon to render the fat. Do not burn. Remove the bacon to a plate lined with paper towels. Pour the fat into a heatproof container. Chop the bacon and set aside. If there are burnt bacon pieces in the pan, wipe out the pan.

Turn up the burner to medium-high. Add the bacon fat. (It should cover the bottom of the pan, but if not, add a little oil.) When the bacon fat begins to lightly smoke, add the onions and sweet potatoes. Do not stir. Turn the heat down to medium and cook for 3 to 5 minutes. Shake the skillet to release the hash and use a wooden spoon to stir, being careful not to mash. Cook an additional 3 minutes. Add the chopped bacon, green onions, thyme, salt, and pepper. Sauté for 30 seconds.

Remove the pan from the heat and add the bourbon. Return the pan to the heat. Be careful as this will flame up. Give the skillet a good shake to release any food stuck to the bottom of the pan. When the flame is gone, use a wooden spoon to scrape the bottom of the pan. Spoon the mixture into a serving bowl or plate. Garnish with thyme and green onions, if desired.

Serve with any beef, pork, chicken, turkey, lamb, or duck entrée. Smoked meats go great with this dish. It can also be served with breakfast.

>> MAKES 4 SERVINGS.

TUCK'S SWEET POTATO HASH FROM EDLEY'S BAR-B-QUE

2 slices thick-cut bacon

½ cup white onion, cut into small cubes

2 cups sweet potatoes, peeled and cut into small cubes

2 stalks green onions, chopped (only greens), plus extra for garnish

2 teaspoons chopped fresh thyme, plus extra for garnish

Salt and black pepper to taste

1 tablespoon apple bourbon (or regular bourbon, in a pinch)

KY ALE BEER CHEESE SPREAD FROM DUDLEY'S ON SHORT

24 ounces (2 cans) amber ale beer*
1 pound grated white Cheddar cheese
1 pound grated Gruyere cheese

1 tablespoon hot smoked Spanish paprika
Salt to taste
Cayenne pepper to taste

Pour the beer into a large bowl. Add the cheeses and allow it to soak at room temperature for at least 1 hour. Drain off the excess beer and reserve. Blend the cheeses in a food processor along with the smoked paprika, salt, and cayenne pepper to taste, adding the reserved beer to reach the desired consistency. Serve with Country Ham Gritters (see page 136 for recipe).

>> MAKES 4 CUPS.

* Dudley's uses KY Ale.

GRANDMOTHER'S BAKED BEANS FROM HALCYON, FLAVORS FROM THE EARTH

1 pound dried great Northern beans
½ teaspoon baking soda
4 ounces bacon, cut into ½-inch strips*

1 cup sugar cane crystals
2 tablespoons butter

Place the beans in a large pot and cover with water. Soak overnight. Drain and cover with 3 inches of fresh water. Add the baking soda and cook over medium heat until tender, 1 ½ to 2 hours.

Preheat the oven to 300 degrees. Stir the bacon strips and sugar into the beans and then transfer to a casserole dish. Top with butter and bake for 3 to 4 hours, or until the water has evaporated considerably.

>> MAKES 12 SERVINGS.

* Use Benton's bacon if you can get it.

SMOKED GOUDA GRITS FROM IVYWILD

2 cups stone-ground (not instant) grits, soaked, skimmed, and drained as per directions on package

3 cups water

4 cups (1 quart) heavy cream, divided

1 tablespoon salt

1 teaspoon black pepper

4 cups (15 ounces) shredded smoked Gouda cheese

In a saucepan over medium-high heat, bring the grits, water, and 3 cups of cream to a boil. Reduce the heat to low and simmer until tender, 20 to 30 minutes. Add the salt and pepper. Stir in the cheese one handful at a time. Add the remaining cream and remove the pan from the heat. Adjust the consistency with more cream or water as needed.

>> MAKES 8 SERVINGS.

SKILLET GREEN BEANS FROM IVYWILD

4 quarts water

2 tablespoons kosher salt

2 pounds fresh green beans, trimmed and strings removed

Ice bath made from 4 quarts water with 4 quarts ice added

2 tablespoons olive oil

2 tablespoons butter

Salt and black pepper to taste

Bring the water to a rolling boil in a large pot over high heat. Add the kosher salt. Return to boil. Drop the green beans in and blanch for 2 minutes. Strain the beans from the boiling water and immediately plunge into the ice bath. Stir the beans in the ice to cool quickly. Let the beans sit in the ice bath for 10 minutes, then drain completely. Cut the beans into 2- to 3-inch segments.

Heat a cast-iron skillet or heavy-bottom skillet over medium-high heat. Once the skillet begins to smoke, add the olive oil followed immediately by the green beans. Be careful since any water on the green beans can splatter in the hot oil. Slowly stir the beans in the oil to coat. Turn the beans occasionally until they have the desired amount of dark char. Remove from the heat and stir in the butter. Season with salt and pepper and serve warm.

>> MAKES 8 SERVINGS.

POTATO SALAD FROM MEMPHIS BBQ COMPANY

2 pounds Yukon gold potatoes
1 pound uncooked bacon
½ bunch chives
1 cup sour cream

½ cup ranch seasoning mix
2 teaspoons salt or to taste
2 teaspoons black pepper or to taste
¼ cup milk

Fill a large pot with water and bring to a boil over high heat. Dice the potatoes, leaving the skin on, and place into the boiling water. Boil until tender, 20 to 30 minutes or until a fork easily pierces the potatoes. Drain and place in a large bowl. Cook the bacon in a skillet over medium heat. Once it's crisp, remove from the pan and place on a plate lined with paper towels to cool. Crumble the bacon and add to the potatoes. Dice the chives and add to the potatoes. Add sour cream, ranch seasoning mix, salt, and pepper and stir to incorporate. Add the milk as needed to adjust the consistency. Refrigerate at least 1 hour before serving.

>> MAKES 6 SERVINGS.

BLACK-EYED PEAS FROM TANGLEWOOD ORDINARY COUNTRY RESTAURANT

2 tablespoons sugar
2 ¼ tablespoons salt
2 bay leaves
2 tablespoons high-quality ham base bouillon

½ onion, chopped
½ pound ham scraps (salt-cured ham)
2 pounds dried black-eyed peas*

Fill an 8-quart pot half full with water and add the sugar, salt, bay leaves, ham base bouillon, onion, and ham scraps. Bring to a low boil over medium-low heat, then simmer carefully for 20 to 30 minutes. Add the dried black-eyed peas and 2 more quarts of water. Peas should be covered with water by at least 2 inches to spare. Simmer until the peas are soft, 2 to 3 hours. Stir occasionally, adding water as needed so that peas remain covered as they absorb the water and soften. Strain out the water and remove the bay leaves before serving.

>> MAKES 12 SERVINGS.

* Overnight soaking of the cleaned raw peas is a variation that can produce a more tender product. The peas will burn, so carefully heating after the initial boil is required. Lots of stirring is best.

3 CHEESE BAKED MACARONI FROM NOFO @ THE PIG

1 pound elbow macaroni, cooked according to box directions and drained

1 cup blue cheese

1 cup Parmesan cheese

2 cups shredded Cheddar cheese

3 large eggs, slightly beaten

2 cups heavy cream

1 teaspoon salt

1 teaspoon black pepper

1 teaspoon garlic powder

2 cups bread crumbs

Preheat the oven to 325 degrees. Grease a 14 x 10-inch baking pan.

Place the drained macaroni in a large bowl and add the blue, Parmesan, and Cheddar cheeses, eggs, cream, salt, pepper, and garlic powder. Stir to combine. Pour the mixture into the baking pan and cover with the bread crumbs. Bake for 30 to 45 minutes until done.

>> MAKES 8 SERVINGS.

LADY PEAS, RICE, AND TOMATOES FROM RESTAURANT EUGENE

2 tablespoons peanut oil

4 ounces smoked bacon, cubed

1 Vidalia onion, thinly sliced

2 cups fresh lady peas

2 bay leaves

3 cups chicken stock

⅛ teaspoon salt

2 cups cooked Carolina gold rice

4 tablespoons chopped fresh parsley

2 ripe tomatoes, chopped, juice reserved

Salt and freshly ground black pepper to taste

Pour the peanut oil in large pot over medium-high heat and add the bacon. Cook until browned. Add the onion and cook until color just begins to show, 8 to 10 minutes. Add the peas, bay leaves, chicken stock, and salt. Bring to a boil. Reduce to a simmer and cook until tender, about 15 minutes. When tender, fold in the rice, parsley, and tomatoes. Adjust the seasoning with salt and black pepper. Remove the bay leaves before serving.

>> MAKES 4 SERVINGS.

HOPPIN' JOHN (PEAS AND RICE) FROM SOUTHERN SOUL BBQ

1 tablespoon olive oil

2 tablespoons finely diced pork fatback

½ large sweet onion, finely chopped

2 cloves fresh garlic, minced

Salt and black pepper to taste

½ tablespoon dried thyme

½ tablespoon dried basil

½ pound smoked sausage*

1 large vine-ripe tomato, roughly chopped

6 cups (1 ½ quarts) good-quality ham or pork stock (see page 61 for recipe)

2 pounds fresh (cooked), frozen, or canned and drained black-eyed peas

1 smoked ham hock

4 cups cooked white rice

Cornbread for serving

Butter for serving

Heat a cast-iron Dutch oven over medium-low heat and add the olive oil. When the olive oil is shimmering, add the fatback and cook until brown and crispy, 6 to 8 minutes. Add the onion, garlic, salt, and pepper and sweat the onion for 15 minutes. Add the thyme, basil, sausage, and tomatoes and cook down for 15 minutes, stirring constantly. Stir in the ham stock and black-eyed peas, increase the heat to medium-high, and bring to a boil. Add the ham hock, cover, and reduce the heat to low to simmer for 1 hour, adding more stock if needed. Add cooked rice to the pot and stir. Hoppin' John is ready to eat. Serve in big bowls with a side of crispy skillet cornbread and butter.

>> MAKES 12 SERVINGS.

* Southern Soul BBQ prefers their fresh Italian, but most any variety will do.

STEWED TOMATOES FROM TANGLEWOOD ORDINARY COUNTRY RESTAURANT

¼ cup (½ stick) margarine or butter

⅔ cup sugar

1 (28-ounce) can chopped tomatoes, drained, or 3 cups chopped fresh plum tomatoes

1 cup Homemade Seasoned Croutons (recipe follows)

Preheat the oven to 350 degrees.

Melt the butter in a medium bowl and whisk together with the sugar. In another medium bowl place the tomatoes and squeeze by hand into 1-inch chunks. Add the tomatoes to the butter and sugar and mix together. Spoon into a deep 9 x 13-inch casserole dish and bake until thoroughly heated, about 45 minutes. Stir. Fold in the croutons. Return to the oven for 10 to 15 minutes. Serve when the croutons have softened.

>> MAKES 8 SERVINGS.

HOMEMADE SEASONED CROUTONS

3 to 4 day-old biscuits

1 teaspoon granulated or powdered garlic

1 teaspoon dried basil

1 teaspoon dried thyme

Olive oil

Preheat the oven to 350 degrees.

Cut day-old biscuits into cubes and spread in a single layer on a baking sheet. Season with the garlic, basil, and thyme. Sprinkle with olive oil and bake until crispy, 8 to 10 minutes.

LOUISIANA HOT SAUCE DEVILED EGGS FROM TOUPS' MEATERY

12 large eggs

4 tablespoons Louisiana hot sauce, divided

2 tablespoons Worcestershire sauce

5 tablespoons mayonnaise

5 tablespoons horseradish

2 tablespoons Creole mustard

¼ teaspoon wasabi powder

24 slices pickled jalapeño peppers

¼ pound bacon, cooked and crumbled, or 3 ounces caviar (if you really want to show off)

Place the eggs in a large saucepan, cover with water by about an inch, and bring to a boil over medium heat. When a boil is reached, remove the pan from the heat and let stand for 15 minutes. Crack the shells of the eggs as you transfer them to a bowl of ice water (this makes them much easier to peel). Chill the eggs for 10 minutes and peel them very carefully to avoid damaging the whites.

Cut each egg in half with a very sharp knife. Scoop the yolks into the bowl of a food processor and gently place the whites in a large bowl. In a small bowl mix 2 tablespoons of the hot sauce with the Worcestershire and pour over the egg whites. Very gently mix the egg whites with the hot sauce mixture so they are completely coated. Let the eggs stand for 10 minutes and carefully drain off any excess.

Arrange the whites, cut sides up, on a serving plate. In the food processor, put the remaining 2 tablespoons of hot sauce, mayonnaise, horseradish, Creole mustard, and wasabi powder and blend with the egg yolks until smooth. Pipe an equal amount of the yolk mixture into each of the egg whites, top with a slice of pickled jalapeño, and garnish with bacon.

>> MAKES 2 DOZEN DEVILED EGGS.

COLLARD GREENS FROM NOFO @ THE PIG

1 ham hock
3 quarts water
3 bunches collard greens (approximately
4 ½ pounds)

1 teaspoon ground red pepper
½ cup firmly packed brown sugar
2 cups cider vinegar

Place the ham hock in a saucepan and add the water. Bring to a boil over medium-high heat and then reduce the temperature to low and simmer for 3 hours, reducing the liquid by half. Add more water if needed. Add the collards, increase the heat to medium, and cook for 1 hour. Add the red pepper and brown sugar, and cook for 1 additional hour. Add the cider vinegar at the end.

>> MAKES 12 SERVINGS.

SWEET POTATO CASSEROLE FROM CHEF'S MARKET

5 pounds sweet potatoes, peeled
1 ¼ pounds pecans, chopped
1 cup all-purpose flour
¾ cup (1 ½ sticks) butter, melted
8 cups (2 pounds) firmly packed brown sugar
2 ½ cups sugar

¾ cup heavy cream
¾ tablespoon ground cinnamon
¾ tablespoon vanilla extract
5 large eggs
1 cup (2 sticks) butter, melted

Preheat the oven to 300 degrees.

Bring a large pot of water to a boil over high heat. Add the sweet potatoes to the water and boil for 20 minutes at full boil.

While the potatoes are cooking, make the topping. In a medium bowl place the pecans, flour, butter, and brown sugar and mix.

Remove the pan of sweet potatoes from the heat and drain. Put the sweet potatoes in a large bowl. Add the sugar and beat with a hand mixer on high speed for 5 minutes. Add the heavy cream, cinnamon, vanilla, and eggs and beat on low speed for another 5 minutes. Add the butter in slowly while continuing to beat the mixture on low for a few more minutes. Spoon into a 9 x 13-inch baking pan and sprinkle the top with the pecan mixture. Bake for 1 hour.

>> MAKES 12 SERVINGS.

PEACHES AND CREAM CORN SALAD FROM ST. JOHN'S RESTAURANT

4 ears bi-color corn, husked and silks removed
Canola oil
Sea salt and white pepper to taste
1 red onion, small diced
1 jalapeño pepper, deseeded and small diced
2 green onions, tops and bottoms finely chopped

1 tablespoon fresh chopped chives
2 tablespoons fresh basil, gently torn
2 cups sungold tomatoes, cut in half (or your favorite cherry tomato)
Salt and pepper to taste
½ cup Red Wine Vinaigrette (recipe follows)

Preheat a grill or grilling pan to medium heat (300 to 350 degrees). Rub the corn with canola oil and salt and then grill on all sides until slightly browned. Let cool. Slice the kernels off the cob into a medium bowl. Add the onion, jalapeño, green onions, chives, basil, tomatoes, salt and pepper, and vinaigrette. Stir to combine. Refrigerate until ready to serve.

>> MAKES 4 SERVINGS.

RED WINE VINAIGRETTE

¼ cup red wine vinegar
1 tablespoon Dijon mustard
1 teaspoon minced red onion

Salt and white pepper to taste
1 cup canola oil

In a small bowl whisk together the vinegar, Dijon, onions, salt, and pepper. Then slowly pour the oil into the vinegar mixture while constantly whisking. If it gets too thick, add a teaspoon or two of water.

>> MAKES ABOUT 1 ½ CUPS.

LIMA BEAN CASSEROLE

1 (14-ounce) package frozen lima beans, cooked according to package directions and drained
1 tablespoon butter
¼ cup finely chopped celery
¼ cup finely chopped onion

1 (10.75-ounce) can mushroom soup
1 ½ cups shredded Cheddar cheese, divided
1 (2-ounce) jar diced pimientos
1 cup bread crumbs
¼ cup slivered almonds

Preheat the oven to 350 degrees. Lightly grease a 2-quart casserole dish.

Place the lima beans in a medium bowl. Place the butter in a small saucepan over medium heat. Add the celery and onions, stirring until softened. Add the celery mixture to the lima beans and stir in the mushroom soup, 1 cup of cheese, and pimientos. Stir the mixture to combine and spoon into the baking dish. In a small bowl mix the bread crumbs, remaining ½ cup of cheese, and the slivered almonds together and sprinkle over the beans. Bake for 25 to 30 minutes or until bubbly and the crumbs are golden brown.

>> MAKES 6 TO 8 SERVINGS.

CENTRAL BBQ BAKED BEANS FROM CENTRAL BBQ

3 (28-ounce) cans baked beans
½ red bell pepper, chopped
½ green bell pepper, chopped
¼ cup firmly packed brown sugar
1 tablespoon minced fresh garlic
½ tablespoon cayenne pepper

1 tablespoon chili powder
1 onion, diced
¼ teaspoon white pepper
½ cup prepared mustard
½ cup barbecue sauce (check out the Memphis Barbecue Sauce on page 46)

Preheat the oven to 275 degrees.

In a large bowl combine the beans, red peppers, green peppers, brown sugar, garlic, cayenne pepper, chili powder, onions, white pepper, mustard, and barbecue sauce, stirring well. Pour into a 2-quart casserole dish and bake until the vegetables have become tender, 1 ½ hours.

>> MAKES 12 SERVINGS.

SQUASH PICKLES

6 (1-pint) canning jars (with lids and rings)
⅔ cup salt
3 quarts water
8 cups yellow squash, thinly sliced
2 cups sugar

2 cups white vinegar
2 teaspoons mustard seeds
2 medium onions, thinly sliced
2 green bell peppers, thinly sliced

Dissolve the salt in water in a large bowl. Add the squash. Keep the squash submerged in the water, using a plate to hold the squash down. Cover for 3 hours.

Fill a water bath canner with water and bring to a boil over high heat. Place the jars in the rack and gently lower into the water. Allow to gently boil for at least 15 minutes. Place the lids and rings in a small saucepan filled with water and bring to a low boil over medium heat.

Drain the squash and set aside. Place the sugar in a large stainless steel pot. Add the vinegar and mustard seeds and bring to a boil over medium-high heat, stirring occasionally until the sugar dissolves. Add the squash, onions, and green peppers and return to a boil. As soon as it returns to a boil, remove the pot from the heat and pack the squash and cooking liquid into hot sterilized jars and close with sterilized rings and lids. Process in a water bath for 5 minutes to seal.

>> MAKES 6 PINTS.

CREAMY CORN DIP

2 tablespoons butter
2 cups whole kernel corn
1 red bell pepper, finely chopped
2 tablespoons finely chopped onion
2 teaspoons finely chopped garlic
1 (8-ounce) package cream cheese, softened
6 slices bacon, cooked and crumbled

¼ cup mayonnaise
1 jalapeño pepper, seeded and finely chopped (1 to 2 tablespoons)
¼ teaspoon salt
¼ teaspoon black pepper
1 cup shredded Cheddar cheese
Corn chips for serving

Preheat the oven to 400 degrees.

Melt the butter in a 9-inch ovenproof skillet over medium heat. Add the corn, red peppers, onions, and garlic. Sauté until the vegetables are tender. Reduce the heat to low and add the cream cheese, bacon, mayonnaise, jalapeño, salt, and pepper.

Continue to cook, stirring constantly until the mixture is combined. Sprinkle with the Cheddar cheese and bake for 10 to 12 minutes or until the cheese is melted. Serve warm with the corn chips.

>> MAKES 12 TO 14 SERVINGS.

Place the potatoes in a saucepan and cover with water. Add the salt and bring to a boil over high heat. Reduce the heat to a low boil and allow to simmer for 12 to 15 minutes or until the potatoes are almost tender. Add the peas and cook until the vegetables are tender. Drain the water. Add the butter and black pepper. Serve immediately or refrigerate and reheat when ready to serve.

>> MAKES 6 TO 8 SERVINGS.

FRESH GREEN PEAS WITH NEW POTATOES

1 pound new red or white potatoes, scrubbed but not peeled

1 teaspoon salt

2 cups fresh green peas

¼ cup (½ stick) butter

½ teaspoon black pepper

MAC 'N' CHEESE FROM THE CASK AND LARDER

12 ounces Havarti cheese

3 ounces Gouda cheese

3 ounces Parmigiano-Reggiano cheese

6 tablespoons butter

⅓ cup all-purpose flour, sifted

4 cups (1 quart) whole milk

4 ounces IPA (India Pale Ale) beer, a good hoppy-flavored one

4 tablespoons Pickled Mustard Seeds (recipe follows), optional

1 teaspoon kosher salt

¼ teaspoon ground white pepper

1 teaspoon hot sauce

1 pound dry elbow macaroni, cooked according to package directions

Ham-Cheddar Crumble (recipe follows)

Shred the Havarti and Gouda cheeses and grate the Parmigiano-Reggiano. Set aside to allow the cheese to warm to room temperature while preparing other ingredients.

Melt the butter in a medium saucepan over medium heat. Whisk in the flour until fully combined, reduce heat to medium-low, and continue cooking, stirring often until the raw flour taste is cooked out and the flour is a light blond color, 10 to 15 minutes. Whisk in the milk and bring to a simmer, stirring often, until the mixture has thickened to wallpaper paste consistency, about 5 minutes. Whisk in the cheeses and beer until just combined and remove from the heat.*

Fold in the Pickled Mustard Seeds, if desired. Season to taste with the salt, white pepper, and hot sauce. Combine the pasta with the cheese sauce in a serving bowl or casserole dish and sprinkle the Ham-Chedddar Crumble over the top. Serve immediately.

If serving later, put in an oven-safe casserole dish. When ready to serve, preheat the oven to 375 degrees, add the crumble, and cook until just warmed through.

≫ MAKES 8 SERVINGS.

NOTE: Any combination of good melting cheeses can be substituted for the Havarti and Gouda.

* It is important not to overheat the cheese sauce mixture as it can become gritty and bring out the bitter flavor of the beer.

PICKLED MUSTARD SEEDS

1 cup white vinegar
2 tablespoons kosher salt
½ cup water

½ cup sugar
4 tablespoons dried yellow mustard seeds

Combine the vinegar, salt, water, and sugar in a small saucepan and simmer on medium heat to dissolve the salt and sugar. Add the mustard seeds. Reduce heat to medium-low and simmer until the seeds soften and nearly double in size, about 30 minutes. Pour into a container and refrigerate. This will keep indefinitely in the refrigerator.

HAM-CHEDDAR CRUMBLE

½ cup very finely diced country ham or bacon bits

½ cup cheese straw crumbs*

Preheat the oven to 375 degrees.

Place the ham or bacon bits in a single layer on a baking sheet and cook until crisp, about 10 minutes. Cool and combine with the cheese crumbs.

≫ MAKES 1 CUP.

* Crumbled cheese crackers or goldfish will work as a substitute.

FRIED DILL PICKLES

1 cup all-purpose flour
¼ cup cornstarch
1 teaspoon baking powder
½ teaspoon salt
1 cup ice water

1 large egg yolk
2 tablespoons dill pickle juice
Vegetable oil for frying
4 cups drained dill pickle slices

Stir the flour, cornstarch, baking powder, and salt together in a large bowl. Make a well in the center and add the ice water, egg yolk, and dill pickle juice. Stir until smooth. Cover the bowl and refrigerate 30 minutes.

Heat at least 2 inches of oil in a deep fryer or in a large skillet over medium-high heat. Dip the pickles in the batter to coat evenly and fry in batches until the pickles float to the surface and are golden brown. Place on a plate lined with paper towels to drain. Serve hot.

>> MAKES 12 SERVINGS.

FRIED APPLES

¼ cup (½ stick) butter
8 medium Granny Smith apples (skin on), chopped

½ cup brown sugar
1 teaspoon ground cinnamon
⅛ teaspoon ground nutmeg

Melt the butter in a heavy skillet over medium-low heat. Add the apples, brown sugar, cinnamon, and nutmeg. Sauté for 15 to 20 minutes or until the apples are tender.

>> MAKES 6 SERVINGS.

BACON CHEDDAR CORN PUDDING

¼ cup (½ stick) butter

3 large eggs

¼ cup all-purpose flour

1 ¼ cups heavy cream

1 (8.5-ounce) can creamed corn

½ teaspoon salt

1 ½ cups fresh or frozen corn kernels

1 cup cooked, chopped bacon

¼ teaspoon freshly ground black pepper

1 ½ cups shredded sharp Cheddar cheese

Preheat the oven to 375 degrees.

Place the butter in a 1 ½-quart casserole dish and put the dish in the oven to melt the butter. In a small bowl beat the eggs until foamy. In a large bowl place the flour and stir in the cream until thickened. Add the beaten eggs, followed by the creamed corn, salt, corn kernels, bacon, and pepper, stirring thoroughly after each addition. Pour the mixture into the buttered casserole dish and stir to incorporate the butter.

Bake for 10 minutes and then stir. Bake another 10 minutes and stir. Then bake an additional 20 minutes without stirring. Remove the pan from the oven and sprinkle with the cheese. Return to the oven and bake an additional 10 minutes or until the cheese has melted.

>> MAKES 8 SERVINGS.

ENTRÉES

Sorghum Bacon Glaze from The MacIntosh

Gulf Shrimp with Tasso Cream Sauce and Old-Fashioned Cornbread from
   Felicia Suzanne's

Spice-Marinated Pork Porterhouse from Louis's at Sanford's

Chicken Fried Pork Chops from Delta Bistro

The Brookville Burger from Brookville Restaurant

Bacon Meatballs from Chef and the Farmer

Roasted Pork Shoulder with Pepper Sauce from NoFo @ the Pig

BLTA Bites from Chef's Market

Pork and Chorizo Meatballs with Pozole Broth from Pasture

Fried Green Tomato BLT from Stella's Kentucky Deli

Chopped Pork Barbecue from Comfort

Cocina Criolla Roast Pork Shoulder from Restaurant Eugene

Porchetta Tonnato from FIG

Braised Pork Belly with Juniper and Ginger Beer over Stone Ground Grits from Comfort

Oysters Rockefeller from Doc Crow's Southern Smokehouse and Raw Bar

Slow-Roasted Pork Shoulder with Gumbo Sauce from IvyWild

Mike's Meatloaf from Table 100

Three Little Pigs Slider with Spicy Pickled Slaw from Fox Brothers Bar-B-Que

Braised Cuban Pork Butt from The Green Room

Louis's Shrimp and Grits with Bacon from Louis's at Sanford's

Double-Cut Pork Chop with Dirty Rice and Cane Syrup Gastrique from Toups' Meatery

Spicy Open-Faced BBQ Sandwich from Mama J's Kitchen

Caramelized St. Louis Pork Ribs with Mustard BBQ Sauce from Soby's
New South Cuisine

Martin's Redneck Taco from Martin's BBQ

The PBLT Sandwich from Hammerheads

Pork Shoulder Sausage from Poole's Downtown Diner

BBQ Crunch Burger from Memphis BBQ Company

Bacon-Wrapped Stuffed Grilled Shrimp from Memphis Barbecue Company

Dr Pepper Glazed Ham from Purple Parrot Cafe

Smoked Onion and Sage Sausage from St. John's Restaurant

Molasses-Glazed Ham Steaks from Purple Parrot Café

Sweet Tea Glazed Pork Loin with Farro Peach Salad from Ruka's Table

Brined Pork Chops from High Cotton

Pork Porterhouse with Kumquat Marmalade from The Ravenous Pig

Peanut Crusted Pork Wiener Schnitzel from Restaurant Eugene

Country Cuban Mixto Sandwiches with Pimento Cheese from Something Different

Black Jambalaya from Crescent Pie and Sausage Company

Raspberry Glazed Pork with Mango Salsa from Chef's Market

Chicken Fried Bacon and Cheddar Waffles from Swine Southern Table and Bar

Grilled Ham, Cheese, and Bacon Sandwiches

Sweet and Spicy Bacon-Wrapped Chicken Tenders

Smothered Southern Pork Chops

Pecan-Crusted Cornbread Pork Loin

Pork Tchoupitoulas from Ruffino's

Tamale Pie Casserole from City Grocery

Ham and Tomato Pie

Cornmeal Fried Green Tomato, Bacon, Pimento Cheese Stack-Up from
Cotton Creative Southern Cuisine

Fried Pork Cutlets

SORGHUM BACON GLAZE FROM THE MACINTOSH

This glaze is great drizzled over grilled pork chops, baked pork roast, or smoked tenderloin.

1 small yellow onion, medium dice
1 carrot, medium dice
2 celery stalks, medium dice
1 bay leaf
1 whole star anise
¼ pound smoked bacon, chopped
3 cups port wine

3 cups red wine
1 cup sorghum molasses, divided
1 gallon pork stock (see page 61 for recipe) or chicken stock
¾ cup bourbon
Salt to taste
Black pepper to taste

In a large skillet over medium heat add the onions, carrots, celery, bay leaf, star anise, and bacon and sweat until the vegetables are lightly caramelized, 5 to 7 minutes. Add the port and red wine and cook until nearly all of the liquid is dissolved. Add ½ cup of the sorghum molasses and cook until slightly thickened. Add the pork stock. Remove the pan from the heat and add the bourbon.

Return the pan to the stove and bring the entire mixture to a boil. Once boiling, reduce heat to low and simmer, letting the entire mixture reduce by ½ to ¾. This should take 10 to 20 minutes. Season with the salt and pepper. Stir in the remaining ½ cup sorghum. Strain and let cool for at least 30 minutes. Refrigerate until ready to use. This will keep for up to a week.

>> MAKES 8 SERVINGS.

GULF SHRIMP WITH TASSO CREAM SAUCE AND OLD-FASHIONED CORNBREAD FROM FELICIA SUZANNE'S

1 ½ tablespoons olive oil

16 medium to large Gulf head-on shrimp, peeled and deveined

Salt to taste

Crushed red pepper flakes to taste

2 ounces tasso ham,* small diced, browned, and drained

1 ¼ cups heavy cream

1 tablespoon roughly chopped fresh cilantro leaves

4 (4-inch) squares cornbread, cut diagonally and toasted

2 ounces goat cheese

1 tablespoon chopped green onions

Pour the oil into a large sauté pan over medium-high heat. In a large bowl place the shrimp and season with the salt and red pepper flakes. Add the shrimp to the pan and sauté for 1 minute. Add the tasso and continue to sauté for 1 minute more. Pour the cream into the pan and bring to a boil. Reduce the heat to low and simmer until the cream becomes thick and coats the back of a spoon, 5 to 10 minutes. Add the cilantro to the pan and mix well.

TO SERVE: Arrange two slices of the cornbread in the center of each plate like a butterfly's wing. Spoon the shrimp mixture over the cornbread. Crumble the goat cheese over the shrimp and garnish with green onions.

>> MAKES 8 SERVINGS.

* If you can't find tasso ham, feel free to substitute smoked ham.

In a small bowl combine the garlic, salt, black pepper, sage, juniper berries, cloves, mace, thyme, nutmeg, paprika, cinnamon, basil, marjoram, savory, dried sage, peppercorns, and bay leaves. Spread the rub on both sides of the chops. Put the meat into a pan in one layer. Cover and refrigerate for at least 12 hours, but no more than 24 hours or the meat will be too salty.

Preheat a grill over medium-high heat and preheat the oven to 450 degrees. Remove the spice rub from the meat with paper towels. Brush both sides of the chops with the oil. Grill the chops over moderate heat for 8 minutes. Turn the meat and cook to your taste, about 10 minutes longer for medium. Alternatively, broil the chops in the oven for 4 minutes. Turn the meat and broil 4 minutes longer. Then bake the chops until cooked to your taste, about 10 minutes for medium.

>> MAKES 6 SERVINGS.

SPICE-MARINATED PORK PORTERHOUSE FROM LOUIS'S AT SANFORD'S

6 cloves garlic, minced

¼ cup coarse salt

5 teaspoons freshly ground black pepper

1 ½ tablespoons chopped fresh sage (or 1 ½ teaspoons dried)

24 juniper berries, crushed

½ teaspoon ground cloves

½ teaspoon ground mace

½ teaspoon dried thyme

½ teaspoon grated nutmeg

½ teaspoon paprika

¼ teaspoon ground cinnamon

¼ teaspoon dried basil

¼ teaspoon dried marjoram

¼ teaspoon dried savory

¼ teaspoon dried sage

¼ teaspoon peppercorns

2 bay leaves

6 (1 ½-inch thick) pork loin chops with the tenderloin

4 teaspoons vegetable oil

CHICKEN FRIED PORK CHOPS FROM DELTA BISTRO

4 (8-ounce) bone-in center-cut
loin pork chops

2 cups buttermilk

Canola oil for frying

2 cups panko bread crumbs

½ teaspoon cayenne pepper

½ teaspoon salt

Place the pork chops in a shallow dish and pour the buttermilk over the chops. Cover and refrigerate for 2 hours.

Pour 1 inch of oil into a large skillet over medium heat or preheat a deep fryer to 350 degrees.

In a shallow bowl use a fork to stir together the bread crumbs, cayenne, and salt. Remove the pork chops from the buttermilk and dredge in the seasoned bread crumbs. Fry the pork chops for 8 minutes on each side if using a skillet, or for 14 to 16 minutes in a deep fryer.

≫ MAKES 4 SERVINGS.

THE BROOKVILLE BURGER FROM BROOKVILLE RESTAURANT

Bacon Marmalade

¼ cup canola oil

1 pound bacon, chopped

2 medium onions, diced

2 tablespoons chopped fresh oregano
(or ¾ tablespoon dried)

¼ cup honey

¼ cup Worcestershire sauce

4 cups cider vinegar

Burger

Vegetable oil for coating the grill

12 ounces ground sirloin

2 ounces favorite melting cheese (Swiss,
Cheddar, and Jack are great choices)

½ tablespoon butter

1 large egg

1 hamburger bun

TO MAKE THE BACON MARMALADE: Heat the oil in a medium saucepan over high heat. Once it starts to smoke, add the bacon and onions, reduce the heat to medium, and cook, stirring often to prevent burning, about 20 minutes. Drain the excess grease from the pan. Add the oregano and honey and cook for 5 more minutes. Add the Worcestershire and vinegar. Bring to a boil, reduce to a simmer, and cook until thick, 2 to 3 hours, stirring occasionally. Remove from the heat and let cool. Spoon into a 1-quart jar and store in the refrigerator for up to 1 week.

TO MAKE THE BURGER: Preheat the grill to medium-high heat and coat the grates with oil. Make two 6-ounce patties, put the cheese in the middle, and seal together. Grill the burger to the desired doneness (medium-rare is when the cheese starts to melt inside). Heat the butter in a small frying pan over medium heat. When the foam subsides, break the egg into the pan and cook until the whites are set.

TO SERVE: Place the burger on the bottom bun, spoon ⅓ cup bacon marmalade on top, and cover with the egg. Serve immediately.

>> MAKES 1 BURGER.

BACON MEATBALLS FROM CHEF AND THE FARMER

1 cup bread crumbs

½ cup milk

1 pound ground pork

¾ pound bacon, ground*

¼ tablespoon grated garlic (1 clove)

¾ tablespoon grated ginger (12-inch piece)

¾ tablespoon chopped fresh sage

¾ tablespoon chopped fresh oregano

¾ teaspoon black pepper

¼ teaspoon salt

1 large egg

Preheat the oven to 350 degrees. Grease 2 baking sheets.

Combine the bread crumbs and milk in a small bowl and allow the bread crumbs to soak while you gather the remaining ingredients.

In the bowl of an electric mixer with a paddle attachment combine the pork, ground bacon, garlic, ginger, sage, oregano, black pepper, salt, egg, and bread crumb mixture. Mix until evenly incorporated. Do not overmix. Form the meat into ¾- to 1-ounce balls, about the size of a golf ball, and place ½ inch apart on the baking sheets. Roast the meatballs for about 15 minutes or until slightly firm and golden brown. Serve over creamed greens or pasta.

≫ MAKES 8 SERVINGS (BETWEEN 30 AND 45 MEATBALLS).

* Chef Vivian uses Benton's bacon, but feel free to use your favorite good-quality bacon instead.

ROASTED PORK SHOULDER WITH PEPPER SAUCE FROM NOFO @ THE PIG

3 jalapeño peppers
1 small sweet onion, chopped into large chunks
1 (12- to 14-pound) pork shoulder

¼ cup salt
24 hamburger buns
Pepper Sauce (recipe follows)

Preheat the oven to 300 degrees.

Place the jalapeños and onion in the bowl of a food processor and grind to a paste. Cover the top side of the pork shoulder with the paste and salt liberally. Place in a roasting pan and roast until the meat reaches an internal temperature of at least 190 degrees and pulls apart easily, 3 to 5 hours. Serve 8 ounces of roast pork on a bun and top with the Pepper Sauce.

>> MAKES 24 SANDWICHES.

PEPPER SAUCE

1 teaspoon vegetable oil
2 tablespoons minced onion
2 teaspoons crushed red pepper flakes
1 teaspoon black pepper

1 teaspoon sugar
3 teaspoons salt
2 cups white vinegar
1 cup water

In a medium saucepan over medium heat add the oil and sweat the onions until they become translucent. Add the red pepper flakes, black pepper, sugar, salt, vinegar, and water. Bring to a boil, remove from the heat, and allow to cool.

>> MAKES 3 CUPS.

BLTA BITES FROM CHEF'S MARKET

12 slices white bread

¾ cup fresh basil

½ cup mayonnaise

4 slices applewood smoked bacon
(cooked and chopped)

1 cup micro greens or thinly
sliced Romaine

3 grape tomatoes (quartered)

1 avocado, diced

Preheat the oven to 350 degrees. Grease a mini muffin pan.

Cut 3-inch rounds out of each slice of bread. Use a rolling pin or your hand to gently flatten the bread. Press the bread rounds into 12 cups of the mini muffin pan to form a bowl shape. Bake the bowls for 5 to 8 minutes until golden. Finely chop the fresh basil and place in a small bowl. Add the mayonnaise and stir to combine. Once the bread cups cool, add the chopped bacon to each cup. Next add the basil mayo. Add the greens, and finish with a quartered grape tomato and a small piece of diced avocado.

>> MAKES 12 APPETIZERS.

PORK AND CHORIZO MEATBALLS WITH POZOLE BROTH FROM PASTURE

Meatballs

2 pounds fresh Mexican chorizo, removed from casing and crumbled

2 pounds ground pork

4 large eggs

1 cup fresh bread crumbs

6 green onions, sliced thin

1 clove garlic, minced

2 red jalapeño peppers, seeded and finely diced

1 tablespoon fresh cilantro, minced

Salt and black pepper to taste

Pozole Broth

1 tablespoon vegetable oil

1 small white onion, finely diced

1 small carrot, finely diced

2 celery stalks, finely diced

3 garlic cloves, minced

2 guajillo chilies, ground (you can substitute ancho chilies)

4 sprigs fresh thyme, minced

2 bay leaves

4 cups pork stock (see page 61 for recipe) or chicken stock

½ cup tomato juice

Juice of 3 lemons

¼ cup masa or finely ground cornmeal

Salt and black pepper to taste

Hot sauce to taste

TO MAKE THE MEATBALLS: Preheat the oven to 375 degrees. Line a baking sheet with parchment paper.

Combine the chorizo, ground pork, eggs, bread crumbs, green onions, garlic, jalapeños, and cilantro in a large bowl. Season to taste with salt and pepper. Portion the mixture into 2-ounce balls and place on the baking sheet. Bake for 20 minutes.

TO MAKE THE POZOLE BROTH: Heat a large saucepan over medium heat. Add the oil to the pan, then the onions, carrots, celery, and garlic. When the vegetables become translucent, in 4 to 5 minutes, add the guajillo chilies, thyme, and bay leaves. Cook for about

3 more minutes, then add the stock, tomato juice, and lemon juice. Simmer for about 15 minutes, then whisk in the masa. Simmer for another 5 minutes, remove the bay leaves, and season to taste with salt, pepper, and hot sauce.

TO SERVE: Arrange 3 to 4 meatballs in a bowl and ladle ½ cup of the pozole broth over top.

» MAKES 8 SERVINGS.

NOTE: For a heartier version, spoon a helping of grits in the bowl before adding the meatballs and broth.

FRIED GREEN TOMATO BLT FROM STELLA'S KENTUCKY DELI

This is their take on the classic sandwich. They lightly fry their tomatoes on a flat-top grill, which emulates old-fashioned cast-iron skillet frying. In the home, a cast-iron skillet will yield the best results.

Fried Green Tomatoes

2 tablespoons bacon fat, oil, or butter for frying, divided
1 cup white cornmeal*
2 teaspoons salt
2 teaspoons garlic powder
1 teaspoon freshly ground black pepper
1 cup buttermilk
2 medium green tomatoes, sliced ⅕-inch thick

Basil Mayonnaise

¼ cup fresh basil
1 cup mayonnaise

Sandwiches

8 slices hearty sandwich bread
16 slices cooked bacon
4 large green leaf lettuce

TO MAKE THE FRIED GREEN TOMATOES: Place a cast-iron skillet over high heat and lightly grease with your oil of choice. Mix the cornmeal, salt, garlic powder, and pepper together in a shallow pan or plate. Pour the buttermilk into another shallow bowl. Submerge the tomato slices in the buttermilk and then dredge thoroughly in the seasoned cornmeal mix to coat. Be sure to press the tomato slices into the mix on both sides to get an even coating. Remove any clumps as these will lead to uneven frying. Place the tomatoes in the hot pan and cook approximately 2 minutes, until the bottom begins to brown. Add more oil to the pan if needed. Flip the tomatoes and cook 30 seconds to 1 minute, or until browned. Plan for 2 to 3 tomato slices per sandwich.

TO MAKE THE BASIL MAYONNAISE: Finely chop the basil. Spoon the mayonnaise into a small bowl and add the basil. Stir to combine and store in the refrigerator until you are ready to use.

TO MAKE THE SANDWICHES: Toast the bread. Spread the inner sides of slices with basil mayo and then stack the bacon, green tomatoes, and lettuce on one side. Close the sandwiches and slice on the diagonal.

≫ MAKES 4 SANDWICHES.

* Use Weisenburger Mill if you are in Kentucky.

CHOPPED PORK BARBECUE FROM COMFORT

Pork

¼ cup kosher salt
¼ cup paprika
2 tablespoons brown sugar
1 tablespoon granulated garlic
1 tablespoon onion powder
1 tablespoon chili powder
1 tablespoon black pepper
1 (6- to 8-pound) Boston butt

Sauce

2 cups cider vinegar
½ cup tomato juice
¼ cup ketchup
2 tablespoons Worcestershire sauce
1 tablespoon granulated garlic
1 tablespoon molasses
1 tablespoon crushed red pepper flakes

TO PREPARE THE PORK: Heat a smoker with hickory and oak to 225 degrees. Combine the kosher salt, paprika, brown sugar, garlic, onion powder, chili powder, and black pepper, and massage the rub into the Boston butt. Place the meat on a rack in the smoker, and let cook for about 12 to 13 hours, or until an internal temperature of 190 is reached.

TO MAKE THE SAUCE: In a large pot combine the vinegar, tomato juice, ketchup, Worcestershire, garlic, molasses, and red pepper flakes and bring to a boil over medium heat.

TO ASSEMBLE THE DISH: When the pork is done, remove the excess fat and bone and chop to desired consistency. Dress the pork with the sauce and serve hot.

≫ MAKES 12 SERVINGS.

COCINA CRIOLLA ROAST PORK SHOULDER FROM RESTAURANT EUGENE

Mix the Creole seasoning, salt, and sugar together in a small bowl. Pat the pork dry and rub the mixture all over the pork. Cover with plastic wrap and refrigerate for 18 hours.

Preheat the oven to 300 degrees.

Place the pineapple, jalapeños, onions, garlic, and bay leaves in a large roasting pan. Place the roast on top of the fruit and vegetables. Pour the chicken stock around the base of the roast and the orange juice over the top. Roast for 6 to 7 hours, basting every 30 minutes. Let rest for 30 minutes. Serve with Lady Peas, Rice, and Tomatoes (see page 193 for recipe).

≫ MAKES 12 SERVINGS.

1 cup Creole seasoning

½ cup kosher salt

½ cup sugar

1 (8- to 10-pound) whole bone-in pork butt

4 cups diced fresh pineapple

3 jalapeño peppers, sliced

2 onions, peeled and cut into eighths

12 garlic cloves, peeled

2 fresh bay leaves

2 cups chicken stock

1 cup orange juice

PORCHETTA TONNATO FROM FIG

Sauce

4 (5-ounce) cans quality oil-packed tuna

6 large egg yolks

2 ounces lemon juice

1 ounce white wine vinegar

2 tablespoons Dijon mustard

2 tablespoons capers, rinsed

6 black anchovies, canned in oil, drained

6 shakes hot sauce

3 cups extra-virgin olive oil

1 cup chicken stock

Salt and white pepper to taste

Pork

2 pounds boneless pork tenderloin, trimmed of excess fat

3 cups unsalted chicken stock, chilled

12 black peppercorns

4 cloves garlic

4 bay leaves

4 small sprigs fresh rosemary

8 sprigs fresh thyme

Optional Garnishes

Chopped olives

Capers

Chives

Shallots, minced and rinsed

Sliced radishes

Baby arugula

Fleur de sel

Fresh-squeezed lemon juice

TO MAKE THE SAUCE: Drain and save the oil from the tuna. Place the tuna, egg yolks, lemon juice, white wine vinegar, Dijon, capers, anchovies, and the hot sauce in a blender and puree. With the blender running, slowly stream in the olive oil. Make sure to go slow to maintain the emulsification. If it gets thick enough that it is not spinning freely, add the chicken stock ¼ cup at a time until it is thick and creamy, but not runny. Adjust the seasoning with salt and white pepper. Use a light touch with additional salt since capers and chicken stock can already be salty.

TO MAKE THE PORK: In a large pot cover the tenderloin with cold chicken stock, peppercorns, garlic, bay leaves, rosemary, and thyme. Slowly bring the stock to a boil. With a large spoon skim off any foam that develops on the surface of the stock. Reduce to a gentle simmer and cover. After an hour, check the internal temperature of the pork. Remove the pot from the heat when the tenderloin reaches 136 degrees. Remove the tenderloin from the pot to a plate, cover with aluminum foil, and allow the meat to rest for 15 minutes. Strain the stock and allow it to cool while the tenderloin rests. Add the pork back to the stock.

TO SERVE: Arrange the sauce on a plate, and shave the pork paper thin (or as thin as you can get) and form in rosette style. Serve with garnishes as desired.

>> MAKES 4 SERVINGS.

BRAISED PORK BELLY WITH JUNIPER AND GINGER BEER OVER STONE GROUND GRITS FROM COMFORT

· ·

2 sprigs fresh thyme

2 sprigs fresh rosemary

2 sprigs fresh sage

2 tablespoons juniper berries, lightly crushed

¼ cup olive oil

Salt and black pepper to taste

1 (3- to 4-pound) pork belly

¼ cup vegetable oil

1 large white onion, peeled and roughly chopped

2 large carrots, peeled and roughly chopped

4 celery stalks, leaves removed and roughly chopped

1 head garlic, split

2 fresh or dried bay leaves

1 cup red wine

2 bottles ginger beer

6 cups pork stock (see page 61 for recipe or use 6 cups of ham base or chicken stock)

Stone-Ground Grits (recipe follows)

Arugula for garnish

Extra-virgin olive oil for garnish

Lemon juice for garnish

Combine the thyme, rosemary, sage, juniper berries, olive oil, salt, and pepper in a large bowl, and add the pork belly. Roll the belly in the marinade, cover with plastic wrap, and refrigerate for at least 3 hours but no more than 6.

Preheat the oven to 375 degrees. Heat a heavy-bottomed ovenproof pan over medium heat. Remove the belly from the marinade (reserve the marinade), pat dry, and season well with salt and pepper. Pour the oil into the pan and carefully sear the belly on both sides until well browned. Remove the belly and reserve. Add the onions, carrots, celery, garlic, bay leaves, and reserved marinade and cook until lightly browned.

Deglaze the pan with the wine, add the ginger beer, and scrape the pan to release the browned bits. Add the stock and the belly, cover, and place in the oven for 3 hours until fork-tender. Time will vary depending on the size of the belly. Strain the braising liquid from the bottom of the pan through a chinois. Skim all the fat from the liquid and reduce by 40 percent over medium-high heat.

When ready to serve, gently reheat the belly in the jus. Serve over the grits, pour a bit of jus over the top, and garnish with arugula tossed in a bit of extra-virgin olive oil and lemon juice.

>> MAKES 8 SERVINGS.

STONE-GROUND GRITS

3 cups whole milk
3 cups chicken stock
1 ½ cups stone-ground grits*

½ cup (1 stick) butter
Salt and black pepper to taste

Pour the milk and stock into a large saucepan and bring to a boil over medium-high heat. Reduce the heat to low and simmer and slowly whisk in the grits. Simmer, stirring often, for approximately 45 minutes. If the grits are still hard, cook until tender. Stir in the butter and season to taste with salt and pepper.

>> MAKES 8 SERVINGS.

* Comfort uses Byrd Mill.

OYSTERS ROCKEFELLER FROM DOC CROW'S SOUTHERN SMOKEHOUSE AND RAW BAR

2 cups Béchamel Sauce (recipe follows)
4 ounces Pernod or other absinthe (such as Herbsaint)
1 pound bacon, diced and cooked crisp
2 cups spinach, chopped and cooked

1 cup grated Parmesan cheese
24 raw oysters on the half shell
Sea salt to taste
Freshly ground pepper to taste

In a large saucepan over medium heat, bring the béchamel sauce to a simmer, add the Pernod, and bring to a boil to cook off the alcohol. Stir in the bacon and spinach. Remove the pan from the heat and fold in the Parmesan cheese. Cool the mixture in the refrigerator for 1 hour.

Preheat the oven to 350 degrees.

Place the oysters in a single layer on a baking sheet. Sprinkle with salt and pepper. Top the oysters with the sauce, coating them completely. Bake for 12 minutes. Serve immediately.

≫ MAKES 6 SERVINGS.

BÉCHAMEL SAUCE

2 tablespoons butter
2 tablespoons flour
1 ¼ cups whole or 2% milk, warmed

Salt to taste
Freshly ground pepper to taste

Melt the butter in a heavy-bottomed saucepan over medium heat. Stir in the flour and cook, stirring constantly, until the paste cooks and bubbles a bit, but don't let it brown, about 2 minutes. Add the warm milk, continuing to stir as the sauce thickens. Bring the mixture to a boil. Add salt and pepper to taste, lower the heat, and cook, stirring for 2 to 3 minutes more. Remove the pan from the heat. To cool this sauce for later use, cover the surface with wax paper or pour a film of milk over it to prevent a skin from forming.

≫ MAKES ABOUT 1 ¼ CUPS.

Liberally salt the shoulder all over, using 1 teaspoon of salt per pound of meat. Wrap or cover tightly and let rest in the refrigerator for 24 to 48 hours. This will allow the salt to permeate the meat thoroughly.

Preheat the oven to 275 degrees.

Sprinkle the pork with pepper at a rate of ½ teaspoon for every pound of meat. Place the shoulder in an oven-safe roasting bag and close with a twist tie. Place in a large roasting pan and cook until tender, about 5 hours. Carefully split open the roasting bag to release steam and allow the roast to cool to room temperature. Refrigerate overnight. (You can skip this step and eat your roast right away if you don't mind the roast falling apart on you—it will still be delicious! If you want to have neat "steaks" of pork roast, you will need to chill it before cutting.)

Remove the roast from the refrigerator. Preheat a heavy-bottomed or cast-iron skillet over medium-high heat until it just starts to smoke.

Preheat the oven to 350 degrees.

Cut the chilled roast into 6- to 8-ounce portions. Sear each steak in the skillet on all sides. Place in a baking pan and bake for 8 to 10 minutes, or until heated through. Serve with Gumbo Sauce over the top of the pork.

>> MAKES 2 TO 3 SERVINGS FOR EACH POUND OF SHOULDER.

SLOW-ROASTED PORK SHOULDER WITH GUMBO SAUCE FROM IVYWILD

¼ cup kosher salt

1 (12- to 14-pound) boneless pork shoulder

⅛ cup black pepper

Gumbo Sauce (recipe follows)

GUMBO SAUCE

½ cup (1 stick) butter

¾ cup all-purpose flour

¼ cup olive oil

2 large onions, finely chopped in food processor

3 green bell peppers, finely chopped in food processor

2 red bell peppers, finely chopped in food processor

½ celery stalk, finely chopped in food processor

¼ cup minced garlic

1 (12-ounce) can tomato paste

4 cups white wine

1 gallon chicken stock, plus more if needed

8 bay leaves

2 tablespoons Italian seasoning

1 (16-ounce) package smoked sausage, sliced thin

Sea salt to taste

¼ cup gumbo filé

Melt the butter in a heavy-bottomed saucepan over medium heat. Stir in the flour. Continue to stir constantly and watch carefully for 45 minutes to an hour, or until the roux turns a rich chocolate brown. Remove the pan from the heat and set aside. (You can make this in larger batches and freeze at this point.)

Heat the olive oil in a large heavy-bottomed pot over medium-high heat. Add the onions, green and red peppers, and celery and sauté until very soft and starting to blacken, about 20 minutes. Add the garlic and stir for 10 seconds (it will turn bitter if you don't move quickly). Add the tomato paste and stir frequently for 5 to 10 minutes until dark orange, caramelized, and starting to burn. Stir in the wine and cook until the wine has reduced by half. Add the chicken stock, bay leaves, Italian seasoning, and sausage. Bring to a boil, reduce the heat to low, and simmer 1 hour.

Raise the heat to medium-high and return to a boil. Stir in the roux. (It's okay if it has cooled and breaks apart.) Reduce the heat to low and simmer 1 hour. Stir periodically to prevent the roux from burning. Add more chicken stock as needed to prevent scorching. Add the sea salt if needed, but be careful not to oversalt. Use a coarse strainer or pair of tongs to remove the bay leaves and sausage, leaving a smooth, velvety sauce. Whisk in the filé. Serve immediately

>> MAKES 2 QUARTS.

Preheat the oven to 350 degrees.

Add the butter to a large skillet over medium heat. When the butter has melted, add the onions and garlic and cook until softened. Remove from the heat and allow to cool.

Place the ground beef and pork and the cooled onions in a large bowl. Put the eggs and the drained rolls in a blender and mix. Add to the meat mixture. Add the parsley, Worcestershire, salt and pepper, and Dijon mustard. Use your hands to mix all ingredients and knead very well. Form into two loaves and place in 9-inch loaf pans. Cook for 45 to 60 minutes, checking after 45 minutes for an internal temperature of 160 degrees.

» MAKES 12 SERVINGS.

MIKE'S MEATLOAF FROM TABLE 100

2 tablespoons butter

3 cups chopped onions

1 tablespoon minced garlic

2 ¼ pounds ground beef

2 ¼ pounds ground pork

5 large eggs

8 white rolls, soaked in milk and drained

1 cup chopped fresh parsley

Dash of Worcestershire sauce

Salt and black pepper to taste

4 tablespoons Dijon mustard

THREE LITTLE PIGS SLIDER WITH SPICY PICKLED SLAW FROM FOX BROTHERS BAR-B-QUE

•••••••••••••••••••••••••• *photo on page 124* ••••••••••••••••••••••••••

This delectable little sandwich allows for plenty of flexibility and is a treat for a tailgater or as an appetizer. Smoke your own butt or buy some smoked shoulder. Make the slaw at least a day in advance for the best flavors. The barbecued pork belly really takes this dish over the top.

Spicy Pickled Slaw

1 cup cider vinegar
1 cup sugar
1 head green cabbage, shredded
1 red onion, thinly sliced
2 jalapeño peppers, seeded and minced
2 bay leaves
Salt and black pepper to taste

Pork

1 (8-ounce) piece pork belly*
1 cup dry rub, divided (see page 52 for recipe)
2 tablespoons sugar
1 (4- to 6-pound) pork butt (or 2 pounds smoked shoulder from your favorite barbecue joint)
1 bottle of your favorite barbecue sauce
2 tablespoons butter, softened
12 slider buns
1 pound bacon, cooked crisp and drained on paper towels

TO MAKE THE SPICY PICKLED SLAW: Pour the cider vinegar in a pot and bring to a boil over medium heat. When it comes to a boil, whisk in the sugar and remove the pan from the heat. In a large bowl add the cabbage, red onions, and jalapeños and pour the hot vinegar mixture over top. Make sure all of the slaw is completely covered by stirring a couple of times. Add the bay leaves, cover, and let sit for at least 5 to 6 hours or overnight in the refrigerator. Taste and adjust seasoning if necessary. Remove the bay leaves before serving.

TO MAKE THE PORK: Slice the pork belly vertically down the middle, cutting it into two pieces. Mix 4 tablespoons of dry rub and the sugar together and coat both pieces of the belly completely. Wrap with plastic wrap and let it sit in the refrigerator for 8 hours or overnight.

Preheat a smoker to 225 degrees. Use the remaining rub to liberally coat the pork butt. Smoke for 8 to 12 hours or until the pork reaches an internal temperature of 190 to 195 degrees.

Remove the pork belly from the plastic wrap and place on the smoker to cook for 5 hours, until it is tender to the touch. Pour

1 cup of the barbecue sauce into a small bowl and baste the belly until completely coated. Cook for 1 more hour, or until the internal temperature reaches 160 degrees. Remove the belly from the smoker and let it rest on a plate covered with aluminum foil for 30 to 45 minutes. Remove the pork butt and wrap in plastic wrap and aluminum foil and set in a warm oven or cooler until ready to serve. If you're in a hurry, pick up 3 pounds of smoked shoulder from your local pit master instead.

TO ASSEMBLE THE SLIDER: Spread softened butter on the buns and toast under a broiler. Pull the pork off the butt, placing a small amount on the bottom slider bun. Next, use a sharp knife to slice the belly into ½-inch slices. Take 2 to 3 slices of pork belly and place on top of the pulled pork. Cut the crispy bacon in half to fit on top of the pork belly. Spoon the pickled slaw on top of the bacon. Drizzle a little barbecue sauce over the slaw and add the top slider bun.

>> MAKES 12 SERVINGS.

* You can special order pork belly at most grocery stores or from a butcher, or find it at your local international market.

BRAISED CUBAN PORK BUTT FROM THE GREEN ROOM

Rub

2 ½ tablespoons ground cumin
2 ½ tablespoons dried oregano
¼ cup minced garlic
1 teaspoon cayenne pepper
2 tablespoons salt
1 tablespoon freshly ground black pepper
1 (6- to 8-pound) whole pork butt

Marinade

2 cups orange juice
1 onion, halved
2 limes, halved and juiced
2 lemons, halved and juiced
1 orange, halved and juiced

Preheat the oven to 350 degrees.

TO MAKE THE RUB: Mix the cumin, oregano, garlic, cayenne pepper, salt, and black pepper in a small bowl. Rub the pork butt with the mixture until the butt is completely covered.

TO MAKE THE MARINADE: Pour the orange juice into a large pan with sides tall enough to cover the pork butt. Add the onion, the lime, lemon, and orange juices, the juiced fruit, and the pork butt to the pan. Cover with aluminum foil and cook for 5 hours, or until the pork is easily pulled apart with a fork.

>> MAKES 6 SERVINGS.

LOUIS'S SHRIMP AND GRITS WITH BACON FROM LOUIS'S AT SANFORD'S

6 slices bacon

1 cup finely chopped onion

⅓ cup finely chopped celery

½ cup finely chopped green bell pepper

2 cloves garlic, minced

1 sprig fresh thyme or ¼ teaspoon dried thyme

2 bay leaves

⅓ cup white vermouth or dry white wine

8 tablespoons all-purpose flour

4 cups fish or shrimp stock (or bottled clam juice in a pinch)

2 tablespoons tomato paste

2 cups heavy cream

Salt and black pepper to taste

Hot sauce to taste, optional

6 tablespoons butter

1 ½ pounds medium shrimp (31/35), peeled and deveined

Creamy Grits (recipe follows)

In a large skillet over medium-high heat, cook the bacon until crisp. Remove to a plate lined with paper towels to drain, reserving the fat in the skillet. Add the onions, celery, green peppers, and garlic to the bacon fat and cook for 4 to 5 minutes. Add the thyme and bay leaves and cook for another minute. Increase the heat to high and add the vermouth and cook until it evaporates, 2 to 3 minutes.

Lower the heat to medium, add the flour to the pan, and stir to prevent lumps. Be sure to scrape up any of the browned bits that are stuck to the bottom of the pan. Cook the flour for a few minutes to brown it. Add the stock and tomato paste and mix quickly with a whisk to avoid lumps. When the mixture starts to bubble, add the cream. Return to a simmer and taste for salt and pepper. At this point, you can also add some hot sauce if you like. Slowly simmer the sauce for another 4 to 5 minutes while you cook the shrimp. Remove the bay leaves before serving.

In a cast-iron skillet melt the butter over medium-high heat. When the butter starts to bubble, add the shrimp. Stir-fry the shrimp until they are just about half cooked, 3 to 4 minutes. Sprinkle with salt and pepper. Quickly pour the simmering sauce over the shrimp and cook for another 2 minutes. Spoon the shrimp and sauce over Creamy Grits and garnish with the cooked bacon, either whole or chopped.

>> MAKES 6 SERVINGS.

CREAMY GRITS

8 cups (2 quarts) whole milk
2 cups quick-cooking grits (not instant)
Salt and black pepper to taste

1 cup heavy cream
¾ cup (3 sticks) plus 1 ½ tablespoons butter, softened

Bring the milk to a simmer in a saucepan over medium heat. Add the grits and the salt and pepper. Stir until it returns to a simmer. Lower the heat and let cook for 12 minutes, stirring often. Add the cream and soft butter, stirring gently to incorporate. When the mixture returns to a simmer, remove the pan from the heat.

>> MAKES 6 SERVINGS.

NOTE: If you want to use stone-ground grits, use 4 cups water and 4 cups milk. The cooking time will probably need to be lengthened to up to 45 minutes. Taste the grits often and add a little hot water if necessary. When the grits are soft, add the cream and butter and serve.

DOUBLE-CUT PORK CHOP WITH DIRTY RICE AND CANE SYRUP GASTRIQUE FROM TOUPS' MEATERY

Pork Chops

½ gallon water
1 cup firmly packed dark brown sugar
1 cup kosher salt
2 bay leaves
Ice
4 double-cut pork chops
Salt and black pepper to taste

Dirty Rice

1 tablespoon canola oil
1 tablespoon all-purpose flour
½ pound ground brisket*
½ pound ground pork

1 ½ teaspoons salt
1 teaspoon cumin
1 teaspoon black pepper
1 teaspoon paprika
1 teaspoon cayenne pepper
¾ cup chicken stock, divided
3 cloves garlic, crushed
3 cups cooked white rice
1 tablespoon butter

Cane Syrup Gastrique

1 cup good maple syrup**
1 cup cider vinegar***
Chopped green onions for serving

TO MAKE THE PORK CHOPS: Combine the water, brown sugar, salt, and bay leaves in large pot and bring to a boil. Then add ice until you have exactly 1 ½ gallons of brine. Place the pork chops in the brine and leave in the refrigerator 24 to 48 hours to brine.

When you're ready to cook the chops, prepare your grill for indirect grilling over medium heat (300 to 350 degrees). Pat the pork chops dry with paper towels. Then liberally salt and pepper both sides of the pork chop and grill to 145 degrees or preferred temperature. Allow the chops to rest for 5 minutes.

TO MAKE THE DIRTY RICE: Heat the oil in a small skillet over medium-high heat. Add the flour and whisk for 8 to 10 minutes, until a dark roux forms. Set aside while you brown the meats.

Place the brisket and pork in a medium bowl and season with the salt, cumin, black pepper, paprika, and cayenne pepper. Heat a thick-bottomed Dutch oven over medium-high heat. Add the meat mixture and brown. Continue cooking until a fond of brown bits develops on bottom of the pan. Pour ½ cup of the chicken stock into the pan and stir the fond with a wooden spoon to scrape up all the flavorful bits. Add the crushed garlic and the dark roux and cook for 20 minutes, adding the remaining ¼ cup chicken stock as needed to keep the meat mixture from drying out. Add the cooked white rice and butter and mix well.

TO MAKE THE CANE SYRUP GASTRIQUE: Pour the syrup and vinegar into a small saucepan over medium-high and bring to a boil. Simmer over low and reduce by half. Watch closely as it tends to burn.

TO SERVE: Place a generous scoop of dirty rice on each plate. Then add the warm pork chop and spoon the cane syrup gastrique generously over the top. Garnish with chopped green onions.

>> MAKES 4 SERVINGS.

* Grind with an electric mixer attachment or ask your butcher to grind it for you.

** Toups recommends using Steen's Cane Syrup, available online.

*** Toups recommends using Steen's Cane Vinegar, available online.

Wash the whole pork shoulder. In a large baking pan stir together the rub, mustard, and black pepper. Place the shoulder in the pan and rub the mixture over the entire surface of the shoulder. Add the water and vinegar to the bottom of the pan, cover with aluminum foil, and refrigerate overnight.

Preheat the oven to 350 degrees.

Bake the shoulder for 3 hours covered. Once done, remove the bone and excess fat. Let the shoulder cool to room temperature. Place the oil in a large skillet over medium-high heat. Add the green peppers and onions and cook for 5 minutes until the onions are translucent and the peppers are soft. Pull the shoulder meat and place in a large bowl. Add the barbecue sauce, garlic powder, and hot sauce and toss to combine. Place the pulled barbecue on the bottom half of a toasted bun. Top with the sliced sautéed peppers and onions. Sprinkle with crushed red pepper to taste if desired. Serve immediately.

》 MAKES 10 TO 12 SERVINGS.

SPICY OPEN-FACED BBQ SANDWICH FROM MAMA J'S KITCHEN

1 (5- to 6-pound) whole pork shoulder

¼ cup Carolina Pork Shoulder Rub (see page 54 for recipe)

¼ cup dry mustard

¼ cup black pepper

2 cups water

½ cup white vinegar

1 tablespoon vegetable oil

2 green bell peppers, sliced

1 large onion, sliced

2 cups barbecue sauce

⅛ teaspoon garlic powder

1 teaspoon hot sauce

8 hamburger buns, toasted

Crushed red pepper flakes to taste, optional

CARAMELIZED ST. LOUIS PORK RIBS WITH MUSTARD BBQ SAUCE FROM SOBY'S NEW SOUTH CUISINE

Barbecue Sauce

2 cups South Carolina Mustard Barbecue Sauce (see page 39 for recipe)

¼ cup Worcestershire sauce

2 tablespoons prepared horseradish

2 tablespoons hot sauce

Ribs

3 racks St. Louis-style pork ribs (½ rack per person)

½ cup hot sauce

1 cup firmly packed brown sugar

2 tablespoons salt

FOR THE BARBECUE SAUCE: Whisk together the Mustard Barbecue Sauce, Worcestershire, horseradish, and hot sauce. Refrigerate until needed.

FOR THE RIBS: Preheat the oven to 350 degrees. Place the whole rib racks in a roasting pan or saucepot. (Cut the racks in half if they don't fit in your pan.) Cover them with the hot sauce, brown sugar, and salt. Add enough water to cover and top with aluminum foil. Cook the ribs for about 2 hours or until they are tender enough to just about fall off the bone. Remove the pan from the oven and uncover it. Allow the ribs to sit until they are cool enough to handle, but not more than 30 minutes. Carefully remove the racks from the liquid and place flat on a platter or baking sheet. Refrigerate to cool completely, 1 hour to overnight.

TO SERVE: Heat the grill to medium. Cut the ribs into double-cut portions (two bones per piece). Baste the ribs with the barbecue sauce and place on the grill. Heat until the ribs are hot, basting every 5 minutes or so. Take care not to burn the sauce.

>> MAKES 6 SERVINGS.

MARTIN'S REDNECK TACO FROM MARTIN'S BBQ

½ cup corn muffin mix (plus additional ingredients from box)

4 tablespoons melted butter, divided

20 ounces pulled pork, divided

16 ounces cole slaw, divided

1 ½ cups Memphis BBQ Sauce (see page 46 for recipe), divided

Preheat a griddle or skillet over medium-high heat. Prepare the cornbread batter according to directions with the mix. Make 4 hoe cakes by dropping the batter by ½ cupfuls and cooking for 2 minutes and 45 seconds each. Carefully flip with a spatula. Use a brush to spread 1 tablespoon melted butter on top of each hoe cake and cook for an additional 2 minutes. Plate the hoe cakes and top each with 5 ounces pulled pork, 4 ounces slaw, and 3 ounces barbecue sauce.

》 MAKES 4 SERVING.

THE PBLT SANDWICH FROM HAMMERHEADS

Brine

1 gallon water
1 cup bay leaves
½ cup black peppercorns
2 cups sugar
1 ½ cups salt
½ cup Italian seasoning
1 (4- to 5-pound) slab raw pork belly

Hammerhead's Secret Rub

1 cup firmly packed brown sugar
¼ cup coarse black pepper
2 tablespoons plus 2 teaspoons sea salt
2 tablespoons plus 2 teaspoons garlic salt
½ cup finely chopped fresh rosemary

Sandwich

24 slices Texas toast
12 thick slices tomato
Lettuce or salad greens
Mayonnaise

TO MAKE THE BRINE: In a large bucket combine the water, bay leaves, peppercorns, sugar, salt, and Italian seasoning. Add the pork belly to the brine and refrigerate for 1 to 2 days.

Prepare a charcoal grill for indirect cooking.

TO MAKE HAMMERHEAD'S SECRET RUB: In a medium bowl combine the brown sugar, pepper, salt, garlic salt, and rosemary. Remove the pork belly from the brine and pat dry. Rub the pork belly with the rub and smoke for 6 to 8 hours over indirect heat. The grill temperature should be a consistent 225 degrees.

Preheat the oven to 200 degrees. Put the smoked belly in a roasting pan. Cover and roast for 8 to 10 hours. Chill, then slice ½ to 1 inch thick. Heat a cast-iron skillet over medium-high heat and sear each piece for 5 minutes or until crispy on the outside. Serve on slices of Texas toast with tomato slices, lettuce, and mayonnaise.

>> MAKES 12 SERVINGS.

PORK SHOULDER SAUSAGE FROM POOLE'S DOWNTOWN DINER

12 pounds pork butt

7 tablespoons sea salt

3 tablespoons red chili flakes

2 tablespoons fennel seeds, toasted

½ cup fresh sage leaves, lightly packed

3 tablespoons freshly ground black pepper

½ teaspoon fresh nutmeg

Remove any bones from the pork butt and cut into strips that will fit in a grinder. In a large bowl place the sea salt, chili flakes, fennel seeds, sage leaves, black pepper, and nutmeg and add the strips of meat. Toss to combine.

Prepare an electric mixer with the grinder attachment and grind the strips once. Place the ground meat in the bowl of the electric mixer and use the paddle attachment to combine the mixture until it becomes tacky. At this point you can cook and serve immediately or store in an airtight container in the refrigerator for up to 4 days or freeze in portions for up to 2 months. To serve, form into patties and cook in a skillet over medium-high heat, turning occasionally, until the internal temperature reaches 165 degrees, about 10 minutes.

≫ MAKES 12 POUNDS.

BBQ CRUNCH BURGER FROM MEMPHIS BBQ COMPANY

2 (4-ounce) ground beef patties

2 teaspoons seasoning salt

2 slices Cheddar cheese

1 bun

1 tablespoon Memphis BBQ Sauce (see page 46 for recipe)

Lettuce, tomato, onion, pickles, for dressing the burger

4 large barbecue pork rinds

Heat a cast-iron skillet or flat-top griddle over medium-high heat. Sprinkle the burger patties with about ½ teaspoon seasoning salt on each side, then place in the skillet. Cook for 2 minutes and then flip over and continue to cook for 1 ½ more minutes. Place the cheese slices on the patties and allow to melt as the patties finish cooking. Toast the bun if desired. Then add ½ tablespoon barbecue sauce to each half. Dress the bottom bun with lettuce, tomatoes, onions, and pickles, and then stack the burger patties on the bottom bun. Top with the pork rinds, then the top bun.

≫ MAKES 1 BURGER.

Peel and devein the shrimp, leaving the tails on. Preheat one side of a gas grill to 350 degrees or set up a charcoal grill for indirect and direct cooking by piling the charcoal to one side. Place the bacon strips right on the grates on the indirect side, cover with the lid, and cook until they are about halfway done. Don't overcook them; they must remain flexible. Set aside to cool.

Slice the cream cheese into ¼ x ¼ x ½-inch slices. Cut the stems of the peppers, slice them in half lengthwise, and remove the seeds. Place a strip of cream cheese on the shrimp's back where the vein was. Place a strip of jalapeño on top of the cream cheese, wrap with a strip of bacon, and hold it in place with a toothpick or two. Place the bacon-wrapped shrimp on the indirect side of the grill, cover with the lid, and cook until the shrimp is pink throughout, about 5 minutes. Remove and brush generously with the Thai sweet chili sauce and serve.

>> MAKES 4 SERVINGS.

BACON-WRAPPED STUFFED GRILLED SHRIMP FROM MEMPHIS BARBECUE COMPANY

20 (16/20) Gulf shrimp

20 slices bacon

1 (8-ounce) package cream cheese

1 (12-ounce) jar whole pickled jalapeño peppers

¼ cup Thai sweet chili sauce

Toothpicks

DR PEPPER GLAZED HAM FROM PURPLE PARROT CAFE

24 ounces Dr Pepper

2 tablespoons good grape jelly*

2 bay leaves

2 tablespoons Pickapeppa sauce**

1 teaspoon minced garlic

2 tablespoons minced shallot

5 whole cloves

1 cinnamon stick

1 tablespoon fresh orange zest

¼ cup freshly squeezed orange juice

2 teaspoons lemon zest

2 teaspoons lime zest

1 (10- to 12-pound) cured smoked ham

1 teaspoon dry mustard

1 cup firmly packed light brown sugar

1 cup water

Prepare the grill for medium-low heat (250 to 300 degrees) cooking and soak 4 cups of wood chips.

In a small saucepan combine the Dr Pepper, jelly, bay leaves, Pickapeppa sauce, garlic, shallot, cloves, cinnamon stick, orange zest, orange juice, lemon zest, and lime zest. Place over medium heat and simmer 30 minutes. Strain the liquid and discard the solids. Return the mixture to the stove and reduce to ¾ cup liquid.

Place the ham on a V-shaped baking rack in a disposable roasting pan. Using a paring knife, cut shallow slits in a criss-cross pattern on the top of the ham. Spoon 2 tablespoons of the glaze over the top of the ham. Combine the dry mustard and brown sugar in a small bowl. Press the mixture over the entire surface of the ham. Pour 1 cup of water into the bottom of the roasting pan. Add the wood chips to the charcoal as needed or if using a gas grill place the wood chips in aluminum foil and wrap up. Poke holes in the foil to allow the smoke to escape. Place over indirect medium-low heat and cover with the lid.

Cook until the internal temperature of the ham reaches 165 degrees. Spoon 1 to 2 tablespoons of the glaze over the ham every 15 to 20 minutes, until all the glaze is gone. Cover as much of the surface of the ham as possible. Allow the ham to rest for 20 to 30 minutes before carving.

≫ MAKES 12 SERVINGS.

* Use Mayhaw or Muscadine if you can find it.

**A Jamaican condiment made with vinegar, tomatoes, onions, raisins, ginger, peppers, garlic, cloves, thyme, and mangoes that can be found near the marinades and other sauces.

SMOKED ONION AND SAGE SAUSAGE FROM ST. JOHN'S RESTAURANT

1 tablespoon whole black pepper
2 teaspoons crushed red pepper flakes
1 tablespoon rubbed sage
3 ½ pounds pork shoulder, cubed
¾ pound pork fat, cubed
2 tablespoons plus 1 ½ teaspoons kosher salt

1 teaspoon sugar
1 garlic clove, minced
1 cup Smoked Onions (recipe follows)
½ cup red wine, chilled
1 tablespoon red wine vinegar, chilled

Grind the whole pepper, red pepper flakes, and rubbed sage in a spice grinder until uniform. In a large bowl combine the pork shoulder, pork fat, salt, sugar, ground spices, garlic, and smoked onions. Mix all the ingredients until well combined. Freeze the pork mixture in a single layer on a baking sheet, arranging the pork fat around the outside with the pork shoulder in the center. Chill until the fat is slightly frozen and the pork shoulder is firm, at least 1 hour. Also freeze the grinder attachment for a hand grinder or an electric mixer fitted with the medium die blade until very cold.

Position the bowl of an electric mixer into a larger bowl filled with ice. Grind the pork mixture into the bowl. Work as quickly as you can to keep everything cold and not let the fat soften. Mix the sausage in the bowl of an electric mixer with a paddle attachment on low speed until the sausage comes together. Add the wine and red wine vinegar and mix on medium speed for at least 1 minute, until the sausage is tacky. Sausage can be formed into patties, wrapped in caul fat, or stuffed into casings at this point and refrigerated up to 1 month. Cook by boiling, grilling, or pan frying.

≫ MAKES 12 SERVINGS.

SMOKED ONIONS

Small handful of hickory chips
2 tablespoons canola oil
2 large onions, diced small

Salt and black pepper to taste
1 ½ tablespoons sherry vinegar
1 ½ tablespoons sugar

Soak the hickory chips in a cup of water for at least 30 minutes. Heat the oil in a medium sauté pan over medium-low heat. Add the onions with a pinch of salt and pepper and cook, stirring often, for 20 minutes or until the onions are tender and a dark, rich color. Reserve the pan and place the cooked onions in a small pan suited for smoking.

Start a small fire on a charcoal grill and add the hickory chips to the top of the coals after they have turned gray and the fire is hot. Place the pan of onions on the grate, cover, and smoke for 10 to 15 minutes, stirring every 5 minutes. Add the smoked onion back to the reserved pan and add the sherry vinegar and sugar. Reduce until slightly thickened. Season to taste.

» MAKES ½ CUP.

MOLASSES-GLAZED HAM STEAKS FROM PURPLE PARROT CAFE

¾ cup orange juice
½ cup molasses
1 teaspoon garlic powder
1 teaspoon onion powder

1 teaspoon crushed red pepper flakes
1 teaspoon Worcestershire sauce
2 (1-pound) bone-in ham steaks

In a saucepan over low heat, cook the orange juice for 2 minutes and turn off the heat. Then whisk in the molasses, garlic powder, onion powder, red pepper flakes, and Worcestershire. Allow to cool.

Place the ham steaks in a baggie and pour in the marinade. Seal the bag and refrigerate the ham for 2 to 3 hours, turning once or twice to make sure all surfaces are covered.

Remove the bag from the refrigerator 1 hour before grilling. Remove the steaks from the marinade and pour the remaining marinade into a small saucepot. Place the liquid over medium heat and simmer until reduced by half. Using a small paring knife, make small slits through the fat on the outer perimeter of the ham steaks.

Prepare a grill over direct medium heat and cook the ham until it turns brown and crispy, 2 to 3 minutes per side. Turn once while cooking. While the ham is grilling, brush the surfaces with the reduced marinade. Remove the ham from the grill and cut into serving-size pieces; drizzle with any remaining marinade.

» MAKES 6 TO 8 SERVINGS.

SWEET TEA GLAZED PORK LOIN WITH FARRO PEACH SALAD FROM RUKA'S TABLE

1 gallon sweet tea (to taste)
4 (8-ounce) portions pork loin

Salt and black pepper to taste
Farro Peach Salad (recipe follows)

Put the sweet tea in a large pot over medium-low heat and reduce to 1 cup. This could take up to 1 hour. It's ready when it becomes a thick, honey-like consistency. Place your pork loins on a baking sheet and season with salt and pepper to taste.

Preheat a grill pan over medium-high heat or prepare an outdoor grill for medium-high cooking. Place the pork loins on the grill and baste with the sweet tea glaze until cooked to at least 145 degrees or desired temperature. Remove the chops from the grill and serve with Farro Peach Salad.

» MAKES 4 SERVINGS.

FARRO PEACH SALAD

1 cup farro
2 cups chicken stock
1 to 2 peaches, sliced

Fresh lemon juice to taste
Extra-virgin olive oil to taste
Salt and black pepper to taste

Bring the farro and chicken stock to a boil in a large pot over high heat. Once boiling, reduce the heat to medium, cover, and cook for 30 minutes or until the farro is cooked and tender. Drain the farro from the pot and transfer to a pan to cool. Once cooled, add the peaches, lemon juice, olive oil, and salt and pepper to taste. Toss the salad and serve or keep refrigerated until ready to serve.

» MAKES 4 SERVINGS.

Place the pork chops in a deep pan and add just enough water to cover the chops. This should take 6 to 7 cups depending on the size of your chops. Strain the water out of the pan into a large saucepan. Place the chops in the refrigerator until you're ready to brine them.

Add the sugar, peppercorns, rosemary, thyme, and salt and bring to a boil over high heat. Turn off the heat and allow the brine to cool, then chill in the refrigerator. Pour the chilled brine over the chops and weigh them down with a small plate if necessary to keep them submerged. Brine in the refrigerator for 24 hours.

Remove the pork chops from the brine. Grill them over medium-high on a gas or charcoal grill until the internal temperature reaches at least 145 degrees, about 5 minutes per side depending on the thickness. Allow the chops to rest 5 to 10 minutes on a plate covered with foil before serving.

>> MAKES 8 SERVINGS.

BRINED PORK CHOPS FROM HIGH COTTON

8 pork chops

6 to 7 cups water

½ cup firmly packed brown sugar

4 teaspoons black peppercorns

4 teaspoons fresh rosemary

2 sprigs fresh thyme

½ cup plus 1 teaspoon salt

PORK PORTERHOUSE WITH KUMQUAT MARMALADE FROM THE RAVENOUS PIG

½ gallon water
½ cup coarse salt
¼ cup sugar
5 sprigs thyme
3 whole cloves
½ tablespoon black peppercorns
½ tablespoon fennel seeds
½ tablespoon coriander seeds

½ tablespoon whole allspice
Zest of 1 orange
3 fresh or 1 dry bay leaves
3 cloves garlic, smashed
6 (20-ounce, 1-inch-thick) porterhouse pork chops*
Canola oil for searing
Kumquat Marmalade (recipe on next page)

Combine the water, salt, sugar, thyme, cloves, peppercorns, fennel seeds, coriander seeds, allspice, orange zest, bay leaves, and garlic in a large pot over medium-high heat. Bring to a boil, stirring frequently to dissolve the salt and sugar. Cool the brine completely before using.

Place the pork chops in a deep pan and cover with the brine. Cover the pan and refrigerate for 6 hours. Remove the pork from the brine and pat dry.

Preheat the oven to 400 degrees.

Heat a large sauté pan over high heat. Add enough canola oil to coat the bottom of the pan in a thin layer. When the oil begins to smoke, add the pork, one or two chops at a time, taking care not to crowd the pan. Sear on both sides until evenly browned. Transfer the chops to the oven and cook until the internal temperature registers 145 degrees, about 20 minutes. Set the pork aside and let rest for 15 minutes. Garnish with the Kumquat Marmalade.

≫ MAKES 6 SERVINGS.

* Also called center-cut pork chops.

KUMQUAT MARMALADE

2 cups cider vinegar
1 cup sugar
Coarse salt to taste

Pinch of crushed red pepper flakes
2 cups thinly sliced kumquats, seeds removed

Combine the vinegar, sugar, salt, and red pepper flakes in a small saucepan. Whisk together until the sugar is dissolved and simmer over medium-high heat until the liquid is reduced and syrupy, 8 to 12 minutes.

Add the kumquats and simmer until the mixture is thick and syrupy and coats the back of a spoon, about 20 minutes.

≫ MAKES 3 CUPS.

Preheat the oven to 250 degrees.

Pour the oil into large heavy-bottomed skillet over medium-high heat. Add the butter and heat until the foam subsides.

Combine the all-purpose flour and 2 tablespoons of the peanut flour in a shallow dish. Combine the remaining peanut flour with the bread crumbs in another shallow dish. Place the eggs in a third shallow dish. Season the cutlets with salt and pepper. Dredge in the flour and shake off the excess, then dredge through the egg, and then the bread crumbs. Add a schnitzel to the pan and brown, 2 to 3 minutes on each side. Transfer to a plate lined with paper towels and place in the oven to keep warm. Repeat with the other schnitzels. Serve with Redeye Gravy.

>> MAKES 4 SERVINGS.

PEANUT CRUSTED PORK WIENER SCHNITZEL FROM RESTAURANT EUGENE

3 tablespoons sunflower or canola oil

3 tablespoons butter

½ cup all-purpose flour

½ cup light peanut flour, divided

1 cup fine dry bread crumbs

3 large eggs, lightly beaten

1 ½ pounds pork tenderloin cutlets, cut into 4 large pieces and pounded thin as for scaloppini

Salt and freshly ground black pepper

Redeye Gravy (see page 139 for recipe)

COUNTRY CUBAN MIXTO SANDWICHES WITH PIMENTO CHEESE FROM SOMETHING DIFFERENT

Pimento cheese spreads all start with four basic ingredients: cheese, mayonnaise, pimentos or red peppers, and seasonings. The artistry and individualism is in the details, and they are hotly debated and often guarded by devotees. The spread is usually based on sharp Cheddar cheese, but other cheeses can be used for flavor and texture, such as Parmesan, Asiago, cream cheese, processed cheese spread, or American cheese, depending upon personal preference and what is on hand.

Something Different uses sharp Cheddar and adds a bit of Asiago to boost flavor. Duke's mayonnaise is preferred by most artisans. But Gill doesn't want the mayonnaise flavor to detract from the cheese, so he adds cream cheese and sour cream along with a minimal amount of mayonnaise to achieve the proper spreadability. Something Different prefers fire-roasted red peppers to pimientos because Gill says he likes the flavor and texture.

Pimento Cheese

1 pound shredded sharp Cheddar cheese
½ pound shredded Asiago cheese
1 pound cream cheese, softened
½ cup sour cream
½ cup mayonnaise
2 (4-ounce) cans diced fire-roasted red peppers, drained
1 teaspoon seasoned salt
2 tablespoons Pickapeppa sauce
½ teaspoon hot Hungarian pepper

Sandwiches

2 (12-inch) loaves Cuban or Italian hard bread rolls
2 tablespoons butter, softened
1 tablespoon prepared mustard
1 pound country ham, thinly sliced
8 ounces smoked ham, thinly sliced
8 slices Genoa salami, optional
Sliced dill pickles

TO MAKE THE PIMENTO CHEESE: In the bowl of an electric mixer with a paddle attachment, add the Cheddar, Asiago, cream cheese, sour cream, mayonnaise, red peppers, salt, Pickapeppa sauce, and Hungarian pepper and blend on low speed until the preferred consistency is achieved.

TO MAKE THE SANDWICHES: Slice the loaves in half and then split horizontally. Butter the outside faces. Spread the mustard on one face of each piece of bread and top each slice of each sandwich with ¼ of the country ham, smoked ham, salami, pimento cheese, and dill pickles. Assemble both slices of each sandwich. In a large skillet set over medium heat, cook the sandwiches for 5 to 6 minutes under the weight of another heavy skillet or a can with a weight on it until crispy and browned. Remove the weight and flip the sandwiches for another 3 to 4 minutes. Alternately, cook the sandwiches individually in a panini maker for 5 to 6 minutes.

>> MAKES 12 SERVINGS.

BLACK JAMBALAYA FROM CRESCENT PIE AND SAUSAGE COMPANY

¼ cup vegetable oil

1 pound smoked sausage, sliced into wedges

3 celery stalks, diced small

2 poblano peppers, diced small

1 yellow onion, diced small

½ pound braised pork or pulled smoked shoulder

½ pound boneless and skinless roasted chicken thigh meat

1 (12-ounce) can black-eyed peas

4 ¼ cups stock (chicken, pork, or beef)

2 tablespoons chopped fresh oregano

2 tablespoons chopped fresh parsley

2 tablespoons chopped fresh thyme

1 tablespoon kosher salt

1 teaspoon freshly ground black pepper

1 teaspoon granulated garlic

1 teaspoon cayenne pepper

2 cups parboiled rice

Place vegetable oil in a 4-gallon saucepan over medium heat. Add the sausage and cook until it sizzles and curls, about 10 minutes. Add the celery, poblanos, and onions and cook until golden brown, 6 to 8 minutes. Then add the braised pork and cook 15 minutes, stirring frequently (every other minute or so). Add the chicken, stir, and cook for another 10 minutes. Add the black-eyed peas and cook another 10 minutes. Then add the stock and bring to a simmer. Add the oregano, parsley, thyme, salt, black pepper, garlic, and cayenne pepper. Add the rice and bring to a simmer. Cover and reduce the heat to low and cook until the rice is soft, about 30 minutes.

>> MAKES 12 SERVINGS.

RASPBERRY GLAZED PORK WITH MANGO SALSA FROM CHEF'S MARKET

Pork

5 ounces frozen raspberries

¼ cup red currant jelly

2 tablespoons sugar

1 ½ teaspoons lemon juice

⅛ teaspoon finely grated lemon peel

Dash of salt

1 cup firmly packed brown sugar

1 ⅔ cups honey

4 cups whole-grain Dijon mustard

1 (2 ½- to 3-pound) pork loin

Mango Salsa (recipe follows)

Preheat the oven to 300 degrees.

In a large bowl combine the raspberries, jelly, sugar, lemon juice, lemon peel, salt, brown sugar, honey, and Dijon. Place the pork loin on a baking sheet. Generously brush the raspberry glaze all over the pork. Cook for 1 hour and 25 minutes. Remove from the oven and let sit for 10 minutes. Slice about ¼ inch thick and place on a serving tray. Garnish with the Mango Salsa.

>> MAKES 12 SERVINGS.

MANGO SALSA

2 ½ cups chopped pineapple

½ cup chopped fresh cilantro

3 small papaya, peeled, seeded, and cut into bite-size pieces

32 ounces frozen mango, thawed (use fresh if in season)

1 cup firmly packed brown sugar

1 cup dried cranberries

¼ cup rice wine vinegar

2 cups shredded coconut

Mix the chopped pineapple, cilantro, papaya, mango, brown sugar, cranberries, vinegar, and coconut in a large bowl. Refrigerate until ready to use.

>> MAKES 8 SERVINGS.

CHICKEN FRIED BACON AND CHEDDAR WAFFLES FROM SWINE SOUTHERN TABLE AND BAR

½ pound slab smoked bacon, cut into
½ x 3-inch slices

2 tablespoons hot sauce

¼ cup honey

¼ seedless watermelon, cut into cubes

¼ cup bourbon

1 cup maple syrup

Canola oil for frying

1 ½ cups buttermilk

1 ½ cups all-purpose flour

2 teaspoons kosher salt

1 teaspoon freshly ground black pepper

1 cup waffle mix (plus box ingredients)

1 cup grated sharp Cheddar cheese

Place the slices of bacon in a saucepan and add enough water to just cover. Bring to a boil, then turn the heat down to a simmer and cook for 45 minutes. Allow the bacon to cool in this liquid.

In a small bowl mix the hot sauce and honey. Place the diced watermelon in a large bowl and pour the honey mixture over the watermelon. Marinate for 10 minutes. Pour the bourbon into a small saucepan over medium heat. Bring it to a boil and then very carefully ignite the bourbon with a long lighter. Let the flames burn out, add the maple syrup, and take off the heat.

Fill a small fryer or a large saucepot halfway with canola oil and heat to 350 degrees. Once the bacon is cool, drain and reserve the liquid for other uses (cooking beans, greens, etc.). Place the bacon in a shallow dish. Cover with the buttermilk and allow to marinate for about 20 minutes. In a large bowl mix the flour, salt, and pepper. One by one, dredge the bacon slices in the seasoned flour and place on a baking sheet.

Fry the bacon in batches until crisp and golden brown. Remove to a plate lined with paper towels and season with a bit of kosher salt.

Preheat a waffle iron. Prepare the waffle mix according to the box recipe. Spray a little nonstick spray on the iron, then spoon ¼ cup batter, sprinkle the Cheddar cheese, and top with ½ cup batter. Cook the waffle according to the waffle iron's suggested time. When finished, remove the waffle and cut into four wedges.

Arrange the waffle slices on a large plate and top with the bacon and marinated watermelon cubes. Drizzle with the bourbon-infused maple syrup and serve with whipped cream if desired.

≫ MAKES 4 SERVINGS.

GRILLED HAM, CHEESE, AND BACON SANDWICHES

8 slices sourdough bread
¼ cup (½ stick) butter, softened
4 slices Swiss cheese
4 slices Cheddar cheese

12 slices cooked smoked bacon
8 slices baked ham, sliced
2 large tomatoes, sliced into 8 slices
4 slices Provolone cheese

Heat a large skillet over medium-low heat. Place 4 slices of bread on the cutting board and spread half of the softened butter on the top side of each slice. Lay the buttered side of 2 pieces of bread down in the skillet. Top each piece with 1 slice each of the Swiss and Cheddar cheeses, 3 slices of bacon, 2 slices of ham, 2 slices of tomato, and a slice of Provolone cheese. Top with the other two bread slices, buttered side up. Cook until the bread browns and the cheese is slightly melted, about 3 minutes per side. Repeat with the other 2 sandwiches. Serve hot.

>> MAKES 4 SERVINGS.

SWEET AND SPICY BACON-WRAPPED CHICKEN TENDERS

8 boneless, skinless chicken breast tenders
8 thick slices bacon

½ cup firmly packed brown sugar
2 tablespoons chili powder

Preheat the oven to 350 degrees.
Wrap each chicken tender with a strip of bacon and secure with toothpicks. Mix the brown sugar and chili powder in a small bowl and roll each tender in the mixture. Place the chicken on a baking sheet and bake for about 35 minutes, until the chicken is fully cooked and the bacon is crisp. If you want the bacon crispier, you can place the tenders under the broiler to crisp, just keep a close eye on them. Let cool for a couple of minutes and roll in the remaining sugary sauce that is in the pan. Remove the toothpicks before serving.

>> MAKES 4 SERVINGS.

Season the pork chops on both sides with the poultry seasoning, salt, and pepper. Heat the oil in a large frying pan over medium heat. When the oil is hot, brown the pork chops well, about 5 minutes on each side. Remove the chops from the pan and reserve on a plate. Pour off the excess oil and place the pan back on the stove over medium heat. Add the butter and the onions, along with a big pinch of salt. Sauté for about 10 minutes or until the onions are well browned. The onions should caramelize for best results. Stir in the garlic and cook for 1 minute. Stir in the flour and cook for 2 additional minutes. Add the chicken broth, buttermilk, and water.

As the mixture comes to a simmer, use a spoon to scrape any browned bits from the bottom of the pan. Turn the heat to low and let the onion gravy gently simmer for 15 minutes. Add a splash of water if it seems to be getting too thick. Add the pork chops and any juices back into the pan and coat with the gravy. Cook for about 10 more minutes. Taste and adjust seasoning if needed.

>> MAKES 4 SERVINGS.

SMOTHERED SOUTHERN PORK CHOPS

4 large pork chops, about
1 ½ inch thick

1 teaspoon poultry seasoning

Salt and freshly ground black pepper to taste

2 tablespoons vegetable oil

1 tablespoon butter

1 large yellow onion, sliced

2 cloves garlic, finely minced

2 tablespoons flour

1 ½ cups chicken broth

¼ cup buttermilk

¼ cup water

PECAN-CRUSTED CORNBREAD PORK LOIN

¾ cup pecans

1 ¼ cups crumbled cornbread

2 tablespoons butter

1 tablespoon finely chopped garlic

2 pounds pork tenderloins

Salt and black pepper to taste

3 tablespoons Dijon mustard

Preheat the oven to 400 degrees. Oil a shallow 9 x 13-inch baking pan.

In a food processor combine the pecans and cornbread and process until the pecans are finely chopped. Melt the butter in a skillet over medium heat. Add the garlic and cook for 1 minute. Stir in the pecan and cornbread mixture. Set aside to cool slightly.

Pat the pork dry and sprinkle with salt and pepper. Place in the baking pan. Spread the mustard thickly over the tenderloins and pat the crumb mixture onto the mustard. Roast in the middle of the oven for 15 minutes. Tent the pork loosely with foil to prevent the crust from burning and continue to roast until a thermometer inserted diagonally into the center of the meat registers 160 degrees. This should take about 15 minutes longer. Let the pork stand 10 minutes before slicing.

≫ MAKES 6 SERVINGS.

PORK TCHOUPITOULAS FROM RUFFINO'S

A Creole interpretation of surf and turf. Barbecued shrimp was invented at Pascal's Manale Restaurant in the 1950s. Ruffino's version uses a compound butter for an emulsified sauce. The flavors of New Orleans-style barbecue (butter, pepper, and Worcestershire) go great with pork or beef.

Compound Butter

2 cups (4 sticks) butter, cut into ½-inch cubes, softened

1 tablespoon black pepper

2 tablespoons Creole seasoning

3 tablespoons Worcestershire sauce

2 tablespoons chopped garlic

Juice of 1 ½ lemons

2 tablespoons minced fresh rosemary

Chops and Shrimp

4 (10- to 12-ounce) bone-in pork chops, frenched*

Fine sea salt and freshly ground black pepper to taste

2 tablespoons butter

1 tablespoon olive oil

16 (10/15) shrimp, headless, peeled, and deveined

4 ounces Abita Amber beer or similar amber beer

TO MAKE THE COMPOUND BUTTER: Place the butter, black pepper, Creole seasoning, Worcestershire, garlic, lemon juice, and rosemary in the bowl of a food processor. Blend until completely smooth and well blended. Lay a sheet of plastic wrap on the counter and place the compound butter on the wrap and form into a log. Twist the ends to seal. Refrigerate for at least 2 hours until hardened.

TO MAKE THE CHOPS AND SHRIMP: Allow the chops to sit at room temperature for 1 hour. Preheat the oven to 350 degrees.

Heat a cast-iron skillet or French steel pan over medium-high heat. Generously season the chops with sea salt and black pepper. Melt the butter in the hot pan and add the chops. Do not touch for 5 minutes. Turn the chops over. A nice crust should have formed. Place the whole pan in the oven and cook about 6 minutes for medium. Check for doneness and remove from the oven. Allow to rest for 5 to 10 minutes.

Heat the olive oil in a sauté pan over medium-high heat. Season the shrimp with salt and pepper. Add the shrimp and cook until the shrimp begin to turn pink. Deglaze the pan with the beer. Lower the heat and whisk in the compound butter 1 tablespoon at a time until it is creamy and you have enough sauce for plating. You should use about half of the compound butter.

TO SERVE: Place each pork chop in the center of a heated plate and top with four shrimp. Ladle the sauce over the shrimp and chops. This sauce goes great with mashed potatoes, creamy polenta, or grits for sopping up the sauce.

>> MAKES 4 SERVINGS.

* Frenching means to trim the meat away from the rib to expose 1 1/2 to 2 inches of bone. You can ask your butcher to do this for you.

ENTRÉES

TAMALE PIE CASSEROLE FROM CITY GROCERY

Delta-style tamales are a staple food of Mississippi. Chef John Currence has developed a casserole recipe that gives you all the flavors of this Delta favorite without having to worry about all those individual tamales in corn husks.

Dark Beer–Braised Pork Shoulder

2 tablespoons salt

3 tablespoons black pepper

1 ½ tablespoons ground cumin

1 tablespoon Ancho chili powder

½ tablespoon ground coriander

½ teaspoon ground cinnamon

1 (3-pound) bone-in pork roast

4 tablespoons olive oil

10 cloves garlic, minced

2 yellow onions, sliced thin

2 jalapeño peppers, sliced thin

32 ounces dark lager or porter beer

3 cups beef broth

Casserole Filling

2 tablespoons butter

1 tablespoon minced garlic

½ cup diced yellow onion

1 cup chopped green or red bell pepper

1 cup chopped fresh tomato

1 teaspoon salt

½ tablespoon black pepper

Zest and juice of 1 lime

2 cups chopped dark beer-braised pork shoulder

¼ cup chopped fresh cilantro

Tamale Batter

1 ½ cups buttermilk

2 ¼ cups chicken broth

½ cup amber lager*

1 cup yellow cornmeal

¾ cup whole-kernel corn

½ cup masa flour

1 ½ teaspoons salt

2 teaspoons black pepper

2 teaspoons sugar

1 teaspoon chili powder

3 tablespoons melted butter

4 tablespoons sour cream

1 large egg

1 ¼ cups shredded sharp Cheddar cheese, divided

TO MAKE THE DARK BEER-BRAISED PORK SHOULDER: Preheat the oven to 325 degrees.

Combine the salt, pepper, cumin, Ancho powder, coriander, and cinnamon in a small bowl. Rinse the pork shoulder, pat dry, and rub generously with the spice mix.

In a roasting pan or Dutch oven large enough to hold the pork roast, heat the olive oil over medium-high heat, until almost smoking. Place the pork in the pan, brown on all sides, and remove to a plate. In the same pan add the garlic, onions, and jalapeños, and sauté until transparent. Return the pork to the pan and stir in the beer, loosening the crispy bits from the bottom of the pan with a wooden spoon. Add the beef broth, bring to a simmer, cover with a lid or aluminum foil, and braise in the oven for 4 hours, or until the meat falls away from the bone.

TO MAKE THE CASSEROLE FILLING: Melt the butter in a medium pot over medium heat. Add the garlic, onions, and peppers and cook until transparent, about 5 minutes. Add the tomatoes, salt, pepper, and lime zest and juice and simmer until the tomatoes have cooked down to a sauce and begun to dry, about 10 minutes. Stir the pork into the sauce until well combined, remove the pot from the heat, and let cool 10 minutes. Stir in the cilantro.

TO MAKE THE TAMALE BATTER: In a saucepan over medium heat, combine the buttermilk, chicken broth, and beer and bring to a simmer. Whisk in the cornmeal, corn, masa flour, salt, pepper, sugar, and chili powder, and stir until very thick. Remove the mixture from the heat, stir in the butter and sour cream, and let stand 3 minutes, stirring to cool. Blend in the egg and set aside.

TO ASSEMBLE THE CASSEROLE: Preheat the oven to 350 degrees.

Heat a 10-inch cast-iron skillet in the oven for 10 to 15 minutes. Remove the skillet from the oven and pour half of the tamale batter in the skillet, or enough to fill it ⅓ deep. Spoon the pork filling onto the batter (the pork should fill the pan ⅔ deep) and sprinkle half of the Cheddar cheese over the filling. Cover the cheese layer with the rest of the cornmeal batter and sprinkle the remaining Cheddar on top. Bake the casserole for 45 minutes, or until the top is golden brown and a cake tester inserted in the center of the casserole comes out clean.

>> MAKES 8 SERVINGS.

NOTE: You can braise the pork shoulder up to 2 days in advance.

* City Grocery uses Dos Equis Dark.

HAM AND TOMATO PIE

Preheat the oven to 425 degrees.

Sauté the ham and green onions in a large nonstick skillet over medium heat for 5 minutes or until the ham is brown and any liquid evaporates.

Prick the bottom and sides of the piecrust, then brush the bottom of the piecrust evenly with the mustard and sprinkle with half of the cheese. Spoon the ham mixture evenly over the cheese and top with a single layer of sliced tomatoes. In a small bowl beat the egg and half-and-half until blended and pour over the tomatoes. Sprinkle evenly with basil, pepper, and the remaining cheese. Bake on the lowest oven rack for 20 minutes or until lightly browned and set. Cool on a wire rack 20 minutes before serving.

>> MAKES 6 TO 8 SERVINGS.

8 ounces diced cooked ham

½ cup sliced green onions

1 (9-inch) frozen unbaked piecrust

1 tablespoon Dijon mustard

1 cup (4 ounces) shredded mozzarella cheese, divided

2 medium tomatoes, thinly sliced

1 large egg

⅓ cup half-and-half

1 teaspoon chopped fresh basil

¼ teaspoon black pepper

CORNMEAL FRIED GREEN TOMATO, BACON, PIMENTO CHEESE STACK-UP FROM COTTON CREATIVE SOUTHERN CUISINE

6–8 slices applewood smoked bacon

Smoked Mayonnaise

3 large egg yolks
1 teaspoon liquid smoke
1 tablespoon Dijon mustard
2 tablespoons cider vinegar
1 cup canola oil
1 teaspoon kosher salt, or to taste
1 tablespoon freshly ground black pepper

Pimento Cheese

1 pound Cheddar cheese
1 teaspoon cayenne pepper
1 (2-ounce) jar diced pimentos
1 tablespoon Smoked Mayonnaise
1 tablespoon cream cheese, softened
⅓ teaspoon garlic powder

Fried Green Tomatoes

Vegetable oil for frying
2 cups yellow cornmeal
1 cup all-purpose flour
1 teaspoon cayenne pepper
2 teaspoons kosher salt
½ cup cornstarch
4 cups (1 quart) buttermilk
4 large eggs
3 to 5 large green tomatoes
Kosher salt to taste
Freshly ground black pepper to taste
Creole seasoning to taste
Fresh chives for garnish

Preheat the oven to 350 degrees.

Cook the bacon on a baking sheet lined with aluminum foil in the oven until crisp, 15 to 18 minutes.

TO MAKE THE SMOKED MAYONNAISE: In a food processor place the egg yolks, liquid smoke, mustard, and vinegar. Blend until smooth. Slowly add the canola oil until thick (if it appears too thick, add 2 tablespoons water to thin it down). Season the mayonnaise with kosher salt and pepper. Store in a sealed container in the refrigerator for up to 2 months.

TO MAKE THE PIMENTO CHEESE: Grate the cheese into a large bowl and add the cayenne pepper, pimentos, Smoked Mayonnaise, cream cheese, and garlic powder. Mix well and spoon into a container. Cover and leave at room temperature.

TO MAKE THE FRIED GREEN TOMATOES: Fill deep fryer with vegetable oil and preheat to 350 degrees.

In a shallow bowl mix the cornmeal, flour, cayenne pepper, salt, and cornstarch.

In another shallow bowl whisk the buttermilk and eggs together. Slice the green tomatoes about ¼-inch thick, and season both sides with salt, pepper, and Creole seasoning. Dip the tomatoes into the buttermilk mixture and then into the cornmeal mixture. Coat well and shake off excess cornmeal. Place in the fryer and cook until golden brown, 3 to 5 minutes.

TO SERVE: Place 3 slices of tomatoes on each plate. Top each tomato with 1 teaspoon pimento cheese. Cut each bacon slice into 3 pieces and top each tomato. Finish by spooning the smoked mayonnaise on top of the bacon. Finely slice chives to garnish.

≫ MAKES 4 SERVINGS.

FRIED PORK CUTLETS

½ cup olive oil
1 ½ cups panko bread crumbs
½ cup grated Parmesan cheese
¼ teaspoon salt

2 large eggs, beaten
1 (1 ¼-pound) pork tenderloin, sliced ¾ inch thick, and pounded to ¼ inch thick

Heat the oil in a large skillet over medium-high heat. Combine the panko, Parmesan, and salt in a shallow dish. Place the eggs in another shallow dish. Coat the pork slices in the beaten eggs, then in the panko mixture. In batches, cook the pork until golden and cooked through, 2 to 3 minutes per side.

≫ MAKES 4 SERVINGS.

DESSERTS

Bacon Ice Cream Coke Float from Brookville Restaurant

Bacon Peanut Butter Cookies

Candied Bacon from Chef's Market Cafe

White Chocolate and Coconut Bread Pudding from Felicia Suzanne's

Buttermilk Pie from Something Different

Grapefruit Chess Pie

Blackberry Crisp

Candied Bacon Brownie from Nose Dive

Caramel Brownies with Brown Sugar Icing

Molasses Gingerbread from Something Different

Maple Bacon Brittle Ice Cream

Southern Peach Cobbler with Bacon Confetti from Mama J's Kitchen

Sweet Tea Pie

BACON ICE CREAM COKE FLOAT FROM BROOKVILLE RESTAURANT

1 pound bacon, sliced
4 cups (1 quart) heavy cream
6 large egg yolks
1 cup sugar
1 teaspoon salt
1 teaspoon vanilla extract
1 (2-liter) cola

Preheat the oven to 400 degrees.

Cook the bacon in the oven on a baking sheet for 17 to 18 minutes or until crispy. Place on a plate lined with paper towels to drain. Put the heavy cream in a plastic container and add the hot cooked bacon. Place in the refrigerator and allow to infuse for 24 hours.

The next day place the yolks, sugar, salt, and vanilla in a medium bowl and whisk until they are pale yellow. Put the cream into a large saucepan and heat over medium. Bring to a simmer. Whisk 1 cup of the cream at a time into the yolk mixture. If you add it all at once, the eggs will curdle. Place the custard back in the saucepan over medium heat and bring to 185 degrees (this should take 7 to 10 minutes).

Strain the custard into a large bowl and cool over an ice bath to speed the cooling process. Using an ice-cream machine, churn the custard per the manufacturer's instructions. Once churned, transfer the ice cream to a container and place in the freezer to set up. Once solid, scoop the ice cream into a tall glass and fill with cola. Brookville prefers to use Mexican coke made from cane sugar.

» MAKES 10 SERVINGS.

BACON PEANUT BUTTER COOKIES

1 cup peanut butter
½ cup sugar, plus sugar to roll the cookie dough in
½ cup firmly packed light brown sugar

1 large egg
1 teaspoon vanilla extract
1 teaspoon baking soda
8 slices bacon, cooked and crumbled

Preheat the oven to 350 degrees. Line a baking sheet with parchment paper.

In the bowl of an electric mixer, blend the peanut butter, sugar, and brown sugar until well combined. Add in the egg, vanilla, and baking soda and continue to mix for another few minutes. Add in the chopped bacon and mix to incorporate. Sprinkle some sugar on a plate. Roll the dough into 1 ½-inch balls and drop into the sugar, rolling to coat. Place the cookies on the baking sheet. Gently press down the cookies using the tines of a fork. Bake for 10 to 12 minutes, until very lightly browned. Cool cookies completely on a cooling rack.

» MAKES 16 COOKIES.

CANDIED BACON FROM CHEF'S MARKET CAFE

1 cup firmly packed light brown sugar
1 tablespoon yellow cornmeal

10 slices thick-sliced applewood smoked bacon

Preheat oven to 350 degrees.

Line a baking pan with heavy aluminum foil and spray a wire baking rack with nonstick cooking spray. In a medium bowl combine the brown sugar and cornmeal. Dip each piece of bacon into the brown sugar and cornmeal mixture to coat heavily and place onto the baking rack. Bake until the bacon is red/brown, 15 to 20 minutes depending on bacon thickness. Remove to a cooling rack, as the bacon will not crisp until it cools. Serve at room temperature.

» MAKES 10 SERVINGS.

Preheat the oven to 350 degrees. Butter a 9 x 9-inch baking pan (about 10 cups).

In a large bowl whisk the eggs until well beaten. Add the brown sugar and Coco Lopez, and whisk until smooth. Whisk in the salt, vanilla, half-and-half, and whiskey. Fold in the bread cubes. Spoon half of the batter into the prepared pan. Sprinkle the chips and coconut over the batter. Spoon the remaining batter into the pan. Bake until the pudding is set in the center, about 60 minutes. Remove from the oven and cool slightly before serving.

» MAKES 16 SERVINGS.

* Felicia Suzanne uses Wonder Bread.

WHITE CHOCOLATE AND COCONUT BREAD PUDDING FROM FELICIA SUZANNE'S

1 tablespoon butter

8 large eggs

2 cups firmly packed light brown sugar

2 (12-ounce) cans Coco Lopez cream of coconut

Pinch of salt

1 tablespoon vanilla extract

4 cups (1 quart) half-and-half

½ cup whiskey

2 loaves white bread, crusts removed and cubed*

2 cups white chocolate chips

1 pound shredded fresh coconut

BUTTERMILK PIE FROM SOMETHING DIFFERENT

1 ½ cups sugar

½ cup (1 stick) butter, softened

3 large eggs, beaten

1 teaspoon vanilla extract

½ cup buttermilk

½ cup sour cream

¼ cup all-purpose flour, heaping

1 deep-dish 9-inch piecrust

Preheat the oven to 350 degrees.

Cream the sugar and butter in the bowl of an electric mixer. Add the eggs and vanilla and mix well. Add the buttermilk, sour cream, and flour and mix well. Pour into the piecrust. Bake for 45 to 50 minutes, or until firm and caramelized on top. Top should be slightly crusty and brown.

≫ MAKES 6 TO 8 SERVINGS.

NOTES: The addition of sour cream adds body and prevents separation into layers, resulting in a consistency reminiscent of chess pie.

To make a lighter version, separate the eggs and beat the whites to a soft peak and fold into the mixture.

Preheat the oven to 350 degrees.

In a medium bowl whisk together the sugar, flour, cornmeal, salt, butter, milk, grapefruit rind, grapefruit juice, lemon juice, and eggs until blended. Pour into the piecrust. Bake for 40 to 45 minutes or until the center is set. Cool on a wire rack.

>> MAKES 6 TO 8 SERVINGS.

GRAPEFRUIT CHESS PIE

1 ½ cups sugar

1 tablespoon all-purpose flour

1 tablespoon yellow cornmeal

¼ teaspoon salt

¼ cup (½ stick) butter, melted

¼ cup whole or 2% milk

2 teaspoons grated grapefruit rind

⅓ cup fresh grapefruit juice

1 tablespoon lemon juice

4 large eggs, lightly beaten

1 (9-inch) piecrust

Preheat the oven to 375 degrees. Grease two 1 ½-cup custard dishes.

Put the berries in a medium bowl. In a small bowl combine the sugar, cornstarch, water, and lemon juice until smooth. Pour over the berries and stir to coat. Divide between the 2 dishes. In a small bowl combine the oats, flour, brown sugar, and cinnamon. Add the butter and mix until crumbly. Sprinkle evenly over the berries and bake for 20 to 25 minutes or until the filling is bubbly and the top is golden brown.

>> MAKES 2 SERVINGS.

BLACKBERRY CRISP

2 cups fresh or frozen blackberries

¼ cup sugar

2 teaspoons cornstarch

2 tablespoons water

1 teaspoon lemon juice

½ cup quick-cooking oats

¼ cup all-purpose flour

¼ cup firmly packed brown sugar

½ teaspoon ground cinnamon

¼ cup (½ stick) butter, softened

Vanilla ice cream, optional

CANDIED BACON BROWNIE FROM NOSE DIVE

4 large eggs

1 teaspoon vanilla extract

2 cups sugar

½ tablespoon salt

1 cup canola oil

2 tablespoons light corn syrup

4 ounces unsweetened baking chocolate

1 ⅓ cups all-purpose flour

⅓ cup dark cocoa

1 teaspoon baking powder

¾ cup semisweet chocolate chips

1 ½ cups Candied Bacon (see recipe on page 280)

Preheat the oven to 350 degrees.

In the bowl of an electric mixer with a paddle attachment, whip the eggs, vanilla, sugar, and salt until thick and pale. Incorporate the oil and corn syrup. Melt the baking chocolate over a double boiler while mixing the other ingredients. Stir the chocolate in the bowl until smooth.

In a small bowl combine the flour, cocoa, and baking powder and add to the egg mixture. After everything is combined, add in the melted chocolate, chocolate chips, and Candied Bacon. Pour the batter into a 9 x 13-inch pan. Bake for 30 minutes. Insert a toothpick in the center and check if it comes out clean. If not, bake for another 5 to 10 minutes until the toothpick comes out clean. Cool on a wire rack and cut into 3 x 3-inch squares.

>> MAKES 12 SERVINGS.

CARAMEL BROWNIES WITH BROWN SUGAR ICING

½ cup (1 stick) butter, softened
4 cups (1 pound) firmly packed brown sugar
3 large eggs
1 ½ cups all-purpose flour
1 teaspoon baking powder

½ teaspoon salt
1 teaspoon vanilla extract
2 cups pecans, chopped
Brown Sugar Icing (recipe follows)

Preheat the oven to 325 degrees. Grease and flour a 9 x 13-inch baking pan.

Cream the butter and brown sugar together in the bowl of an electric mixer. Add the eggs and beat until mixed. In a small bowl mix together the flour, baking powder, and salt and add to the butter mixture. Beat to combine. Add the vanilla. Stir in the pecans. Pour into the greased pan. Bake for 30 minutes. Cool before icing with the Brown Sugar Icing and allow icing to cool before cutting.

>> MAKES 16 SERVINGS.

BROWN SUGAR ICING

¾ cup firmly packed brown sugar
⅔ cup white sugar
1 tablespoon dark corn syrup

½ cup heavy cream
¼ cup (½ stick) butter

Mix the brown sugar, white sugar, corn syrup, heavy cream, and butter together in a medium saucepan over medium heat. Bring to a boil and cook to a soft ball stage (230 degrees), stirring occasionally. Pour over the cooled brownies.

>> MAKES 1 CUP.

MOLASSES GINGERBREAD FROM SOMETHING DIFFERENT

1 cup (2 sticks) butter, softened
1 ½ cups sugar
4 large eggs
1 ½ cups molasses
1 cup buttermilk
3 cups all-purpose flour
1 teaspoon salt

2 teaspoons cola
2 teaspoons ground ginger
2 teaspoons ground cloves
2 teaspoons ground cinnamon
2 teaspoons ground allspice
1 cup hot water
Lemon Hard Sauce (recipe follows)

Preheat the oven to 350 degrees. Grease and flour a 9 x 9-inch baking pan.

Cream the butter and sugar together in the bowl of an electric mixer. In a medium bowl add the eggs, molasses, and buttermilk and mix well. Combine the flour, salt, cola, ginger, cloves, cinnamon, and allspice. Slowly add the flour mixture to the sugar mixture and mix until smooth. Stir in the hot water. Pour into the pan and bake for about 30 minutes until a toothpick inserted in the center comes out clean. Serve warm with the Lemon Hard Sauce.

≫ MAKES 8 SERVINGS.

LEMON HARD SAUCE

½ cup (1 stick) butter, softened but not melted
½ cup powdered sugar

1 teaspoon vanilla extract
2 tablespoons lemon juice

Combine the butter, powdered sugar, vanilla, and lemon juice in a small bowl and blend well. Drizzle over individual slices of gingerbread.

≫ MAKES 8 SERVINGS.

MAPLE BACON BRITTLE ICE CREAM

3 large egg yolks
¼ cup sugar
Pinch of salt
1 cup whole or 2% milk

1 cup maple syrup
2 cups heavy cream
Bacon Brittle (recipe follows)

In a medium bowl whisk the egg yolks, sugar, and salt until pale yellow. Transfer to a saucepan and whisk in the milk. Cook over medium heat, stirring, until almost simmering and thick enough to coat a spoon. Stir in the maple syrup. Transfer to a bowl and refrigerate until cold, about 30 minutes.

Stir the cream into the chilled custard. Churn in an ice-cream maker according to the manufacturer's directions. Stir in the Bacon Brittle during the last 5 minutes of churning.

» MAKES 8 SERVINGS.

BACON BRITTLE

1 tablespoon butter, plus more for the jelly-roll pan
3 strips smoked bacon

1 cup sugar
½ teaspoon baking soda
Pinch of cayenne pepper

Butter a 15 x 10-inch jelly-roll pan. Cook the bacon in a medium skillet over medium heat until crisp, about 5 minutes per side. Transfer to a plate lined with towels to drain. Let the bacon cool, then chop very finely. Cook the sugar in a saucepan over medium-high heat, stirring constantly, until it melts and turns golden, about 4 minutes. Continue to cook, stirring, until light amber, about

2 more minutes. Remove from the heat and immediately stir in 1 tablespoon of butter. Carefully stir in the baking soda, then the bacon and cayenne pepper. Pour onto the prepared pan and let cool until set, about 15 minutes. Break into tiny bite-size pieces.

» MAKES ¾ CUP.

SOUTHERN PEACH COBBLER WITH BACON CONFETTI FROM MAMA J'S KITCHEN

6 (15.25-ounce) cans canned peaches, well drained
2 cups plus 8 tablespoons sugar, divided
¾ teaspoon salt
2 tablespoons plus 2 teaspoons ground cinnamon, divided
½ cup (1 stick) butter or margarine, softened

1 tablespoon fresh lemon juice
¾ cup self-rising flour
3 cups all-purpose baking mix
2 cups water
8 slices bacon
Ice cream or whipped cream

Preheat the oven to 350 degrees.

Place the peaches in a large bowl and combine 2 cups of sugar, salt, 2 tablespoons cinnamon, butter, lemon juice, and flour. Toss the ingredients by hand until mixed. Pour the ingredients into an ungreased 12 x 12-inch baking dish. Mix the all-purpose baking mix and water with 2 tablespoons of sugar. Gently pour the baking mixture over the peach mixture until the peaches are covered, leaving small pocket openings.

In a small bowl combine the remaining 6 tablespoons sugar and 2 teaspoons cinnamon.

Sprinkle a small amount of sugar mixture on top of the batter. Bake for 45 minutes or until golden brown.

Cook the bacon in a skillet over medium-high heat for 8 to 10 minutes, until crisp, and then drain on a plate lined with paper towels. Chop the bacon into small bits like confetti. Serve the cobbler in a deep bowl with ice cream or whipped cream. Sprinkle the bacon confetti bits on top to finish. Serve immediately.

≫ MAKES 12 SERVINGS.

BACON PEANUT BRITTLE

6 slices bacon, diced
2 cups sugar
½ cup (1 stick) butter
½ cup water

⅓ cup light corn syrup
1 teaspoon kosher salt
½ teaspoon baking soda
2 cups roasted, unsalted peanuts

Cook the bacon in a skillet over medium heat until crispy. Drain on a plate lined with paper towels. Spray a 15 x 10-inch jelly-roll pan with nonstick cooking spray. Combine the sugar, butter, water, and corn syrup in a large saucepan over high heat. Bring to a boil and cook for 10 to 12 minutes, until the mixture registers 225 degrees on a candy thermometer.

Remove from the heat and whisk in the salt and baking soda. Stir in the peanuts and cooked bacon. Pour the brittle onto the prepared baking sheet and use a coated spatula to spread it into an even ½-inch thick layer. Let cool completely at room temperature before breaking into pieces.

≫ MAKES 20 SERVINGS.

SWEET TEA PIE

1 cup (2 sticks) butter, softened

2 cups sugar

8 large egg yolks

¾ cup strong orange pekoe tea, cooled

1 teaspoon grated lemon zest

1 tablespoon fresh lemon juice

2 tablespoons all-purpose flour

1 ½ teaspoons cornmeal

¼ teaspoon salt

1 (9-inch) piecrust

Preheat the oven to 350 degrees.

Place the butter and sugar in the bowl of an electric mixer and beat on medium speed until the mixture is light in color. Add the yolks one at a time, beating on low after each addition. Slowly add the tea, zest, and lemon juice. Scrape down the bowl. Add the flour, cornmeal, and salt and mix well. Pour into the piecrust and bake for 50 to 55 minutes until set. Cool completely on a wire rack and then chill for at least 2 hours in the refrigerator.

» MAKES 6 TO 8 SERVINGS

ACKNOWLEDGMENTS

Convincing chefs and pitmasters to part with their sacred secret recipes for this book was much easier than one might expect. Especially considering that the ultra-competitive world of barbecue revolves around secret rubs, sauces, and techniques, the fact that these Southern chefs were willing to share them with the readers of *The Southern Foodie* series is particularly gratifying. I encourage you to visit their dining establishments and thank them in person whenever you can.

I met many of these chefs through various food festivals and Southern Foodways Alliance events around the region. Special thanks to John T. Edge and the staff of the SFA for keeping the flame of Southern food burning and for assembling such wonderful groups of talented and passionate chefs, writers, academians and fans of Southern food to exalt and preserve the heritage of our region.

The hardworking staffs of food festivals like the Atlanta Food and Wine Festival, Charleston Wine and Food Festival, Music City Eats (now named the Music City Food and Wine Festival), and Euphoria in Greenville, South Carolina, offer great opportunities to interact with the South's most talented chefs while sampling their fare in entertaining environments. I suggest that anyone who loves good food and wants to meet the folks who prepare it plan to visit at least one of these festivals every year.

Special thanks to the kind friends who suggested restaurants for inclusion and for helping to make the connections with the talented cadre of chefs. First and foremost is Thomas Williams, whom I call "the nexus of all things Southern and delicious." His support has been invaluable, and I am honored to call him my friend. Others who were particularly helpful include: Cheryl Lemoine, Taryn Scher, Melany Mullens, Sarah Abell, Richard Lewis, Danielle Emerson, Jamie Estes, Jesse Hendrix, Brooke Filosa, Janet Kurtz, Susannah Runkle, Marcus Braham, Lindsay Guidos, John Kunkel, Elizabeth and Jeff Moore, Amanda Staley, Mary Elizabeth Kidd, Jill Allen, Jim Myers, Angie Sicurezza, Gina Boulware, Hunter Territo, Mary Reynolds, Molly McFerran, Becky Tanenbaum, and Gabby McNamara. Please don't let the fact that you are a member of such a long list in any way diminish my gratitude to you all. Just know that you're part of a great group of people who helped make this book possible.

My main partners in pork on this project were Bryan Curtis, Heather Skelton, Teresa Blackburn, and Mark Boughton , a roster of talented editors, a food stylist, and a photographer who were a joy to work with and were so very kind as deadlines came up and went rushing past along the way. Thanks also to Bryan's mom, Patsy Caldwell, for all her help with recipe development. You should all buy her book series (*Bless Your Heart*, *You Be Sweet*, and *Y'all Come Over*) too!

I could always depend on John Egerton, the dean of Southern food writers for inspiration and advice, and he is so missed by the entire food community after his passing in late 2013. John was never afraid to ask the tough questions and encourage all of us to look in the mirror when it came to addressing the heritage of Southern culture and food. His partner in the seminal *Southern Food: at Home, on the Road, in History* project was the talented photographer Al Clayton. After years of only knowing my adopted family, my cousin Jennie Clayton introduced me to the man who it turned out was my long-lost uncle. Finding out that I actually had food writing in my blood has been a wonderful blessing. Thanks to all involved and Uncle Al will also be remembered fondly since his passing.

I'll always be grateful to all the fans of my first book, *The Southern Foodie*, for the warm reception I received at book signings, speaking events, and during my appearances on QVC. Special thanks to David Venable of *In the Kitchen with David* for rewarding my food with his signature "happy dance" and introducing so many QVC fans to *The Southern Foodie*.

On the personal side, I'd like to thank my general practitioner for spotting me a few cholesterol points during my annual physical and to my home office mates, Nellie and Rufus for keeping me company during the writing process. This book probably took twice as long to write because there was usually a poodle in my lap hanging his head across my arm as I typed, but I wouldn't have had it any other way!

Finally, to Lisa Tinsley, I offer my eternal thanks and love. Friends kid that I really must have a tough job traveling around and getting paid to eat and drink. But it's getting to come home to a loving household that actually makes me happiest, and I've even been known to skip a meal to return early to Lisa's arms. In my eyes, a meal at home with her will always be preferable to any haute cuisine.

ABOUT THE AUTHOR

Chris Chamberlain is a food and drink writer based out of Nashville, Tennessee, where he has lived his entire life except for four years studying at Stanford University. He is a regular contributor to *Nashville Scene*, *Nashville Lifestyles*, *Food Republic*, and *Local Palate* and the author of *The Southern Foodie: 100 Places in the South to Eat Before You Die and the Recipes that Made Them Famous*.

A certified barbecue judge, Chamberlain has judged multiple times at the Jack Daniel's World Invitational Barbecue Championship in Lynchburg, Tennessee and the World Food Championship in Las Vegas. He spent a year tracking the barbecue circuit for *Food Republic* where he also writes a continuing series highlighting non-traditional food destinations called "The Hidden South."

He has appeared on television many times as a food commentator on shows like *Eat St.*, *Diners, Drive-ins, and Dives*, *Unique Eats*, *Chow Masters*, and *More at Midday*, and has served as a judge, moderator, and emcee at many cooking competitions and culinary panel discussions.

In his spare time, Chamberlain loves to cook at home, both indoors and outdoors and splits his time between Nashville and Sewanee, Tennessee, where he enjoys spending all day writing on his screened-in porch watching the birds gorge on the feeders while waiting for a pork shoulder to slowly cook for his own gluttonous pleasure.

RECIPE INDEX

LOCATION INDEX

CONTRIBUTOR INDEX